Real-Life Monsters

Real-Life Monsters

A Psychological Examination
of the Serial Murderer

Stephen J. Giannangelo

 PRAEGER

AN IMPRINT OF ABC-CLIO, LLC
Santa Barbara, California • Denver, Colorado • Oxford, England

Library of Congress Cataloging-in-Publication Data

Giannangelo, Stephen J.
  Real-life monsters : a psychological examination of the serial murderer / Stephen J. Giannangelo.
      p. ; cm.
  Includes bibliographical references and index.
  ISBN 978-0-313-39784-4 (hardcopy : alk. paper) —
ISBN 978-0-313-39785-1 (eISBN)
  I. Title.
  [DNLM: 1. Homicide—psychology. 2. Criminal Psychology. WM 605]
  616.89—dc23   2012014963

ISBN: 978-0-313-39784-4
EISBN: 978-0-313-39785-1

16 15 14 13 12   1 2 3 4 5

This book is also available on the World Wide Web as an eBook.
Visit www.abc-clio.com for details.

Praeger
An Imprint of ABC-CLIO, LLC

ABC-CLIO, LLC
130 Cremona Drive, P.O. Box 1911
Santa Barbara, California 93116-1911

This book is printed on acid-free paper ∞

Manufactured in the United States of America

For Mom and Dad–
together again
together always
And for Kathy
thank you for finding me

Contents

Preface

In the early 1960s, as a child growing up in New England, I spent a great amount of time with a riveted focus on the subject of movie monsters. Plastic models, magazines, and the latest horror flick ruled the day for this child. I even managed to convince my slightly skeptical mother to allow me to go to bed early on Saturday evenings, so she could wake me up in time to watch the weekly monster movie shown at midnight. Concerned relatives counseled my mom, thinking that maybe I could turn out, well, odd. Maybe they were right.

Still, for some reason, I never was all that affected by the horrors of the cinema. While interesting, I never did buy into the terror of Frankenstein's Monster, *The Wolf Man,* or the *Creature from the Black Lagoon.* They were interesting, but not real. Later movies came closer: *The Exorcist, The Omen*— these monsters looked a little more like they could be hiding under my bed—but not really. I believe this is what sparked my interest in human psychopathology and extreme abnormal psychology. I wanted to know what real monsters were capable of.

For it's the people who walk among us that strike fear into our hearts. Not the seven-foot tall hulk with bolts in his neck, sewn together with leftover parts from the graveyard—it's the normal-looking scrawny kid who works at the chocolate factory, brings people home, and desperately clings to the idea they might not leave this time. And then eats them. It's not the half-man, half-wolf that howls at the full moon and scours the night for victims—it's the chubby ex-shoe salesman turned contractor, the part-time performing clown, who lures a parade of young, unsuspecting victims to his home. And then buries them in his crawl space.

These are the monsters of real life. This is what real nightmares are made of.

In a 1993 *New York Times* interview, prolific true-crime author Jack Olsen recalled:

we took a field trip to Holmesburg Prison, and I'm 19 years old and we get inside and I see all these guys who look just like me. I thought that criminals looked different. And this is what I attribute my interest in crime to.

I start every book with the idea that I want to explain how this seven or eight pounds of protoplasm went from his mommy's arms to become a serial rapist or serial killer. This is my drive and my compulsion. I think a crime book that doesn't do this is pure pornography.

I had the honor of discussing such issues with Mr. Olsen in 1997. He told me how much he liked my original book about serial murder and said it "was one of the clearer voices" on the subject and taught him plenty. This is high praise from an author I respected immensely. I'd hoped to have Mr. Olsen pen a foreword for this project, but sadly we lost him in 2002. He will be missed. I did need, however, to restate his position about curiosity based on that "seven or eight pounds of protoplasm." I share this compulsion.

This book is a continuation—a 2012 perspective on an idea I developed in my first book, *The Psychopathology of Serial Murder: A Theory of Violence.* It seems the concept stands today, with over a decade's worth of additional information and feedback. In addition, the perspective of this book, unlike those that cover the general subject of serial murderers, is to look specifically at the psychological underpinnings of these monsters that walk among us. The behaviors of these creatures are actually consistent enough to identify, and the goal is to pin down a developmental process that creates them.

The suggestion and presentation of an original theory is, at best, optimistic and ambitious. To attempt to explain a phenomenon such as the psychopathology of the serial killer could easily be described as overwhelming. However, that is the intent of this book, as it was 15 years ago.

The reader must be aware that this book will by no means insinuate an explanation that could be carved in stone. The theory must be considered a starting point, a conclusion based on a limited amount of available knowledge; something to be reexamined and rethought with the passage of time and accumulation of information. Thus, this book continues that process.

The intent is to observe the available information regarding the serial killer, to dissect and apply the consistencies, and to develop a model of pathology. Observed will be clinical viewpoints, existing theory, socio-environmental influences, and actual case histories. All these factors and more are critical to this analysis and will contribute to the thinking about this subject.

The serial murderer is examined in the context of the fourth edition, text revision *Diagnostic and Statistical Manual of Mental Disorders* (*DSM-IV-TR*), the reference published by the American Psychiatric Association. This is not to say that this book speaks only to those in the arena of psychology; quite the contrary. The book encompasses the disciplines of sociology, history, biology, psychology, and law enforcement, to name a few, and attempts to reach anyone interested in the development and the impact of this particular offender on our society.

This book is organized as a review of current clinical perspectives that could be applied to the psyche of the serial killer (Chapter 2); a review of the idea behind biological bases for violence, criminal behavior, and serial murder (Chapter 3); a discussion of sociological observations and environmental factors in the killers' backgrounds (Chapter 4); a discussion of the synthesis of a preliminary theoretical model of pathology (Chapter 5); the analyses of eight case studies in the context of prior assumptions (Chapters 6 and 7); a resulting analysis of an etiological theory (Chapter 8); a fascinating, frank conversation I had with a confessed serial killer sentenced to death row and his insights (Chapter 9), and a conclusion (Chapter 10) with observations and suggestions. Future research is also considered.

The reader should note that references to various serial killers and related nonserial cases will appear throughout the text. For those unfamiliar with a particular case, a brief synopsis of each offender appears in alphabetical order in the Case Briefs of Appendix A. Therefore, each individual will not be footnoted; they are easily referred to in the appendix.

The reader should also note that terms in this book are by no means universal. Various writers have very specific usages for concept terms such as *dissociative* and *deviance,* which very well may not agree with others' usage. Several forms of media use certain terms in a completely generic manner, to the point of losing their intended distinctions. For example, many newspapers and other media continue to use the term *mass murderer* in reference to serial killers, whereas those who study these individuals clearly do not find the terms interchangeable.

Therefore, the reader should direct his or her attention to the Glossary in Appendix B to clarify the use and intention of many of the terms used in this book. They are specifically used within the context of this book's perspective and do not intend to insinuate a universal acceptance of their use.

The reader of this new volume should also be aware that while there are many new and current references, there are a number of older citations of studies and research done many years ago. Some are essential to the historical context and the discussion at hand; many were produced around the same time frame a certain offender was found out and prosecuted; others are classic references that remain important and relevant. I would actually call them essential, when discussing a narrowly viewed and examined subject such as the serial murderer and theories of violence and criminology. The reader should be assured that this work, while retaining much of the classic contributions of the genre, has clearly been reexamined in light of new study, theory, and science.

Clearly, theory about serial killer development will continue to rage. Arguments of guilt and innocence will continue, as in the cases of Wayne Williams, Albert DeSalvo, and Lucy de Berk. Over the years, long-established kill totals evolve as they have with the 2011 victim analysis of John Wayne Gacy. Even the identities of some killers, as famous as the Zodiac Killer and Jack the Ripper, are unknown. "Nobody will ever know—I am as mystified now as I was then," said officers in the Ripper case, according to Honeycombe (2009). I've been lucky enough to view the Black Museum at Scotland Yard, and while some I spoke to were reasonably sure of their belief of Jack's identity, others still did not agree. I just hope this book can aid the readers in making their own informed opinions about these debates and many more.

Maybe we can yet capture the real-life monsters they can't quite convert to the movie screen.

Acknowledgments

The production of a new book is impossible without a host of great friends and respected people who offer input, guidance, and support.

To my friend Cathy Clevenger, my resident attachment disorder expert and long-time professional dealing with the most high-risk young offenders, a great amount of thanks for years of teaching knowledge, expertise and shared experiences, and a fine contribution to this project.

Michael Wilt and Valentina Tursini both contributed greatly to the final stage of making this new book possible. Michael for his help at the beginning and Valentina's professional and tireless efforts in dealing with both my fuzzy proposal and endless questions throughout. And of course Beth Ptalis for taking us to the finish line.

Kate Vernor, for suggestions and references on the research side.

Professor Scott Culhane of the University of Wyoming and Commander Ron Freeman of Duquesne University, for unselfishly offering some terrific research material, and Ron: thanks for the fine quote.

Great thanks to Jessica Senn, who graciously offered her expertise on the line art and figures.

I really should acknowledge Rick, who provided personal insight and an honesty about some difficult issues that must be recognized. These things are rarely discussed in this way.

I still must continue to acknowledge the assistance of those who made contributions to my previous book, without which this work would be impossible. Great thanks still go out to: Karen Kirkendall, Joel Adkins, Ron Ettinger, Karen Klainsek, Judy Rodden, Kim Egger, Dale Lael, Mike Giannangelo, Keith Hanson, Danielle Waller, Bob Craner, Ken Daugherty, Irene Kelly-Pasley, and my friend, mentor, and colleague, Dr. Steven Egger.

And a massive, heartfelt thanks to my amazing wife Kathy Giannangelo, who not only provided unwavering support when I truly thought I'd never get to take a fresh look at this project, but also took on some difficult proofreading and provided additional creative input. This is not to mention her essential IT skills and technical expertise that saved me endless hours of kicking computers and developing further alternate forms of linguistic profanity.

Part I

The Development of a
Serial Murderer

Introduction: An Identification of the Offender

> We continue to be haunted with the fear that people will remember this killer, even glorify him, for the slaughter of our children.
>
> —Families of victims of Danny Rolling

As I peered through the thick glass separating us, I caught a glimpse of my own reflection. I had a look of rapt attention, as if I could not wait to see what happened next. For a moment I was aware of the sad, grey prison walls enveloping us and the stark bleakness of the surroundings. I glanced down and noticed I was literally on the edge of my seat, anticipating what he was about to say, in what direction he might go. My seat was quite a bit different than the stool he sat on, with hardware for shackles attached.

He explained to me why he killed so many women in a short period of time. He quickly agreed he'd do it again if given the chance. He debated whether he should really be considered a psychopath. As he spoke, I couldn't help but think there was nothing about him that would make me consider him a threat if we were on the outside. He tried to understand what would take him from an adventurous young man to what people regarded as a monster.

I'm still trying to understand.

Serial murder. Rarely a day goes by without a fleeting reference to this expression. It's heard on television, in movies, in newspapers, and in everyday conversation. More average Americans know who Jeffrey Dahmer is than Jonas Salk. Everybody's heard of serial killers.

"We fear evil, but we are fascinated by it. We reject the 'Other' as different and dangerous because it's unknown, yet we are thrilled by contemplating sexual excess and violations of moral codes by those who are not our kind" (Zimbardo, 2007, pp. 4–5).

But who are they? What makes a handsome, normal-appearing young law student murder dozens of women? Why does a mild-mannered chocolate factory worker kill, dismember, and cannibalize individuals he found attractive, who came home with him on particular nights? What makes a serial killer kill? More important, what makes him or her in the first place?

The subject of serial murder has been the focus of an inordinate amount of attention, research, debate, and often exploitation in recent years. The sensationalism and emotional response the subject evokes make it an easy target for articles, movies, true crime books, yellow journalism, TV tabloids, and other money-making paraphernalia ranging from comic books to trading cards. However, sifting through this avalanche of sensationalism does yield a lining of true research and scientific study that might suggest answers to just who the serial killer is, and why.

SOME DEFINITIONS OF SERIAL MURDER

The first difficult question is, who exactly is a serial killer? The Federal Bureau of Investigation (FBI) has one definition; various theorists have others. Is it just someone who kills more than one person? A hit man? Is a mercenary a serial killer? What about an abortion doctor? The more the question is asked, the more answers there seem to be.

Credit for the term "serial killer" is given by Ramsland (2005b) to Richard Hughes in his 1950 book, *The Complete Detective*. Robert Ressler, a longtime FBI profiler, is often credited with common usage of the term, after hearing the term *series* in use in England regarding a pattern of crime. He also felt this was comparable to serial adventures in the movie industry (Vronsky, 2004). Different writers and theorists have also quoted other examples of the use of the term in the 1960s and 1970s, while even more have claimed the credit themselves.

Many definitions of serial murder are established by specific parameters, such as victimology, geographic location, and killer–victim relationships. Some feel serial killers must reveal a certain pattern or their victims must represent deeply rooted symbolism. Other theories include sex and dominance.

The FBI states their definition of serial murder, taken from Title 28, Section 540B of the U.S. Code, describes the killing of a series of three victims or more, "having common characteristics such as to suggest the reasonable possibility that the crimes were committed by the same offender or offenders."

According to Brantley and Kosky (2005), the agency makes no reference to "underlying motivation" and the definition is "intentionally broad" in order "to encompass the full array of serial killers" (p. 28).

In 2011, the FBI's Behavioral Analysis Unit (BAU) published the results of a 2005 symposium held in San Antonio, Texas, comprised of 135 scholars, government crime experts, and veteran homicide detectives. This group concluded that serial murder should be defined by the "unlawful murder of two or more victims by the same offender in separate events." This clearly broad definition was intentionally designed out of concern that serial murders were being underestimated (Hargrove, 2011). However, this definition would incorrectly include gang killings, murder for hire, and spree killers, to name a few.

Very specific parameters cause some researchers to eliminate some offenders from a grouping of serial killers based on, possibly, a technicality. Colin Wilson, referring to G.J. Schaefer, stated, "technically speaking, based solely on his convictions, Schaefer could not be labeled a serial killer" because Schaefer had only been convicted of two killings (Schaefer & London, 1997, p. 1). Wilson apparently rigidly adheres to a three-victim minimum standard. It would be difficult to limit those studied as serial killers based on an arbitrary number of kills actually resulting in conviction.

Holmes and DeBurger (1988) listed distinctions they found within a pattern of serial murder. They included almost always a male killer and a female victim; a victim the same race as the killer; a killer whose age is between 25 and 35; no geographic variation in sites; victims of similar status; and a stranger-to-stranger relationship between killer and victim (p. 24). Inasmuch as these variables appeared consistent in their small (44) sample, most of these distinctions are arguable in light of various case histories. For example, while male killer or female victim roles are common, many cases include homosexual male killers and victims. A reasonable modification of this assumption could be male killers and eligible sexual partner victims. The common assumption that killers and victims are usually of the same race can also be disputed. While the general criminological principles state "murderers and victims look remarkably alike" and "murders tend to be overwhelmingly intraracial" (Goode, 2008, p. 153), this seems to be more of a reflection of another conventional wisdom, that the likelihood of murder rises along with the level of intimacy between people. However, serial murder is more often a stranger-to-stranger crime, and too many of the cases tend to have unique features, which causes conflicts in painting with too broad a brush.

Eric Hickey, author of *Serial Murderers and Their Victims* (1991, p. 8), feels a serial killer must be defined in the most general of terms, so as not to eliminate offenders by speculation rather than through verifiable evidence. His definition includes "any offenders who kill over time." Hickey's assertion seems plausible for the most part, except that his all-inclusive population is not usable for purposes of this book. Hickey's demographic approach and breakdown are dissimilar from this book in that there are specific offenders excluded from this consideration, by design. Hickey correctly notes that some serial killer traits can be eliminated from the definition due to "speculation" rather "than verifiable evidence given the current state of serial murder research" (1997, p. 12). The direction of this book is to consider a psychological theory originally formulated by personal speculation, and then to evaluate its merit in the context of verified evidence.

Steven Egger's (1990, p. 4) definition of a serial killer states:

> a serial murder occurs when one or more individuals (males, in most known cases) commit a second or subsequent murder; is relationshipless; is at a different time and has no apparent connection to the initial murder; and is usually committed in a different geographical location. Further, the motive is not for material gain and is believed to be for the murderer's desire to have power over the victims.

Egger's definition also includes a specific consideration of the victims, offering that they may have a symbolic value and insinuating that they are selected often for their perceived vulnerability. He further defines this in his 2002 book, *The Killers Among Us,* where he explains victims typically "include vagrants, the homeless, prostitutes, migrant workers, homosexuals, missing children, single women, elderly women, college students and hospital patients" (p. 5). The assumptions regarding the serial murderer definition in this book will more closely resemble Egger's than any other, differing mainly in reduced consideration of victim status and concentration on the killer's personality, internal motivators, and development. While a certain vulnerable victim is a clear and favorite serial killer target, the sexual interest target is also a substantial one.

The focus here will be on what would appear to be the essence of the phenomenon of this particular criminal. The definition of a serial murderer, which parameters this book will be operating under, will therefore be narrow; much more narrow than most studies of the subject. There will be an attempt to identify a very specific psychological dynamic in theory. Mass murderers and spree killers, for example, are not included, as they appear to involve an entirely different set of psychodynamics.

AREN'T THEY ALL MASS MURDERERS?

This is a critical part of this book. It's routine for the newspapers to refer to serial killers, spree killers, and mass murderers all in interchangeable terms. However, the focus of this book is to correctly and definitely identify the psychological makeup of the serial killer. Why should we care? That will be discussed in the Conclusion.

The fact is there are very different sets of dynamics at work in each type of offender. While a mass murderer in general language is a person who kills a group of people, in more specific terms he or she is the offender who purposefully kills a large group at a single event. George Hennard, who in 1991 drove a truck into a Luby's restaurant in Killeen, Texas, and then executed as many people as possible with a handgun, is a very different psychological case than a calculated cold-blooded predator like Anthony Sowell. The prototypical mass-murdering school shooters or workplace massacres or a violent rampage by a jilted spouse, such as that of Robert Stewart who shot eight elderly nursing home residents in North Carolina in 2009, bear no resemblance in their very public acts as compared to a long-term patient predator who kills many carefully selected victims over time. A spree killer such as Andrew Cunanan leaving a trail of seemingly random victims behind represents an entirely different mind-set than the young photography targets of Rodney Alcala.

Eliminated are murderers of a serial nature who have any financial or other tangible motivation that might render incidental the killing aspect of the crime. Also eliminated from the study is the cult-obsessed type, as the true serial killer—or at least the type this analysis tries to identify—may be drawn to cult activities, but not necessarily. The serial murderer kills because he or she wants to, not because he or she is mindlessly led by a cult. This targeted personality may carry out killings in a serial manner owing to an association with a cult, but not because he or she is merely guided or even controlled by that influence. The specific psychological phenomenon to be identified here is a development of internal factors, owing someone to habitually kill for the implicit thrill, satisfaction, or satiation of the act; or as Herman Mudgett put it: for the "pleasure of killing my fellow beings" (Editors of Time-Life Books, 1992, p. 95). The ultimate control of another human being and the accompanying catharsis are the psychological hallmarks of the individuals to be discussed.

The reader must understand that the focus of this book is to try to identify and characterize the individual who kills for the joy of killing. Unlike Hickey's broader population, this book will consider a smaller, more focused sample set of data, defined by greater consideration of preliminary information. The examination will be of a group of offenders whose need and motivations to kill appear unencumbered by extraneous variables, such as money or outside influence.

THE PROBLEM OF ESTIMATING NUMBERS

The actual prevalence of this type of offender is difficult to pinpoint. Historical estimates have ranged from 6,000+ victims a year (McKay, 1985), to 4,000 a year (Lindsey, 1984), to 3,500 to 5,000 a year (Holmes & DeBurger, 1988). Kenna Kiger noted that active offenders have been estimated as low as 30 to as high as 500, depending on the source of research (Egger, 1990, p. 37). Egger later referenced a disagreement between the FBI and the CNN, who reduced the former's estimate of serial killers between 1977 and 1992 from 331 to 175 after eliminating duplications. An FBI agent quoted in the CNN report guessed at "25, 35, or 40" active at a time, whereas another guessed probably 50–100 (Egger, 2002, p. 68). These figures represent activity in the

United States, as cross-cultural research is extremely limited. There is little agreement, and very little in the way of reliable accuracy in numbers, other than the fact that these killers exist and continue to thrive in our society. Even the aforementioned Texas symposium published in 2011 didn't attempt to rigidly place a number beyond the fact that serial murder is relatively rare in the grand scheme of murder and that there is a consensus that many successful killers have gone undetected (Hargrove, 2011). The FBI stated that approximately 2 percent of homicides reported to Violent Criminal Apprehension Program (ViCAP), on file with the bureau in Quantico, Virginia, are attributed to serial murder. Retired FBI profiler Mark Safarik guessed there were up to two dozen serial killers operating now.

A 2010 *USA Today* report stated, "during the past four decades, at least 459 people may have died at the hands of highway serial killers, FBI statistics show." Suspects included as many as 200 long-haul truck drivers, with at least 10 suspects believed to be involved in 30 or more murders. However, the report went on to state it was very difficult to pin down actual serial killings as opposed to other types of crime, including drug trade. Figuring out how old a particular crime is also is challenging. Many victims included prostitutes, a favorite disposable target of serial killers. A highway rest stop would seem to be an ideal spot for serial killers to operate, with prostitutes engaging in high-risk activity and the highway offering an easy-access escape route. Information continues to be fed to the FBI Highway Serial Killings database, but sorting out the results remains unclear. Still, an agent who oversaw the FBI effort for three years stated, "We seem to have one a week that comes in. . . . They're out there" (Morrison, 2010, pp. 1, 2A).

In 2011, long-haul trucker John Boyer pleaded guilty to the murder of a woman in North Carolina and confessed, without a hint of remorse, to the killings of women in Tennessee and South Carolina, and was suspected in more (Collins & Dalesio, 2011). Investigators were taken aback by the unbridled hatred for women by the man who lived with his mother near Augusta, Georgia. One investigator was greeted in an interview with Boyer by, "What bitch are you here about?"

The media have called attention to the activities of law enforcement agencies in apprehending the perpetrators of these sensational crimes. As well, the direct relationship between the media and serial killers is clear. Gibson (2006) concludes that in all cases of serial killing the "interrelationships between serial killers, law enforcement, the media and the public are complex," media coverage influences the killers as well as the investigation, and "serial killers and serial murder cases influence the media" (p. xvii).

Undeniably, these issues are of critical importance and relevance. However, the direction and perspective of this book is psychological, putting forth a blueprint of the development and motivation of the serial killer. Discussed here are some of the current theories commonly applied to this phenomenon. These theories are then combined with admitted intuition and speculative insight to develop and consider a theoretical model of the psychopathology of the serial killer.

VICTIMOLOGY

Another key element is, when trying to identify a serial murderer, that there must be a presence of a certain link to the victims. Victims of a mass murder generally have no connection other than being in the same place (the wrong place) at the same time, such as the victims at Columbine, Richard Speck, Luby's, or Virginia Tech. A serial murderer, the type that this book attempts to identify as a psychological personality type, generally has a rhyme or reason to his or her victim choice—whether it's physical, pretty young girls with hair parted in the middle for Bundy, or a general sexual target as with Gacy or Dahmer, or disposable sexual surrogates as with Shawcross, or simply a person engaging in a high-risk personal lifestyle who is an easy target that might not be missed (victims referred to as the "less dead" by Steven Egger), victims of killers like Dahmer, Shawcross, and Anthony Sowell. Generally, a thread that ties the victim pool together can be realized when identifying a serial murderer. Some may be carefully stalked, while others could be simply unlucky, found in the wrong place at the worst possible moment, as in the cases of the Zodiac Killer, Gary Ridgway, and David Berkowitz. Victimology, along with psychological state, is usually how a serial murderer is separated from a mass murderer or a spree killer, and is a critical point within the profile assembled of a particular offender.

DO WE KNOW WHAT WE THINK WE KNOW?

Finally, the study of serial murder continues to humble even the most experienced researcher. I was told by Dr. Steven Egger, as renowned an expert on the subject as there is, that the more one studies this subject, the more comes the realization of how little one knows (personal communication, 1993). Competing theory and additional knowledge continue to confound and blur a topic we would all hope could be much more clear.

In 2003, I clipped an article in the *London Guardian* about Lucy de Berk, an accused serial killer nurse from the Netherlands (Osborn, 2003). The case was interesting because not only did she appear to kill at least seven patients in an angel of mercy fashion (and as well was suspected in many more), she fit into many serial killer profiles, both in gender and in behavior. Stories of her "compulsions" from her diary fit neatly into commonly held psychological ideas regarding this type of offender's profile. The FBI published an article in the *Law Enforcement Bulletin* (Brantley & Kosky, 2005) in 2005, analyzing de Berk's case in terms of motivation, behavior, and characteristics. In the context of serial murder in general, Lucy's crimes were viewed as not atypical, especially within the realm of "heath-care worker serial murderers."

Lucy de Berk's patients at the hospital in the Hague seemed to unexpectedly die. Suddenly. A hospital review determined that not only had 8 patients under her care died, but 19 elderly patients had died while under her care in a previous facility. Another died at home after a visit from Lucy. She was arrested for the murder of 13 patients in 2001.

In 2002, the District Attorney's office and the Hague Police Department presented the case to the FBI's BAU at the National Center for the Analysis of Violent Crime. An on-site review resulted in the eventual expert testimony of BAU personnel regarding the motivation, behavior, and psychological characteristics of serial murderers (Brantley & Kosky, 2005). It was noted that female serial murderers kill those in close proximity, including those within custodial care as in the cases of health care serial murderers. Issues including power, recognition, excitement as well as a reduction of stress and tension were discussed as reasons for health care workers, primarily female, to kill.

In Lucy de Berk's case, she repeatedly wrote in her diary about giving in to her compulsions. She wrestled with confusion over her lack of feelings or compassion. She strove to understand her self-described "sociopathic personality" (Brantley & Kosky, 2005). She stated, "I don't even know why I am doing it. . . . I will take this secret with me to the grave. . . . Still, I hope I am helping people by this" (Osborn, 2003, p. 13).

The FBI reported de Berk had established a close relationship in the case of every victim and had been seen in the vicinity of them before their deaths. Oddly, Lucy reported deterioration in the patients, which contradicted other nurses' observations. She had been accused of stealing drugs that happened to be the same ones the victims had been taking. Intoxication of specific drugs was noted in the deaths of at least two little girls.

Lucy was convicted of four counts of first-degree murder for the injection deaths of three babies and an elderly woman and three counts of attempted murder as well as perjury, falsifying a high school diploma, and theft of several books from the prison library. She received life imprisonment. On appeal, she was convicted of seven counts of murder and four counts of attempted murder.

However, after serving six years of a life sentence, de Berk was not only cleared, released, and exonerated of the crimes, she received a personal apology by the country's attorney general Harm Brouwer, and a financial settlement was discussed ("Court Clears," 2010). It was determined during a subsequent retrial that much of the evidence, highly speculative statistics of probability, was faulty and other circumstantial evidence invalid.

An assertion by a statistician that the odds of her being present during each suspicious death were 1 in 342 million was debunked. A witness who testified about hearing incriminating statements recanted. Deaths previously ruled suspicious were now deemed not to have signs of being unnatural. The damning words found in de Berk's diary regarding her compulsions were later explained away as her desire to use Tarot cards, or according to de Berk's daughter were "pure fiction" written for a novel.

Were there serial murders committed in those hospitals in the Netherlands? It is simply impossible to conclude. It is also impossible to ascertain the involvement of anyone at that scene at this point in time. Still, the de Berk case is an example that facts and analysis of both concluded cases and theoretical concepts accepted for years may or may not be accurate, and may continue to evolve.

2

Clinical Diagnoses and Serial Killer Traits

I actually think I may be possessed with demons, I was dropped
on my head as a kid.

—Dennis Rader/BTK

CLINICAL PHENOMENA AND THE SERIAL KILLER

Many syndromes and clusters of personality traits as recognized by the psychological community are noted in the literature regarding serial killers. The following labels and diagnoses are often assigned to these offenders at some point
in their contact with psychologists or psychiatrists, both before and after their
crimes. Also, many law enforcement agencies, in studying this type of offender,
point to the following characteristics and clinical phenomena in an effort to understand the thought and behavior patterns driving these offenders' behaviors.

THE ANTISOCIAL PERSONALITY

Often, serial killers are described as psychopaths or sociopaths, or in more
widely accepted terminology, as having dissocial or antisocial personality disorder (APD). According to the *Diagnostic and Statistical Manual, Fourth
Edition Text Revision* (*DSM-IV-TR*) (American Psychiatric Association
[APA], 2000, p. 706), the criteria for this disorder includes:

A. Pervasive pattern of disregard for and violation of the rights of others,
   occurring since age 15 as indicated by at least three of the following:

1. Failure to conform to social norms with respect to lawful behavior as indicated by repeatedly performing acts that are grounds for arrest.
2. Deceitfulness, as indicated by repeated lying, use of aliases, or conning others for personal profit or pleasure.
3. Impulsivity or failure to plan ahead.
4. Irritability and aggressiveness, as indicated by repeated physicals fights or assaults.
5. Reckless disregard for the safety of self or others.
6. Consistent irresponsibility, as indicated by repeated failure to sustain consistent work behavior or honor financial obligations.
7. Lack of remorse, as indicated by indifference to or rationalizing having hurt, mistreated, or stolen from another.

B. Individual is at least 18 years of age.
C. Evidence of conduct disorder onset before age 15.
D. The occurrence of the behavior is not exclusively during the course of schizophrenia or a manic episode.

These criteria are particularly relevant to the serial killer, as many such offenders share childhoods colored with demonstrations of behavior consistent with criteria for conduct disorder, such as using weapons, physical cruelty to people and animals, forced sexual activity, and fire setting (APA, 2000 pp. 98–99). Key elements shared by the sociopath or the antisocial personality, and the serial killer are a failure to conform to social norms regarding lawful behavior, physical aggressiveness, impulsivity, lack of regard for the truth, manipulativeness, and most important, lack of remorse or empathy. Remorse is reported by some serial killers after commission of some crimes, but never to the point of their changing their behavior or seeking help, such as Dodd, Nilsen, Dahmer, Bundy, and others.

Causal factors for an antisocial personality include a possible biological predisposition (Andreasen, 1984), childhood trauma (shared by the vast majority of serial killers), possible neurological factors in the control of impulsivity regarding serotonin levels in the brain, and heredity. The *DSM-IV-TR* states that APD is more common among the first-degree biological relatives of those with the disorder than among the general population. Adoption studies indicate that both genetic and environmental factors contribute to the risk (APA, 2000, p. 704).

Those diagnosed with antisocial personalities also share deep-seated doubts regarding their own adequacy (Havens, personal communication, 1993). Most antisocial personalities are men, again reflecting serial killer demographics.

It should be noted, however, that it is not enough to simply describe the serial killer as an antisocial personality. The vast majority of the current prison population shares this diagnosis, as well as many average citizens (Politicians? Car salesmen?) who are not incarcerated. Actually, most of us at some time or another could look over the *DSM-IV-TR*'s criteria and recognize a few qualities close to home. This clustering of traits is helpful, however, as it adds to an overall profile and suggests possible consistencies and etiologies, but the criteria should not be overrated.

THE PSYCHOPATHIC PERSONALITY

Antisocial, sociopath, and psychopath are not interchangeable terms, as often commonly used. *Psychopath* is a far more severe psychological condition in terms of symptoms and treatment. According to Blair, Mitchell, and Blair while 80 percent of U.S. inmates reach diagnostic criteria for APD, only 15–25 percent meet the criteria for psychopathy as established by Hare (Blair et al., 2005, p. 19). Psychopaths and sociopaths are not separately listed in the *DSM-IV-TR,* nor are they found in the World Health Organization's ICD-10 classification. Psychopathy was a term used in earlier versions of the *DSM* but gradually fell under the label of antisocial and is considered basically a synonym of antisocial, describing a subject with a lack of empathy and attachment to others while exhibiting manipulative behavior.

The ICD-10 classification of dissocial identity disorder may be meant to mirror the APD listing, but it does mention a little more in the way of behavior, namely that the behavior is not "readily modifiable by adverse experience, including punishment" and a "low threshold for discharge of aggression, including violence," both characteristics sounding closer to a psychopathic personality. Personality traits listed include amoral, antisocial, asocial, psychopathic, and sociopathic (World Health Organization, 2008, p. 345).

This book, however, strongly supports the position that the psychopaths (and sociopaths) are markedly more severe offenders than antisocials, as established by research on their behaviors. Reportedly the *DSM-V,* currently under development, will re-examine the character issues that separate them from mere antisocials.

The psychopathic offender appears to be predisposed for predatory violence and is the classic serial killer personality. Indeed, this type of personality was the subject of J. Reid Meloy's book, *The Psychopathic Mind: Origins, Dynamics, & Treatment* (1988).

The psychopath, according to Meloy, is a personality incorporating both aggressive narcissism and extended chronic antisocial behavior over time. The personal history of psychopaths shows a trail of used, injured, and hurt people as these individuals tarnish their object world in a continuous effort to build their own fragile sense of self. Robert Hare (1993) noted that psychopaths "have little aptitude for experiencing the emotional responses—fear and anxiety—that are the mainsprings of conscience" (p. 76).

In identifying the psychopath, the revised *Hare Psychopathy Checklist* (*PCL-R*:2nd ed.) (Hare, 2003) measures such traits, most if not all of which are found in the serial killer personality:

1. glibness and superficial charm
2. grandiosity
3. continuous need for stimulation
4. pathological lying
5. conning and manipulativeness
6. lack of remorse or guilt
7. shallow affect
8. callous lack of empathy
9. parasitic lifestyle
10. poor behavioral controls
11. promiscuity
12. early behavior problems
13. lack of realistic, long-term goals
14. impulsivity
15. irresponsibility
16. failure to accept responsibility for actions
17. many short-term relationships
18. juvenile delinquency
19. revocation of conditional release
20. criminal versatility

These traits are comparable to those traits found in the antisocial personality, but the checklist goes a step further in identifying internal as well as external characteristics. This clustering is similar to ones observed in Cleckley's classic work *Mask of Sanity* (1941).

The defining trait of the psychopath has to be considered his or her complete lack of empathy, to the point of simply not understanding remorse or the concern for others. He or she may be able to feign remorse and attempt to say the right things, usually through repetition of counseling and time in the system. In 1989, just hours before his execution, Ted Bundy was interviewed by Dr. James Dobson in a video shot on Death Row in Florida entitled *Fatal Addiction*. Much of Bundy's talk attempted to underline a connection between his development as a killer and an exposure to violent pornography. However, when specifically asked about remorse, his rambling three-and-a-half minute answer sounded like the classic psychopath who was grasping for the words to sound like someone who could convince others of his regret. His words were unconvincingly hollow:

DOBSON: [I]s the remorse . . . there?
BUNDY: I know that people will accuse me of being self-serving but we're beyond that now, I mean I'm just telling you how I feel . . . but, through God's help, I've been able to come to the point where I've, much too late, but better late than never . . . feel the hurt and the pain I've been responsible for. Yes, absolutely. In the past few days myself and a number of investigators have been talking about unsolved cases.

Bundy went straight from trying to convince the listener he was remorseful for his murders to essentially selling his value as someone on death row who could help clear unsolved cases, to discussing violence in the media, people with predisposition like his, kids watching TV at home, and could not help but come across as a person who could not understand the concept of remorse beyond a detached attempt at saying what he thought people might want to hear.

During the penalty phase of his trial, Anthony Sowell took the stand and apologized to his victims' families, without much explanation. After he was given the death penalty, a juror later stated, "we found it [his statement] to be completely rehearsed, completely condescending, complete lack of remorse." Another juror reported Sowell winked at her at one point ("Sowell jury: death sentence," 2011). A surviving victim who saw a headless corpse in Sowell's house said, "Does he feel shame? Does he feel anything?" (Seewer & Sheeran, 2011).

The psychopath is more frequently and severely violent than the antisocial personality, and the violence continues until it reaches a plateau at age 50 or so, whereas nonviolent activity drops off sooner (Hare, McPherson, & Forth, 1988). The psychopath is generally regarded as untreatable.

A key aspect of the psychopath in regard to serial killers is that the violence tends to be predatory and primarily on a stranger-to-stranger basis. The violence is planned, purposeful, and emotionless. This emotionlessness reflects a detached, fearless, and possibly dissociated state, revealing a lower level of impulses generated by the autonomic nervous system and a lack of anxiety. The psychopath's general motivation is to control and dominate, and his history reveals no bonds with others.

Sexually, psychopaths continue their grandiose demeanor and are hypoaroused autonomically, which causes them to be continuously seeking sensation. Their attitude is one of entitlement, not reciprocity. This lack of bonding reflects a lack of emotionality and a diminished capacity for love, where sexual partners are partly objects and are devalued. The psychopath also displays a propensity for sadism (Meloy, 1993). Stanton Samenow once noted that the criminal experiences an "adrenaline rush" by "fantasizing about violence, talking about violence, and behaving violently" (2004, p. 102).

It should be noted that psychopaths tend to "engage in more instrumental, goal-driven homicides," whereas "non-pychopathic offenders engage in predominantly reactive, spontaneous violence" (Bartol & Bartol, 2008, p. 271). Regardless of the psychopath's personal goal and lack of empathy, his behavior is planned and purposeful as opposed to emotional and in response to a stimulus.

In 2010, the journal *Psychological Science* noted a study by University of New Mexico psychologists who observed that psychopaths know the difference between right and wrong, but can fail to weigh the difference when making decisions (Monteleone, 2010). It was observed that the psychopathic inmates studied had demonstrated difficulty in making inferences connecting negative consequences to risky situations as well as failing to connect required actions or compensations to behaviors an average person would understand, such as putting gas in a car after borrowing it.

Experiments conducted by researchers at the University of Wisconsin-Madison (UW) demonstrated psychopaths behaving in a manner similar to those suffering brain damage, reported in the journal *Neuropsychologia* (Doherty, 2010). The experiments support the theory that a defect or wiring flaw in a portion of the brain behind the eyes called the ventromedial prefrontal cortex is responsible for psychopathic behavior. This part of the brain has been identified as the origin for emotions like empathy, guilt, and shame. Research involving games played by inmates at the Wisconsin Department of Corrections showed prisoners diagnosed with primary psychopathy who played the games with UW researchers used the same kinds of strategies and made similar decisions to players who had suffered devastating damage, often due to medical conditions such as strokes and tumors, to this portion of their brain. These subjects reportedly had led normal emotional lives until their brains were damaged.

Blair et al. concluded that if an individual's neurocognitive systems involved in the regulation of reactive aggression and emotional learning are impaired at an early age, the individual "will present with the emotional difficulties associated with psychopathy." Affected areas will include socialization that could result in "elevated levels of instrumental aggression" (Blair et al., 2005, p. 141).

Again, it should also be noted, that the psychopath terminology is commonly used interchangeably with the possibly more commonly used term *sociopath*. In the purest of technical considerations, a sociopath is an offender who more likely learned his or her behavior, while the psychopath appears born with the personality. In any case both offenders will look very much alike in the ensuing discussions of this book: marked absence of empathy, manipulative nature, and using other people, an aggressive, predatory pattern of behavior and no regard for consequences.

Both will also display a certain immaturity that seems to go with the psychopath or the sociopath, a dimension of the personality seeming to reflect a holding pattern at a particular age of development, which almost explains the narcissistic, selfish, and uncaring perspective. Dr. Betty McMahon described Danny Rolling as "extremely immature . . . there is a great impairment of empathy. That is something that tends to come with maturity" (Ryzuk, 1994, p. 388). Rolling said once that "something died" at a very young age and he would always be immature and inadequate (Rolling & London, 1996, p. 9).

BORDERLINE PERSONALITY DISORDER

A comparable condition to APD is borderline personality disorder, which includes a pervasive pattern of instability in interpersonal relationships, self-image, affects, and marked impulsivity. This pattern begins by early adulthood and is present in a variety of contexts, as indicated by the presence of at least five of the following (APA, 2000, pp. 706–710):

1. Frantic efforts to avoid real or imagined abandonment.
2. A pattern of unstable and intense interpersonal relationships characterized by alternating extremes of idealization and devaluation.
3. Identity disturbance; markedly and persistently unstable self-image or sense of self.
4. Impulsivity in at least two areas that are potentially self-damaging.
5. Recurrent suicidal behavior, gestures, threats, or self-mutilating behavior.
6. Affective (emotional) instability due to a marked reactivity of mood.
7. Chronic feelings of emptiness.
8. Inappropriate, intense anger or difficulty controlling anger.
9. Transient, stress-related paranoid ideation or severe dissociative symptoms.

Again, this disorder includes a defective sense of identity and extreme instability. The sufferer often views the world and people as "all good" or "all bad" (Baron-Cohen, 2011, p. 55). This description could relate to the large percentage of female serial killers who act as angels of mercy, who attempt to right the world's wrongs, or who seek revenge and owe the world (or some part of it) a payback. Aileen Wuornos was diagnosed by a prison neuropsychologist as meeting all eight of the criteria for borderline personality disorder (Reynolds, 1992).

Although borderline personality disorder is more often (75%) diagnosed in females, it is not exclusively so, as even Jeffrey Dahmer was diagnosed by prison psychiatrists as having features of this disorder (Dvorchak & Holewa, 1991). Arthur Shawcross also exhibited such characteristics, and John Wayne Gacy was described by a forensic psychiatrist, Richard Rappaport, as utilizing borderline personality organization. Rappaport stated that Gacy brought young boys to his home so he could "star in a play scripted by himself," illustrating a primitive ego defense common to borderlines: projective identification (Cahill, 1986, pp. 339–340).

Causal factors in borderline personality disorder include a history of incest or other sexual abuse and a proneness to experience dysphoria, or a generalized feeling of ill-being, as well as abnormal anxiety, discontent, or physical discomfort, commonly thought to be connected to a problem of the limbic system. Dissociative symptoms may occur during extreme stress. Borderline is approximately five times more common among first-degree biological relatives with the disorder than in the general population.

Both APD and borderline personality disorder display gross deviation from normal attachment processes, which results in a disinhibition of violence (Meloy, 1993). The borderline individual will be pathologically attached, whereas at the other end of the spectrum is the antisocial, who is pathologically detached. Pathological attachment development issues often result in personalities that are criminal, and exhibit traits of the sociopath or the psychopath.

DISSOCIATION

Another phenomenon usually considered in the psychology of the serial murderer is the dissociative state or disorder. Dissociation (Egger, 1990) is the lack of integration of thoughts, feelings, and experiences into the stream of consciousness. In other words, it is a mental separation from the physical place of an individual. Dissociation has been cited as an example of spontaneous self-hypnosis (Bliss, 1986, p. 166). The phenomenon has been used to describe peoples' reactions to various traumatic experiences, as well as a precursor to pathologies described in the *DSM-IV-TR,* such as fugues, amnesias, depersonalization, dissociative identity disorder (formerly multiple personality disorder), and posttraumatic stress disorder (PTSD).

The *DSM-IV-TR* (2000) describes general dissociative disorders as a disruption in the usually integrated functions of consciousness, memory, identity, or perception (p. 519). Disorders include depersonalization disorder, with criteria such as experiencing a feeling of detachment from, and as if one is an outside observer of, one's mental processes or body, like one is in a dream. This statement has been made by many serial murderers.

Morton Prince (1975, p. 291) referred to dissociative states as:

a large category of conditions characterized by alteration of the personality. In this category are to be found various types of alteration, some normal and some abnormal, all due to the same processes and mechanisms and therefore fundamentally resembling one another, in that they are all types of depersonalization and repersonalization from the standpoint of the modern conception of the structure of the personality. Specifically, these types are known as sleep, hypnosis, fugues, trance, somnambulisms, multiple personality, etc.

Causality regarding dissociative states includes severe childhood trauma and some evidence of a physical predisposition. Many of those who experience dissociative states are of above-average intelligence, another trait found in many serial killers.

Literature involving serial killers and the possible presence of a dissociative state is extensive:

Jeffrey Dahmer: He couldn't embrace. He couldn't touch. His eyes were dead.

(Dvorchak & Holewa, 1991, p. 32)

Ted Bundy: I looked up at Ted and our eyes locked. His face had gone blank, as though he was not there at all.

(Kendall, 1981)

Bundy himself stated after a murder he would be coming out of a horrible trance or dream.

(Dobson, 1989)

Dayton Leroy Rogers: He seemed to be slipping in and out of a fantasy state [while calling the victim someone else's name] . . . he was all-consumed by the deep mental state he was in.

(King, 1992, pp. 30, 38)

Wayne Nance: He [the victim] looked him straight in the eye. He saw nothing: no glee, no remorse, just a dead gaze.

(Coston, 1992, p. 313)

Bobby Joe Long: It was like a dream me doing it.

(Norris, 1992, p. 125)

Even beyond the serial killer, violent crime continues reports of what would seem to be dissociative states. An Indiana teenager who strangled his 10-year-old brother told his girlfriend he wanted to be just like a fictional TV serial killer and fantasized about killing people since the eighth grade. Andrew Conley described the murder as "watching the murder from outside himself" (Wilson, 2010). A Jamaican American mass murderer on Long Island, Colin Ferguson shot and killed 6 and wounded 19 more while being described as "he had a blank look on his face" (Ramsland, 2005a). In Kansas City, a woman convicted of killing an expectant mother, cutting the baby from her womb and stealing the child, reported being in a dreamlike state during the murder (Duclos, 2008). In 2011, Levi Aron admitted to killing an eight-year-old and dismembering him. Later, he was described in a psychiatric evaluation as, "his mood is neutral, practically blank" ("Levi Aron," 2011).

It should be noted that it's not uncommon for defense attorneys to concoct insanity defenses centered around offenders who don't remember committing an offense. Dissociative states should not be confused with psychotic or delusional episodes or hallucinations. Still, many of these reports of disassociation are plausible especially in the cases of serial killers and others when the reports are made by witnesses' observations.

These episodes indicate a certain level of dissociative process, albeit on a minor scale. Usually, the process does not appear as a full-blown dissociative disorder, such as a psychogenic fugue state or multiple personality disorder and does not enter into the psychopathology of the serial killer. These disorders have not been documented or confirmed with any frequency (if at all) and are often the basis for an attempt at malingering or are used as the basis for an insanity defense (e.g., Bianchi, Gacy).

Drawing a parallel between a psychopathic personality and the dissociated demeanor of the serial murderer, Meloy (1992) noted that "psychopathy is, among other things, a disorder of profound detachment." He added, "from this conscienceless, detached psychology emerges a heightened risk of violence, most notably a capacity for predation" (p. xvii).

DOUBLING

The discussion of dissociation leads to mention of a recent theory in the psychology of rationalizing killing, that of doubling. Robert J. Lifton, in *The Nazi Doctors* (2000, p. 418), refers to doubling as:

> the division of the self into two functioning wholes, so that a part-self acts as an entire self. An Auschwitz doctor could, through doubling, not only kill and contribute to killing but organize silently, on behalf of that evil project, an entire self-structure (or self process) encompassing virtually all aspects of his behavior.

This self process could easily be the phenomenon exhibited when a killer appears to be in a different or detached state, watching what is going on rather than being the direct participant, thus removing himself or herself from the feelings and responsibilities of murder. Lifton speaks of the benefits of doubling, including the connection of the two selves. This connection could allow serial killers to put on a mask of sanity when not participating in crimes, as well as to avoid guilt, which might otherwise be utilized in a typical antisocial personality. Finally, the unconscious dimension of doubling takes place largely outside of awareness, allowing an alteration of moral consciousness. The serial killer who attaches critical importance to his or her acts, and is driven by the fantasy and then the act, can incorporate those acts through this unconscious dimension. It is an active psychological process, a means of adaptation to extremity (pp. 418–430). Robert Ressler, veteran profiler for the FBI, has stated "psychopaths . . . are known for their ability to separate the personality who commits the crimes from their more in-control selves" (1992, p. 154). This sounds very much like Lifton's principles.

James S. Grotstein speaks of the development of a "separate being, living within one that has been preconsciously split off and has an independent existence with independent motivation, separate agenda, etc." and from which can emanate "evil, sadism, destructiveness or even demoniacal possession" (1979, pp. 36–52). He attributes its development to those elements of the self that have been artificially suppressed and disavowed early in life.

The phenomenon of doubling appears to have been observed even by Freud (1938), who coined the term *splitting* to identify dissociation in relation to repression. This was further specified by Kohut (1971, pp. 176–177, 183) by conceptualizing vertical, rather than horizontal, splits in the psyche, noting the "side-by-side existence of cohesive personality attitudes with different goal structures, different pleasure aims, different moral and aesthetic values."

According to Lifton, doubling can include elements considered characteristic of sociopathic impairment, such as a disorder of feelings, pathological avoidance of a sense of guilt, and resort to violence to overcome a masked depression. Murderous behavior may thereby cover a feared disintegration of the self, a concept that appears so critical and so damaged in the view of a serial killer.

NARCISSISTIC PERSONALITY DISORDER

The *DSM-IV-TR* describes the narcissistic personality as that having a pervasive pattern of grandiosity (in fantasy or behavior), with need for admiration and a lack of empathy. The pattern begins by early adulthood, and is present in a variety of contexts, as indicated by at least five of the following (2000, pp. 714–717):

1. Has a grandiose sense of self-importance.
2. Is preoccupied with fantasies of unlimited success, power, brilliance, beauty, or ideal love.
3. Believes that he or she is special and unique and can only be understood by, or should associate with, other special or high-status people or institutions.
4. Requires excessive admiration.
5. Has a sense of entitlement.
6. Is interpersonally exploitative.
7. Lacks empathy.
8. Is often envious of others or believes that others are envious of him or her.
9. Shows arrogant, haughty behaviors or attitudes.

Most of these traits can be found in the serial killer's personality (e.g., Bundy, Wuornos, Alcala, Gacy—and so many more). Aggressive narcissism is pervasive in the classic psychopath and features a pronounced sadistic streak (Meloy, 1992).

All these features were found in Angelo Buono and Kenneth Bianchi, the "Hillside Stranglers." When asked by a prison inmate why he killed all those girls, Buono brazenly declared, "They were no good, they deserved to die. It had to be done" (O'Brien, 1985, p. 301). Many other witnesses, including even Bianchi, noted one of Buono's favorite phrases was "some girls deserve to die."

OBSESSIVE COMPULSIVENESS

Another pattern that seems to emerge with serial killers is the presence of obsessive-compulsive traits. Obsessive-compulsive disorder (OCD) can manifest in *obsessions*, defined as recurrent and persistent ideas, thoughts, impulses, or images, that are experienced as intrusive and inappropriate and that cause anxiety or distress—for example, a parent's horrific impulses to hurt one's child (APA, 2000, p. 457). Additionally, the thoughts, impulses, or images are not simply excessive worries about real-life problems; the person attempts to ignore or suppress such thoughts or impulses or to neutralize them with other thoughts or actions. The person, while owning a sense that the content of the obsession is not the kind of thought he or she would expect to have, recognizes these obsessions as a product of his or her own mind (p. 457).

Also apparent are *compulsions*, defined as repetitive behaviors or mental acts performed in order to prevent or reduce anxiety or distress. The behavior is designed to reduce the distress that accompanies an obsession or to prevent some dreaded event or situation; however, the activity is not connected in a realistic way with what it is designed to neutralize or it is clearly excessive. Also, the person recognizes that his or her behavior is excessive or unreasonable. In the course of the disorder after repeated failure to resist the obsessions and compulsions, the individual may give in to them, no longer experience a desire to resist them and may incorporate them into his or her daily routines (APA, 2000, pp. 457–458).

Similar behavior patterns on a smaller scale (obsessive-compulsive personality disorder) feature a number of diagnostic criteria, four of which are required for diagnosis of the disorder. They include:

1. Preoccupation with details, rules, lists, order, organization, or schedules to the extent that the major point of the activity is lost.
2. Shows perfectionism that interferes with task completion.
3. Is excessively devoted to work and productivity to the exclusion of leisure activities and friendships (not accounted for by obvious economic necessity).
4. Is overconscientious, scrupulous, and inflexible about matters of morality, ethics, or values.
5. Is unable to discard worn-out or worthless objects even when they have no sentimental value.
6. Is reluctant to delegate tasks or to work with others unless they submit to exactly his or her way of doing things.
7. Adopts a miserly spending style toward both self and others; money is viewed as something to be hoarded for future catastrophes.
8. Shows rigidity and stubbornness (APA, 2000, p. 729).

Obsessive-compulsive people often have problems expressing aggressive feelings and so they stifle them, causing an implosion of emotions that could cause great internal damage. They often have a history of stress, are twice as often males, and are often children of people with OCD or personality disorder themselves. The obsessive-compulsive condition often precedes the onset of depression.

Also apparent is a biological link other than the aforementioned heredity. One hypothesis is there are communication difficulties between the brain's frontal lobes and its basal ganglia, buried deep in the lower part of the brain. This creates problems of integrating sensory, motor, and cognitive processes, and results in persistent unwanted thoughts and involuntary actions (Bruno, 1993, p. 147).

It seems that these traits are yet another dimension easily applied to a great number of serial killers, yet often overlooked by the literature. Consider the obsessive rituals of a David Berkowitz, the compulsive habits of a Dayton Rogers or Robert Berdella, the terror of the dreaded event (potentially being alone) of a Jeffrey Dahmer. The obsessive compulsion of killing is easily viewed as a strategy to avoid the distress in store after failing to find a victim when the urge is great. Obsessive-compulsive behavior often shows up in males, and there are strong suggestions of genetic or biological links. Most important, the extreme insistence of these personalities that others follow their rules sounds deadly similar to the emotions of those whose main pathology stem from a need to dominate and control.

Dr. Jonathan Pincus made the observation about serial killers he's studied: "What I find puzzling is the obsessively repetitive features of the details of the crime in serial killing. Each killer has a specific modus operandi. This bespeaks some kind of perverse need that must be satisfied in a particular manner" (2001, p. 129). While Pincus does not specifically refer to the clinical disorder of obsessive compulsiveness, he certainly describes this in the serial killer's nature as well as his need to kill.

A final consideration is the actual process of completing compulsive acts. First, there is the cycle of discomfort and anxiety, followed by the act (which relieves the tension), followed by a period of guilt and/or a reliving of the act. This process mirrors the apparent cycle of a serial killer's activities: the urge, the act, and the cooling-off period. The process can also include post-offense behavior, such as reliving the fantasy that has become reality, getting involved with the investigation, or returning to significant locations (Douglas, Ressler, Burgess, & Hartman, 1986).

POSTTRAUMATIC STRESS

Another condition to be considered is PTSD. Earlier versions of the *DSM* described this condition as experiencing an event outside the range of usual human experience and that would be markedly distressing to almost anyone, which could describe the early experiences of many serial murderers. The *DSM-IV-TR* goes on to note that the essential feature is the development of characteristic symptoms following exposure to an extreme traumatic stressor involving direct personal experience involving death, serious injury, or a threat to the physical integrity of another person. Other diagnostic features include the experience of intense fear, helplessness or horror, the symptoms of reexperiencing of the traumatic event, persistent avoidance of stimuli related to the trauma and a numbing of general responsiveness as well as symptoms of increased arousal (2000, p. 463).

Specific behaviors include recurrent and intrusive recollections of the event, including distressing dreams and dissociative states featuring flashbacks. Persistent avoidance of stimuli associated with the trauma include a detachment or estrangement from other people and a markedly reduced ability to feel emotions, especially those associated with intimacy and also showing diminished responsiveness to the external world, referred to as "psychic numbing" or "emotional anesthesia," usually soon after the traumatic event (2000, p. 464). Victims of PTSD also report an inability to have loving feelings, a sense of a foreshortened future, irritability, outbursts of anger, and difficulty in concentrating.

The childhood trauma that all serial killers seem to share, whether emotional, physical, sexual, or a combination, would most likely fit the description of a distressing event, serious enough to cause these symptoms. Henry Lee Lucas and Andrei Chikatilo are extreme examples. Certainly, the dissociative trances of a Jeffrey Dahmer, Ted Bundy, or an Edmund Kemper could be interpreted as an example of posttraumatic response.

REACTIVE ATTACHMENT DISORDER

If there has been a significant development in the study of serial murder psychopathology since *The Psychology of Serial Murder* was first published, it's the research on reactive attachment disorder. While poor attachment has always been considered, research connecting severe attachment issues and possibly psychopathic or sociopathic behaviors has been clear. From the ATTACh (Association for the Treatment and Training of Attachment in Children, 2011) website:

Many children throughout the world do not benefit from adequate parenting during their early years. Their foundation for healthy development is damaged so they have difficulty in forming loving, lasting, intimate relationships. This condition, known as attachment disorder, can be triggered by abuse, neglect, abandonment, separation from birth parents, birth trauma, maternal depression, chronic illness, frequent moves and placements, and even divorce. Parents find that children with this condition are less responsive to direction, less eager to please and more aggressive. These children are at increased risk for serious psychological problems in adolescence and adulthood.

Attachment pathology is often related to many of the issues discussed in this chapter, such as dissociation, childhood personality disorders, and elements of psychopathology. Children who have been mistreated often develop a disorganized attachment style that is related to dissociation and a lack of sense of self (Ingram & Price, 2010, p. 88). This is considered a defense mechanism created in order to protect the self as a response to trauma. Ingram and Price also reference Ogawa's 1997 observation that insecure attachment, dissociation, a lack of sense of self, and trauma are related to later disassociation in the context of traumatic experiences (p. 89). Connections to later development of borderline personality disorder were also observed.

As well, Ingram and Price observed studies that correlate insecure attachment histories to subjects falsely representing their esteem as overly high to overcompensate for an actual feeling of worthlessness. These behaviors often resembled behavior by those exhibiting narcissistic personality disorders. Also noted is the fact that children's vulnerability to depression increases, particularly when exposed to new interpersonal stressors, if they have developed insecure attachments according to Bowlby's 1980 attachment theory (2010, p. 217).

Licensed clinical social worker and child and adolescent therapist Cathy Clevenger notes that children suffering from severe attachment pathology are stuck in the security phase, as commonly referenced in Abraham Maslow's Hierarchy of Needs. "These children have never learned to trust, never developed empathy," says Clevenger. "They are stuck in survival mode, hoarding food, never experiencing comfort, developing severe control issues because they cannot control their environments or depend on caregivers." Clevenger states that the severely attachment disordered child will often display personality traits similar to the psychopath, most notably manipulativeness, control-oriented behavior, lies and stealing, destructiveness, a lack of impulse control, evidence of the MacDonald triad, hypervigilance, and displays a lack of conscience or remorse (personal communication, 2011; also from the attachment disorder site, 2011).

The most striking confluence of attachment issues and clinical issues related to the serial murderer personality type is the development of a severe lack of empathy, as seen in the APD or most specific, the psychopathic or sociopathic personality found in the serial killer. Ingram and Price observed, "one pathway toward a lack of concern for others might include an early avoidant attachment relationship, instilling a view of others that is threatening or hostile" (2010, p. 92). Ingram noted the correlation between Cleckley's and Hare's research on psychopaths noted previously in this chapter. Children with a history of damaged attachment who are prone to develop problematic impulsivity and severe lack of empathy are highly comparable to the violently narcissistic psychopath or sociopath who exemplifies the nature of the serial murderer.

During his 2011 trial, serial murderer Anthony Sowell made statements about his mother's lack of nurturing when he was a child and talked about his inability to hug his sisters and that he could not hold their hands.

Other Disorders—ADHD, Depression, and Bipolar Disorder

Research has continued to tie attention-deficit hyperactivity disorder (ADHD) to crime. In 2009, a Yale School of Public Health study found that children with ADHD are more likely to commit crimes as adults (Nadelmann, 2009). After controlling for race, education, and income level, Yale School of Public Health assistant professor Jason Fletcher and UW researcher Barbara Wolfe found that certain types of crime were linked to particular symptoms of ADHD in children ages 5 to 12. A report by the Center for Science in the Public Interest showed a strong relationship between ADHD and risk for criminality, even in the absence of childhood conduct problems as some studies connecting hyperactivity and adult psychopathology state ("ADHD: New evidence of crime link," 2007). This echoed a 1997 study that found childhood hyperactivity, even when not combined with conduct problems, is a strong risk for later violence and other issues. Studies show that at least 25 percent of prisoners in U.S. prisons suffered from ADHD (Young, 2010).

Much of the connection appears to stem from impulsive behavior, depression, and engaging in risky behavior. However, it should be noted that it appears when individuals with ADHD commit violent crimes, these acts are more likely to be crimes of spontaneous and reactive aggression rather than carefully plotted out offenses. Such crimes are generally impulsive acts driven by a provocation or conflict (Young, 2010). This would be at odds with the profile of the predatory behavior of the prototypical serial killer. However, these killers do demonstrate a need for power and control, a trait shared by young fire setters with "internal imbalances like attention deficit disorder" (Kolko, 2002, p. 224).

Depression can be connected to crime in a number of ways, often in conjunction with other mental disorders and environmental factors. Also, depression has been connected to magnesium deficiency. The activity of serotonin receptors is affected by changes in magnesium levels. This suggests that part of the high rate of violent crime could be mitigated by ending the magnesium deficiencies (Mason, 1998).

A study from Sweden's Karolinska Institute suggests that bipolar disorder (manic or depressive features) does not increase the risk of committing violent crimes. It states the overrepresentation of individuals with bipolar disorder in violent crime statistics is attributable to concurrent substance abuse ("Bipolar disorder," 2010). Some previous research has also suggested that patients with bipolar disorder are more likely to behave violently. However, it has been unclear if the violence is due to the bipolar disorder per se or caused by other aspects of the individual's personality or lifestyle.

INSANITY: AN UNCLEAR CONCEPT

Not mentioned as yet is the possibility that serial killers are psychotic, insane, or simply mentally ill. This may be an issue of semantics, as many will say that anyone who commits atrocities such as savage rape, torture, murder, dismemberment, or cannibalism, surely must be crazy. The idea is that, for one to be able to kill and handle dismembered body parts, the person must be insane. This is commonly referred to as the *res ipsa loquitur* argument—the theory (actually, the thing) speaks for itself (Masters, 1992). It's a common refrain among defense attorneys. It was the claim by the defense in the Dahmer insanity claim in 1992 and was no different as made by Anthony Sowell's attorney 19 years later—the idea that living in a house with the rotting remains of his murder victims—means the "man is sick in the head" (Sheeran, 2011c).

Some people feel that the insanity defense requirements are purposefully difficult to ensure conviction of violent offenders. This could be a reasonable conclusion in light of changes resulting from the Hinckley case after his attack on Ronald Reagan and his acquittal by reason of insanity in 1983. Tougher requirements resulted including the removal of the volitional prong (conforming conduct) from the prosecution (Packer, 2009) and requiring the defense to provide an affirmative defense in federal cases. Cheney (1992) felt in the Edmund Kemper trial, "everyone [was] afraid to find out that there was something really wrong with the defendant" (p. 190), and she states that the "disparity between medical and legal definitions of insanity perpetuate a fiction which is bizarre and actually harmful, however soothing to some members of the public" (p. 173).

In 2006, Chicago, Illinois serial killer Paul Runge's insanity defense was rejected after a psychologist testified he was a sexual sadist with little control over his impulses to attack women (Coen, 2006). Earlier at trial, Runge's defense attempted to claim he should be exempt from the death penalty because his obsessive-compulsive sexual sadism could be likened to mental retardation, causing him to not be able to process information or learn from mistakes.

Those on the prosecution's side will disagree. E. Michael McCann, prosecuting the Dahmer case, drove home this point to the jury: "Committing an unnatural act, such as having sex with a dead body, does not in itself denote insanity" (O'Donnell, 1992, p. 14). Even the judge at the Dennis Nilsen trial pointed out that "a mind can be evil without being abnormal" (Masters, 1992, p. 269).

What makes the insanity plea so difficult is it is inherently confusing. "It's an attempt to explain rationally the irrational," says William Moffit, an Alexandria, Virginia, defense attorney (Toufexis, 1992, p. 17). The term *insanity* bears little resemblance to common or even what is considered medical usage. Insanity is, actually, only a legal term, and is certainly not found in a diagnostic manual such as the *DSM-IV*.

Generally, the legal test is whether, at the time the crime was committed, the defendant was suffering from a mental defect that made him incapable of telling right from wrong. Some states also consider whether a defendant's mental illness impaired his or her ability to control his or her actions. The Dahmer case hinged on this irresistible impulse defense (Toufexis, 1992).

It is often assumed that the defendant must at least be suffering from a psychosis, not a personality disorder (i.e., APD, which is usually specifically excluded as a defense), to qualify for an insanity defense. Most states mirror the American Law Institute's (ALI) insanity standard, which includes the caveat that the terms mental disease and mental defect "do not include an abnormality manifested only by repeated criminal or otherwise antisocial conduct."

This language was specifically intended to prevent defendants identified as sociopaths or psychopaths from using the defense (Packer, 2009, pp. 12–13).

However, a key point to remember is that even the presence of psychosis is not enough. Merely being schizophrenic does not automatically exculpate one from one's actions. According to the American Law Institute's standard, it must be proven that the accused's mental condition was the reason for his or her not being able to "appreciate the wrongfulness" of his or her actions or be "unable to conform his [or her] conduct to the requirements of the law" (Packer, 2009; Smith & Meyer, 1987, p. 389). Case law in the 1950s required that the criminal act must be considered a product of the mental illness; simply the presence of a mental illness was not enough. Another factor is the varied requirements for meeting standards for insanity in different states or in federal court. Requirements of volition, intent, mens rea, products of mental disease, diminished capacity, impulses, appreciation, substantial capacity, and many other terms vary wildly between different regions and in the minds of different jurors. However, the issue of not guilty by reason of insanity is one for the courts to decide, more specifically, the juries, mainly because the concept of insanity is purely a legal one, not a medical or scientific one, decided eventually in each case by citizen jurists, not by expert witnesses.

In Illinois, for instance, the insanity statute or definition is pretty simple: "§ 5-1-11. Insanity. 'Insanity' means the lack of a substantial capacity to appreciate the criminality of one's conduct as a result of mental disorder or mental defect" (Illinois General Assembly, 2012).

Very few serial killers are found insane, but some (e.g., DeSalvo, Lucas, Chase, Corona, and Kemper) have been diagnosed as psychotic or schizophrenic at some times. All would appear to have some mental disorders. Still, the majority of individuals considered in this book appeared to understand the difference between right and wrong and seemed aware of the circumstances and results of their actions. Essentially all were aware of the law's requirements enough to conceal their actions.

Rodney Alcala made an interesting observation when asked why he bit a victim's breasts during an assault: "You're in an unreasoning situation. Your brain and you just don't know what to do. It's not like do this, do that. You're not reasoning. You've lost your ability to reason. You're not thinking. . . . I raped her" (Lasseter, 2004, p. 19).

Ted Bundy, admitting he was well aware of what he was doing, just made reference to the compulsion:

I don't have a split personality. I don't have blackouts. I remember everything I've done. [After one killing] we went out for ice cream after eating hamburgers. It wasn't like I had forgotten or couldn't remember, but it was just over . . . gone . . . the force wasn't pushing me anymore.

(Kendall, 1981, p. 175)

Dr. Park Dietz (1992b), the widely respected insanity defense expert, noted in a statement following the Dahmer trial:

> If the jury had found Mr. Dahmer insane, it would have been open season for sex offenders, because the core of the defense theory was that sexually deviated men cannot control their behavior. . . . [They] are precisely analogous to the disorders found among most child molesters, serial rapists and serial killers, as well as many of those committing sex offenses.

SUMMARY: THE CLINICAL PERSPECTIVE

In considering the theories brought out in this section, a pattern emerges. It seems that while serial killers show many syndromes as described in the field of clinical psychology, "there is no single diagnostic category [at this time] that fits these individuals. The pathology of serial murderer is a separate diagnostic category" (Apsche, 1993, p. 10). Illinois and Missouri serial killer and rapist Timothy Krajcir simply described himself in a confession as "twisted" ("Sex offender confesses," 2007).

Labels such as antisocial, borderline, narcissistic, and psychopath do apply; phenomena such as dissociation, doubling, posttraumatic stress, and obsessive-compulsive behavior can be observed. Many of these states have overlapping features and etiology. There are shared biological or neurological aspects in most cases, indicating a possible physical factor. For most serial killers, there definitely appears to be a history of physical, sexual, or mental abuses. Finally, and possibly most important, these killers seem to evidence a pervasive lost sense of self and intimacy, an inadequacy of identity, and a feeling of no control. These could all be factors in a pathology that manifests itself in the ultimate act of control—the murder, and repeated murder, of other human beings.

3

Biology and Its Effect on Violent Behavior

I am a mistake of nature. I deserve to be done away with.

—Andrei Chikatilo

BIOLOGICAL PERSPECTIVES

The notion of nature or biology as a key element in social deviance reaches as far back as criminologist Cesare Lombroso in the late 19th century. Lombroso observed the physical correlations between violent (born) criminals and certain animals, or beasts of prey. His distinction between the born criminal and the occasional criminal (one led to criminality owing to illness or difficult situation) marks the predatory nature of the serial killer.

Soon after Lombroso's declarations regarding the inherited nature of criminal tendencies, confirmatory evidence was provided in a book by sociologist Richard Dugdale. Included was a study of a clan led by two sons who married their illegitimate sisters; the results showed that out of more than 700 descendants, only 6 did not become prostitutes or criminals. Another sociologist, Henry H. Goddard, studied a soldier who had fathered a baby by a feeble-minded girl, then married a Quaker girl from an honest and intelligent family. Nearly five hundred of the Quaker girl's descendants were traced, none of whom were criminals; of the same number of descendants of the feeble-minded girl, only 10 percent were normal (Wilson, 1989, pp. 177–179).

Research has grown throughout the years and continued to indicate that aggressiveness and criminality do have a genetic factor (Pervin, 1989).

Identical twins are twice as likely as fraternal twins to be similar in their criminal activity. A close relationship has also been found between antisocial behavior in adopted children and such behavior in their biological parents. A
pioneer in this field, Dr. Adrian Raine of the University of Pennsylvania, states
on his Department of Criminology Faculty profile (2011) that his main area
of interest is "*Neurocriminology*—an emerging sub-discipline of criminology
which applies neuroscience to probe the causes and cures of crime." Dr. Raine
and his colleagues' research focus, which includes "childhood conduct disorder, reactive and proactive aggression, adult antisocial personality disorder,
homicide, and psychopathy," simply continues to pave a path in this explod-
ing arena of research.

One fascinating observation made by Raine and Sanmartin (2001) was a
measure of what might be more influential, deprived family environment or
poor brain functioning. His research included the positron emission tomography (PET) scans of murderers of a control group, a group of deprived (poor
home life) murderers and those from a relatively good household. The PET
scans of the normal or control group and the murderers in the deprived group
looked most alike, whereas the scans of the murderers from the good homes
were markedly different. The inference was that the brain functioning of the
murderers influenced by a bad environment was reasonably normal, but the
killers from a good environment were more influenced by the abnormal, lack
of prefrontal brain functioning than they were by their environments (pp.
43–44). Raine found that the murderers from good homes showed a 14.2
percent rate of reduced functioning of the right orbitofrontal cortex, a brain
area they found was of particular interest. According to Raine, "damage to
this brain area in previously well-controlled adults results in personality and
emotional deficits that parallel criminal psychopathic behavior" or what other
researchers termed "acquired sociopathy" (p. 44).

An analysis of case histories shows a steady pattern of inherited biological and/or physical abnormalities in serial killers. Many such killers, over
the course of their abusive upbringings, suffered head injuries and trauma
directly—for example, Henry Lee Lucas, Albert DeSalvo, and Bobby Joe
Long. Head injuries have been known to cause markedly abnormal personality changes, as well as can affect higher brain functions, such as mediation
of instincts (as in rage, aggression, violence, and sexual gratification). The
cerebral disturbances of some individuals are detected by neurological signs as
temporal lobe epilepsy and electroencephalogram (EEG) abnormalities. John
Wayne Gacy is just one serial killer diagnosed with epilepsy. Others exhibit
irregular EEGs under special circumstances—for example, after drinking alcohol (Levin & Fox, 1985, p. 31). One killer's abnormal EEG was referred to
as a "neurophysiological handicap" that weakened his ability to resist the psy-
chogenetically induced impulse to kill (Revitch & Schlesinger, 1981, p. 22).

There is a striking prevalence of neurological impairment among juvenile
killers. In a study done by Dr. Dorothy Otnow-Lewis, all 14 of the death
row inmates in her sample had a history of symptoms consistent with brain
damage, including head injuries severe enough to result in hospitalization

and/or indention of the cranium. In addition, serious documented neurological abnormalities such as focal brain injury, abnormal head circumference, abnormal reflexes, seizure disorders, and abnormal EEG readings were found (Ewing, 1990, p. 9).

Other neurological signals include epilepsy (as in the case of Gacy), dyslexia, and other learning disorders. A classic example is Bobby Joe Long. His congenital dysfunction of the endocrine system caused him to develop breasts at puberty, and according to Norris (1992), experience a lunar protomenstrual cycle for life. It is noted some experts disagree that such a cycle could even exist. Combined with his brain injuries from a motorcycle accident and four other severe head traumas before the age of 10, this condition must have had an impact on his insatiable sex drive, persistent headaches, and violent personality.

THE MACDONALD TRIAD

Another support for the theory of physical abnormality is the presence of behavior clusters commonly referred to as the *MacDonald triad*. These behaviors include late enuresis (bed-wetting, later than five years of age), fire setting, and animal abuse and torture. MacDonald studied 48 psychotic and 52 non-psychotic patients and found that "very sadistic patients often had [these] three in common in their childhood histories" (Merz-Perez & Heide, 2004, p. 6).

Various researchers since MacDonald's 1963 study have asserted that these characteristics, as well as other displays of impulse control possibly traced to a neurological origin, can be predictive of future violence (Revitch & Schlesinger, 1981, p. 177). As cited in Slavkin (2001), "the co-morbidity of these behaviors and their predictive power in identifying adult criminal behavior have been verified in a number of studies" (Lester, 1975; Prentky & Carter, 1984; Robbins & Robbins, 1967; Rothstein, 1963; Wax & Haddox, 1974). As far back as 1940, Yarnell (cited in Slavkin, 2001) called this grouping an *ego triad,* observing problems with enuresis and cruelty to animals in young fire setters. These specific control issues are further discussed within the context of the triad in Chapter 4.

While MacDonald's study resulted in his observation that very sadistic patients shared the common characteristics of enuresis, fire setting, and torturing small animals, he was not convinced that the appearance of the triad was a valuable predictor of future homicidal behavior (Merz-Perez & Heide, 2004). However, Hellman and Blackman's (1966) study concluded that the triad was important in predicting violent antisocial behavior when noted in childhood. Their argument stated that the voiding represented in enuresis equated in fantasy with damaging and destroying, representing sadism and hostility. They said fire setting was a "manifestation of the type of aggression associated with enuresis" and that the two characteristics were intimately related. Hellman and Blackman also concluded the torture of dogs and cats, which "violated the human bond with pets," was a more significant predictor of future violent behavior than the torture of other small animals such as turtles and flies (pp. 6–7).

Trauma to the Brain

Brain injuries litter the landscape of violent behavior. Earle Leonard Nelson, known as the "Gorilla man," murdered almost two dozen women in the mid-1920s. He was thrown from a trolley when he was 10 and lay comatose for nearly a week. His behavior reportedly became even more bizarre from that point on (Schechter & Everitt, 1997, p. 111). He complained of headaches, memory loss, and was increasingly aggressive.

Dr. Adrian Raine's 1994 brain-scan study, discussed earlier, revealed that adults convicted of violent crimes showed impaired function in a key area of the brain linked to impulse control (Baron-Cohen, 2011; Elias, 1994). The findings add to the growing evidence that biological qualities may predispose a person to violent acts. However, Raine noted, "that doesn't mean these brain functions aren't caused by the environment." Dr. Raine said the impairment could be inborn and/or caused by a variety of experiences, including violent shaking by adults in childhood, concussions, gunshot wounds, or even bad falls.

Dr. Raine did PET brain scans on 22 adults arrested for murder or attempted murder. Each exam was compared to the scan of a matched adult of the same age, but who had never been accused of a violent crime. Findings showed evidence of significantly fewer active cells—meaning lower function in two brain areas crucial to impulse control that are located in the prefrontal cortex. No other brain dysfunctions were found.

Dr. Dorothy Otnow-Lewis, in describing some of the "overkill" of violent offenses found in the case of "Lucky" Larson, compared his actions to a "decorticate cat" (Otnow-Lewis, 1998, pp. 125–126). She explained a cat with a cortex surgically separated from the rest of the brain appears normal at first glance. It purrs and responds to affection. The doctor states the cat's "responses to stimuli that ordinarily would cause expressions of mild discomfort or annoyance are no longer moderated by the frontal cortex." This stimulation causes the cat to become "ferocious, directing its attack at anything it perceives as threatening or uncomfortable." The 54 stab wounds Lucky Larson inflicted on a hapless convenience store clerk, according to Otnow-Lewis and her colleague, Dr. Jonathan Pincus, were the result of "the expression of a limbic system released from higher cortical control" and should not be "held completely responsible for behaviors beyond his control."

Otnow-Lewis's study included testimony about Johnny Garrett, who was executed in Texas in 1992 for the rape and murder of a nun when he was 17. Johnny's cousin stated:

> Grandma hit me in the head with a pipe. . . . Grandma hit Johnny in the head a lot of times. . . . She would just up and hit him with whatever she had close by. . . . Grabbed one of those things that you put in shoes and hit him in the head with that thing until he went to sleep. That's what

she did when she wanted us to go to sleep. She would hit us in the head until we passed out.

(Otnow-Lewis, 1998, p. 263)

Otnow-Lewis drew a comparison between the brain damage of Lucky Larson with another murderer, Marie Moore. She noted that the medical history of Moore underlined a brain disorder. She stated that a computerized axial tomography (CAT) scan revealed "a very striking pattern of frontal lobe atrophy with widening of the interhemispheric fissure and some lesser atrophy of the vermis of the cerebellum," according to the attending neuroradiologist (Otnow-Lewis, 1998, pp. 163–164). Otnow-Lewis wondered if the damage was a result of a car accident Moore was involved in when she was hit by the windshield, or possibly from a previous attack with a baseball bat. Her history also included complaints of blackouts, memory lapses, enuresis, violent episodes, unexplained thefts as a child, buzzing in her ears, passing out, and body numbness (p. 164). At one point, her childhood neurologist declared her problems were emotional, but Otnow-Lewis points to her frontal lobe damage as yet another example of erratic behavior, most notably her shacking-up with a very young man and inferred that their kidnapping, torture, and murder of a young girl was related to brain damage.

The effects of cumulative brain trauma on behavior continue to find their way into the news. Athletes such as college football player Owen Thomas and former National Football League (NFL) Chicago Bears' star Dave Duerson experienced depression, erratic behavior, and committed suicide in 2010 and 2011, respectively. Postmortem brain analyses revealed a degenerative condition described as chronic traumatic encephalopathy (CTE). This condition has been found in more than 20 deceased NFL players (Silcox, 2010) and high school and college football players as well as wrestlers, boxers, and more recently National Hockey League (NHL) players such as Bob Probert and Reggie Fleming, both known for their aggressive, physical play ("Researchers," 2011). In a tragically short period of time, three former enforcers in the NHL died in the summer of 2011: Wade Belak, Derek Boogaard, and Rick Rypien, the latter two in their 20s and Belak only 35. Rypien had suffered from depression for years and Belak, who hanged himself, appeared to as well. Boogaard suffered multiple concussions in his years as a hockey fighter and his family donated his brain to the same Boston University where researchers discovered the evidence of CTE in Fleming and Probert. Former NHL tough guy Stu Grimson commented that if science shows a prolonged career in the role of enforcer has a high correlation to traumatic brain disease, "That's not going to come as a surprise to anybody" (Brady & Allen, 2011, 10C).

Professional wrestler Chris Benoit's story was the most tragic. In 2007 over a three-day period, Benoit strangled his wife and son, and hung himself. While different theories flew regarding his behavior, it was determined that drugs, most notably steroids, were not a causal factor. However, a fellow wrestler contacted Chris Benoit's father and suggested that the cumulative years of brain injury could have led to his crimes. After analysis, West Virginia University head of neurosurgery Julian Bailes stated Benoit's brain was so damaged that "it resembled the brain of an 85-year-old Alzheimer's patient," and said it was something you should never see in a 40-year-old ("Benoit's brain," 2007). The damage was compared to the similar brain results found in the NFL players' studies.

GENETICS AND BEHAVIOR

It has been said that the predatory behavior of prey animals reflects "a neurological basis that is different from that of other kinds" of behavior (Moyer, 1968). In other words, predatory aggression is different from other aggression, in that it "does not show rage and is not interchangeable with fight behavior, but it is purpose-oriented, accurately aimed, and the tension ends with the accomplishment of the goal" (Fromm, 1973, p. 99).

The calm, purposeful behavior of the accomplished serial murderer clearly reflects the actions of a predatory aggressor rather than the behavior of an excited, fight-stimulated organism. This behavior is best described by researchers like Baron-Cohen (2011) and Blair et al. (2005) who describe the nonempathetic, goal-oriented criminal aggression as "instrumental aggression."

The temptation is great to consider a person's history of violence as the main precursor to further violence. However, not every child who is abused becomes a serial killer, just as not every child who is abused develops a multiple personality. Sometimes children in the same family, subjected to the same abuse, take different psychological routes. One may develop a multiple personality and another, although experiencing problems, may not. These mixed results are also true of children raised in parental surrounding that would either suggest the development of a psychopath or not. There is an explanation for these differences, and it appears to be organic. Baron-Cohen (2011) in *The Science of Evil: On Empathy and the Origins of Cruelty* feels this is an indication of the environment interacting with "genes for empathy" in producing the psychopath, genes that evidence exists are associated with scoring on various measures of empathy (pp. 126–127).

So, what about the children of killers, or of rapists? There are few twin studies to ascertain the behavior of siblings raised in different settings involving violence. However, consider the example of Aileen Wuornos, an alcoholic lesbian slayer of seven. Her father was a child molester, a kidnapper, and a "violent sexual predator" (Reynolds, 1992, p. 257). He was also a bed-wetter until age 13. At one point, he escaped from a hospital for the criminally insane, but he eventually hung himself in prison. When she was an infant, he left Aileen and her 15-year-old mother. Little Aileen must have been her father's daughter. Her dad may not have taught her anything, but did he leave the seed of violence?

It should be noted that nearly all the studies of empathy in twins have found a greater correlation on empathy measures in monozygotic or identical twins when compared to dizygotic or nonidentical twins (Baron-Cohen, 2011, p. 128).

Extensive research on biological factors regarding serial killers was conducted by Richard T. Kraus (1995), in an investigation of the Arthur Shawcross case. Kraus noted that the 47, XYY chromosomal karyotype, abnormally elevated urinary kryptopyrroles, and multiple brain injuries "have relevance as identifiable precursors for potential violence in such individuals with a history of behavioral disturbance."

Jacobs, Brunton, and Melville (1965) initiated the first chromosome survey for XYY males, discovering a high incidence of males with the extra chromosome among a criminal population described as dangerous and violent. Later studies (Casey, Segall, Street, & Blank, 1966; Court-Brown, Price, & Jacobs, 1968; Price & Whatmore, 1967) supported these findings, and concluded that "the extra Y chromosome is associated with anti-social behavior . . . and predispose its carriers to increased risk for developing a psychopathic personality" (Kraus, 1995, pp. 11–24). Also of interest were findings by Neilsen et al. indicating that XYY patients might be a "comparatively high risk for committing arson, sexual criminality and a high frequency of violence" (Neilsen, 1970; Neilsen, Tsuboi, Turver, Jensen, & Sachs, 1969). Price and Jacobs (1970) found that "the behavior disorders in these men which may exist in the absence of mental deficiency . . . correlate with a personality disorder . . . [and] points to the existence of a constitutional psychopathic state" (p. 365).

In case reports of children with XYY, the children are described as "enigmatic in their personality development . . . vulnerable to simple threats and stresses that most would shrug off . . . loners . . . isolationists" (Money, 1970). Zeuthen, Hansen, Christensen, and Neilsen (1975) found the children with XYY who "grew up in good homes . . . to a certain extent differed from their siblings"; they were "more impulsive, restless, hot tempered, hyperactive . . . and lacked control of aggressive impulses."

Behavioral Genetics (1982) summed it up: "For the XYY, there seems to be little doubt. The extra Y does create some special risk for developing anti-social behavior." These findings all suggest episodes and characteristics in the histories of most serial killers. It is also true that the XYY violence theory has its supporters and detractors alike.

Kryptopyrrole (referred to as the mauve factor) is an endogenous metabolite that occurs in humans in either very low amounts or not at all. A reading of Arthur Shawcross's kryptopyrrole level revealed the following: "urine kryptopyrrole: H 200.66 mcg/1OOcc. Expected value 0–20" (Olsen, 1993, p. 491). The H was laboratory shorthand for high, already evident by the numbers. Shawcross had more than 10 times the expected highest amount of kryptopyrrole circulating in his body.

When this substance circulates in the body, it forms a stable Shiff base with pyridoxal phosphate (the aldehyde form of pyridoxine or vitamin B6, and then complexes with zinc, thereby depriving the body of these two essential compounds (Pfeiffer, Sohler, Jenny, & Iliev, 1974). Both pyridoxal phosphate and zinc are cofactors at the catalytic site of many enzymes. Decarboxylation reactions normally involve pyridoxal phosphate in the synthesis of various neurotransmitters, such as dopamine, norepinephirine, gamma-aminobutyric acid, and serotonin, while zinc is a cofactor in many enzymes, such as lactate dehydrogenase and alkaline phosphate. In addition, both pyridoxal phosphate and zinc are involved in the biosynthesis of heme, which is essential to life (*Harper's Biochemistry,* 1990). As a result, any deficiencies in pyridoxal phosphate or zinc can result in medical illness and psychiatric disturbance (Kraus, 1995).

In a study of the relationships among kryptopyrrole, zinc, and vitamin B6, Ward (1975) reported that the level of kryptopyrrole can vary in the same individual, increasing when that person is experiencing more stress and falling "dramatically" with large doses of zinc and vitamin B6 with an associated decrease in stress. Pfeiffer (1974) states that urinary excretion of kryptopyrrole is increased by stress of any kind.

O'Reilly, Hughes, Russell, and Ernest (1965) found that the incidence of this condition was "much higher in emotionally disturbed children and adults. than in the general population." A high urinary kryptopyrrole level does appear to correlate with low stress tolerance and loss of control (Kraus, 1995). Thus, it is considered a "biochemical marker of psychiatric dysfunction" and "can identify individuals at high risk for becoming violent."

Kraus's extensive, ground-breaking research in the Shawcross case clearly indicates that there are biological markers for psychiatric disturbance and violence. Also indicated is the aggravation caused by stress at all levels. The XYY research is extensive, whereas kryptopyrrole study continues to be limited regarding serial killers at this time. However, the inference of a biological predisposition is inescapable.

Baron-Cohen's (2011) research on the "empathy genes" resulted in his conclusion that four genes, after genotyping took place, showed "strongly significant association" with the empathy quotient, a measure of empathy in an individual. These genes were: CYPB11B1, a gene from the sex steroid group; WFSI, located in the group related to social–emotional behavior; and two from the "neural growth group, NTRK1 and GARBR3" (p. 138).

Researchers and geneticists at both Massachusetts General Hospital and the Netherlands found a genetic mutation in some men that was more likely to cause them to be aggressive and violent ("Dutch," 1993). Their reports stated that the mutation is associated with abnormal behavior, including attempted rape and exhibitionism (Snider, 1993). They found by urinalysis, the men abnormally metabolized the enzyme monoamine oxidase A (MAOA). In the brain, MAOA breaks down dopamine, serotonin, and noradrenaline, all substances known to affect behavior. When the researchers examined family genes, the men had slightly different coding from unaffected males.

Another thought is, the previously considered personality disorders—APD, borderline personality disorder, and obsessive compulsiveness—all suggest some genetic or biological link in serial killers and further underscore the possibility of a physical defect or disposition. As well, childhood disorders with the closest links to crime (ADHD, oppositional defiant disorder, and conduct disorder) suggest genetic inheritance in recent studies (Rowe, 2002, p. 39).

Unfortunately, as things stand there are still no reliable, predictive tests for the criminal brain at this time. Rowe (2002) and others have suggested the possibility of genes that could be related to criminal disposition, such as the dopamine (D4) receptor, serotonin, and MAOA. Raine's 2000 magnetic resonance imaging tests included testing the resting heart rates and skin conductance levels of subjects in 2000 and found they predicted whether someone had antisocial personality disorder with 77 percent accuracy, a 27 percent improvement over guessing (Rowe, 2002, p. 85). It has been established by multiple researchers that an impaired functioning of the prefrontal cortex of the brain is related to criminal disposition. Still,

> Although modern brain imagining technologies can produce wonderfully detailed images of the living, functioning brain, they cannot pick out the criminally disposed from the nondisposed with anything like a diagnostic level of accuracy.
>
> (Rowe, 2002, p. 71)

According to Stout, "over and over again, heritability studies come up with a statistical finding that has emotionally charged social and political implications—that indeed a person's tendency to possess certain sociopathic characteristics is partially born in the blood, perhaps as much as 50 percent so" (2005, pp. 123–124). However, general acceptance of biological behaviors for criminal behavior continues to be slow, regardless of increasing studies suggesting otherwise. As criminologists Williams and McShane (1999) state regarding public policy, "biological versions have not been very popular in the past half-century," and "until recently there have been few biologically oriented crime policies" (p. 46). Meanwhile, "psychological perspectives have found much more favor with policymakers as a standard approach to criminal behavior."

4

Environment, Background, and Personality

They ain't got, I don't think, a human being alive that can say he
had the childhood I had.

—Henry Lee Lucas

POSSIBLE ETIOLOGICAL FACTORS

In considering the potential ingredients to produce a serial murderer, the literature includes many phenomena in addition to the syndromes described in
the *DSM-IV*. Mental, physical, and sexual abuse; organic damage or biological anomaly; mental and attitude maladjustments; and sexual dysfunction are
but some of the other factors that come into play.

This chapter reviews the issues that seem to consistently color or correlate
with the histories of serial killers. Some issues are included because of an intuitive sense one develops when analyzing the literature; others simply appear
too often in these cases to ignore. Here, the focus is on the environmental
details and the social influences on the development of the serial murderer.
Unlike Chapter 2, which presented clinical psychology's perspective on the
personality types embodied by these offenders, this chapter discusses the external and social issues in their development.

ENVIRONMENTAL FACTORS

Clearly deserving of equal consideration in the development of serial killers
is the matter of environmental setting or history. The trauma experienced by

the majority of the killers in question is legendary. Consider Albert DeSalvo, who watched his father savagely beat his mother, witnessed the murders of drunks in his neighborhood, and was eventually sold along with his sister to a farmer as slaves. Then there is Henry Lee Lucas, who was forced to watch his mother have sex with various men, was beaten mercilessly daily, was made to eat from the floor and steal food, and was brought up as a girl until age seven, wearing long hair and dressing in girl's clothes (Egger, 2002).

Gerald Stano, who confessed to 25 murders of young women in Florida, was linked to at least 40 more. He was the fifth child born to a mother who lost all her children to adoption because of abuse and neglect. When Stano was removed from his home, he was malnourished, physically and emotionally neglected, and functioning at an "animalistic" level (Sears, 1991, p. 37).

There are many less dramatic instances of negative environmental settings, but certainly they are abhorrent enough to cause serious damage to a person's sense of self or to development of an appreciation of the lives of others. The beatings that the father of John Wayne Gacy gave him for his suspected homosexuality and underachievement; the practice of Bobby Joe Long's mother making him live in a hotel room with her, sharing her bed; the ridicule and punishment Edmund Kemper received from his mother and grandmother, questioning his masculinity—are just a few examples. The combination of physical predisposition and environmental stressors helps develop a pattern of maladjustment with two major consequences: a distorted sense of self and a dysfunctional sexual component.

ESTEEM DEVELOPMENT AND SENSE OF SELF

Along with physical abuse, the childhoods of most serial killers are filled with systematic emotional rape that harms their impressionable psyches. This injury prohibits them from developing a healthy sense of self, an understanding of intimacy, or feelings of personal esteem.

Childhood is when these killers develop obsessive and distorted views of their own identities and their ever-increasing need for control. Most have had little, if any, control over themselves or their surroundings as children, and their resulting fear and dread in relation to control issues is understandable, if not predictable. Ingram and Price (2010) make note of research suggesting child mistreatment and other traumas in general have been found to be related to dissociation, and a lack of sense of self (p. 88). Also noted are several ways in which dissociation, a lack of sense of self, trauma, and insecure attachment may be related (p. 89). On the other end of the continuum is an inflated or artificial self-view, characterizing additional personality disorders such as narcissism.

Many of the personality disorders discussed in Chapter 2 involve a distorted sense of self and a lack of control. These disorders can overlap with other issues, such as fear of loneliness, rejection, overreaction to stress, and misuse of alcohol and other substances.

Many killers, such as Kenneth Bianchi, Rodney Alcala, Aileen Wuornos, David Berkowitz, and Ted Bundy, were adopted early in life. Adoption is sometimes viewed by the child as the ultimate form of rejection by his parents. Certainly, Jeffrey Dahmer's tumultuous upbringing and perceived abandonment set into motion his loss of self and his immobilizing fear of being alone.

In a classic 1985 FBI study of sexually oriented murderers (Ressler, Burgess, Depue, Douglas, & Hazelwood, 1985), family histories were found to consistently lack a process for the subjects, as children, to become adults and relate to and value other members of society. Inadequate patterns of relating and infrequent positive interaction with family members were noted. A high degree of instability in the home life, as well as a poor-quality attachment among family members, was also found. Also, interviews showed that most offenders had unsatisfactory relationships with their fathers, while reporting that relationships with their mothers were of highly ambivalent quality. Today, researchers would certainly develop the attachment issues suggested there.

Revitch and Schlesinger (1981) found that, in cases of sexually motivated compulsive gynocide (the murder of women), there was some unhealthy emotional involvement with the mother. They felt that this resulted in a displacement of affect from mother to other women, culminating in a displaced matricide (p. 174). They also quote Freud, who stated that "the sexual instinct itself may not be something simple, that it may be on the contrary, be composed of many components, some of which form perversions. Our clinical observation thus calls our attention to fusions, which have lost their expression in the uniform normal behavior" (1938, p. 175). Revitch and Schlesinger note that in sadistic gynocide there is a fusion of sex and aggression.

The Sexual Component

A consistent factor in the development of the serial killer is the presence of a seriously dysfunctional sexual orientation. This is another issue given varying degrees of importance by different researchers. Some feel it is a key influence, whereas others view it as merely incidental. The position of this author is that deviant sexual motivation clearly has an impact on the killer's psychology, that it is the bridge, the clearest link between mental and physical processes in the psychopathology in question. Dr. David Abrahamson maintains that in "all of what we call senseless or aimless violence, there is a strong sexual element" (Cheney, 1992, p. 210). Defense expert Dr. George Woods, testifying at Anthony Sowell's trial, stated categorically many serial murder cases "have a strong sexual component to them" (Scott, 2011b).

Westley Allan Dodd, the child killer and rapist put to death in Washington State, was certainly on his way to a successful career as a serial sex killer. In his 1992 self-written pamphlet to parents, teachers, and children to warn against people like him (*When You Meet a Stranger*), he claimed to have molested about 25 boys and girls and attempted 40 others. Albert DeSalvo's uncontrollable sex drive seemed to fuel his mania, as he committed an estimated two thousand sexual assaults (Leyton, 1986). Most killers' careers are launched by violent sexual fantasies that lead to the sexual assault preceding the actual murders.

Some murderers do not kill with the overt motivation of sexual activity such as rape or sexual assault (pre- or postmortem) seeming to be a factor; however, other fetishes and sexual paraphilia are usually apparent. Ted Bundy had an abnormal collection of socks and once stated the importance of having more socks than he could ever use. This reflected the foot fetishes of Dayton Rogers and Jerry Brudos, both of whom severed the feet of some of their victims for later enjoyment.

Not to be forgotten is the motive of pure sexual sadism. Sadism, torture, and rape are usually thought of in terms of violence, but the sexual aspects of these crimes should not be overlooked. Freud referred to sadism as a partial drive of the libido, and explained that sadistic desires have no overt connection with sexual strivings, but are unconsciously motivated by them (Fromm, 1973, p. 280). Quite often the crimes of the killer enmesh the violence and sexual excitement of the sadist.

Edmund Kemper was described as a pure sadist by one psychiatrist, a condition presumably fueled by his hatred of his mother. DeSalvo seemed to strike out at women who represented the cold rebuke of his wife, Irmagard. Angelo Buono was a seasoned pro at brutal rape before his first murder for pleasure. Even Richard Ramirez noted in an interview (*Inside Edition,* 1993) that his sexual satisfaction could be reached only through violence.

However, sadistic specialists such as Lawrence Bittaker and Roy Norris just tortured and mutilated for the sheer enjoyment of hearing their victims scream. Bittaker and Norris wanted to stock their own private town of young girls to torture and rape. Herman Mudgett killed just to "hear their cries for mercy" (Editors of Time-Life Books, 1992, p. 95). Dayton Rogers even stopped attacking one victim who ceased screaming and resisting, apparently because she took the whole pleasure out of the act.

Albert Fish was so enthralled with sexual sadism and masochism that he regularly inserted needles in his groin, along with engaging in various other forms of self-mutilation. He looked forward to the electric chair as the "supreme thrill, the only one I haven't tried" (Editors of Time-Life Books, 1992, p. 99). Sexual sadists have displayed interest in activities consistent with the serial murderer, such as:

> selection of strangers as victims; advance selection of a location to which the victim is taken; participation of a partner; careful planning (including impersonation of a police officer); use of a pretext in approaching victims; keeping victims captive . . . sexual bondage . . . performing multiple sex acts . . . intentional torture; murder or serial killings (most often by strangulation); concealing victims' corpses; recording offenses; and keeping personal items belonging to the victims.

> (Dietz, Hazelwood, & Warren, 1990)

There is also the violent homosexual, who combines the components of a decayed, personal loathing sense of self and sexual urges. Homosexuality is barely referenced in the *DSM-IV-TR*, only when the individual experiences "persistent or marked distress about sexual orientation" (APA, 2000, p. 582). Killers who are fueled by a rage and a hatred of their own sexuality include sexually inadequate or homosexual individuals such as serial killers Dean Corll, Westley Dodd, John Wayne Gacy, Andrei Chikatilo, Larry Eyler, possibly Jeffrey Dahmer, Dennis Nilsen, and spree killer Andrew Cunanan. They are prime examples of such violent expression of frustration and rage.

Patrick Kearney, referring to younger homosexuals as "hustlers and phonies," admitted to killing at least 32 young men and boys, ranging from ages 5 to 28. He butchered them for years, later at a rate of one per month, and earned the nickname the "Trash Bag Killer" for his disposal methods of dumping the severed remains in garbage bags (Cartel, 1985, pp. 145, 147). Forensic psychiatrist Richard Rappaport echoed observations of personal rage between killer and victim when he noted that "a serial killer often has an extremely close relationship with his victims. He sees in them characteristics he sees in himself" (Garelik & Maranto, 1984).

Lucas, Toole, Bianchi, Buono, Long, Bittaker, Morris, Dahmer, Bundy, Shawcross, Gacy, Corona, Dodd, Chikatilo, Rader, Alcala, Sowell—the list goes on endlessly of serial killers whose primary interest included some form of sexual activity. More recently, a Canadian Air Force Officer, Col. Russell Williams, entrusted with flying prime ministers and Queen Elizabeth II, was exposed as living a double life: secretly acting as a serial killer as well as practicing a shocking fetish for stealing and photographing himself wearing girls' and women's underwear while masturbating (Noronha, 2010).

A popular theory is that rape and sadism are not acts of sex but of violence. Possibly, but not in all cases. It's probably somewhat dangerous to dismiss the personal sexual preference nature of these offenders. In some extreme cases, acts of torture, rape, necrophilia, and other deviant paraphilic activities may be labeled as acts of violence, but must also be recognized as acts, however distorted, of sex.

Causative aspects of a sexual deviance, usually including some form of paraphilia or sexual activity with a nonconsenting partner (i.e., rape, exhibitionism, or pedophilia), can reflect common psychological characteristics. Social isolation, low self-esteem, and feelings of sexual inadequacy can indicate an emotional immaturity (Costello & Costello, 1992, p. 272).

Sadistic tendencies can sometimes be traced to an early association of emotional feelings in response to someone's inflicting pain, or even torturing an animal. When the experience is a vivid, haunting one, the result may link the inflicting of pain with sexual arousal. Masochism seems to be triggered by early experiences of extreme pain linked with strong emotion, which in some way is associated with a satisfying sexual event (Costello & Costello, 1992, p. 269). Consistent with a diathesis–stress model (see Chapter 5), a predisposing biological component or personality trait must be assumed to cause such events, however powerful, to have lasting effects.

Certainly, the dimension that separates these criminals from ordinary rapists and sexual offenders is the eventual killing of their victims. The act appears far more significant than just a way to cover up a crime or silence a witness. Instead, it was for the expressed pleasure and catharsis of the act itself, whether to dominate, to control, or, as Ted Bundy put it, "to possess them . . . forever."

FANTASY

A deviant and consuming fantasy appears to be the fuel that fires the process. Serial killers seem, at an early age, to become immersed in a deep state of fantasy, often losing track of the boundaries between fantasy and reality. They dream of dominance, control, sexual conquest, violence, and eventually murder. Fantasy would seem to be the place where the killer retreats in a dissociative episode.

Long Island serial killer Joel Rifkin was consumed by violent fantasies. After a childhood of rejection and isolation, he started having daydreams about raping and stabbing women. Inspired by the Hitchcock film *Frenzy*, he became fixated on the idea of strangling prostitutes ("Joel Rifkin biography," 2011). He eventually acted out in this obsession.

Jeffrey Dahmer, in psychiatric interviews, revealed that he fantasized how it would feel to attack a jogger and "sexually enjoy him" (Dietz, 1992a). He thought out his plan of stalking someone in a certain place and subsequently went there with a baseball bat in rehearsal of his plan. After he was imprisoned, Dahmer spoke with Robert Ressler (Ressler & Shachtman, 1997, p. 137), who asked him about fantasy and what was about to happen before he went out to hunt for a victim:

DAHMER: Just . . . using pictures of past victims. The videotapes, the pornography videotapes, the magazines.
RESSLER: But there was a continuation [of the fantasy by] using these things, the skulls, things of that nature?
DAHMER: Right.

At an early age, Edmund Kemper also had fantasies of killing his sisters and other people. He extensively fantasized and carefully rehearsed, going through the motions of picking up hitchhikers before he would eventually carry out his homicidal impulses. Dahmer's and Kemper's activities are examples of Prentky et al.'s (1989) idea of "rehearsal fantasy," a motivator that is practiced in the environment. This rehearsal fantasy is usually associated with dysfunctions such as genital and gender dysphoria, a general feeling of unhappiness and anxiety regarding sexual issues, experienced by both Dahmer and Kemper. It is in the fantasy where the serial killer determines his future victims' goodness of fit, a mental representation of the type of individual needed to fulfill a particular pathological need.

Many studies have supported the role that fantasy plays in motivating the serial murderer. The Prentky et al. (1989) study, in which samples of serial murderers versus single sexual murderers were compared, postulated the role of fantasy as an internal drive mechanism for repetitive (serial) acts of sexual violence. The study's hypothesis was that three items common to serial offenders would be manifested by the existence of a drive mechanism, described as an intrusive fantasy life. They included a high prevalence of paraphilias, documented or self-reported violent fantasies, and organized crime scenes. All three hypotheses were supported by the study.

MacCulloch, Snowden, and Wood (1983, p. 29) found "a pattern of sadistic fantasies that, in repetition-compulsion fashion, were played out repeatedly—initially in fantasy only, later on in behavioral mock trials, and eventually in assaults. The more the fantasies were cognitively rehearsed, the more power they acquired." They found that "once the restraints inhibiting the acting out of the fantasy are no longer present, the individual is likely to engage in a series of progressively more accurate 'trial runs' in an attempt to enact the fantasy as imagined."

The genesis and pervasiveness of such fantasies may result from a failure to master the impulses stimulated by child abuse and trauma, hence the repetitive and compulsive nature of both the fantasy and the serial sexual violence (Grossman, 1991).

Burgess, Hartman, and Ressler (1986) found a fantasy-based motivational model for sexual homicide. Interactive components included impaired development or attachments in early life; formative traumatic events; patterned responses that serve to generate fantasies; a private, internal world consumed with violent thoughts that leaves the person isolated and preoccupied; and a feedback filter sustaining repetitive thinking patterns. In this study, they found evidence of daydreaming and compulsive masturbation in more than 80 percent of the sample, in both childhood and adulthood.

In terms of classical conditioning, Abel and Blanchard (1974) noted that "the repeated pairing of fantasized cues with orgasm results in their acquiring sexually arousing properties." This is consistent with Bandura's (1969) finding that at least three social-learning variables may be important in linking sexual arousal to deviant fantasy: parental modeling of deviant behavior in blatant fashion; repeated associations between the modeled deviant behavior and a strong positive affective response from the child; and reinforcement of the child's deviant response (Prentky et al., 1989).

John Campbell, of the FBI's Behavioral Science Unit, felt that the media promotes fantasy. "We're seeing more serial killers in society because we promote violence through media coverage. The problem with all this attention is that it could have a tendency to foster fantasy—and trigger action" (Davids, 1992, p. 150). Fantasy's role in the serial murderer's life is providing "an avenue of escape from a world of hate and rejection" (Hazelwood & Douglas, 1980).

Given a scenario in which a person has developed no real sense of self, no concept of esteem or self-worth, and no meaningful reciprocal relationships with those around him, he or she is likely to see an avenue of escape from hate and rejection. In this person's fantasy, he or she may remake the present, the past, and the future. He or she may create a world of acceptance and respect. He or she can enjoy the status of a worthwhile person and be a desirable sex partner. Most important, he or she can call all the shots, write all the lines, and fill in all the blanks. The carte blanche control offered in the world of fantasy is priceless—and addicting.

It appears that many serial killers often retreat into their world of fantasy at some point in their developing pathology. They may delve into sexual, violent, graphic scenarios, and use pornography or detective magazines to assist their creative process. Linked with continued masturbation, retreating within themselves, and in self-imposed isolation, they begin down the path of a murderous obsession. Fantasy is also a logical first step toward a dissociative state, a process that allows the serial killer to leave his stream of consciousness for what is, to him, a better place.

Jeffrey Dahmer had sexual fantasies about corpses and open viscera during a formative stage in his life (Dietz, 1992b). John Joubert fantasized about strangling and eating his babysitter when he was age 6 or 7, following established patterns of open masturbation and fantasy about strangling and stabbing young boys in their undershorts (Ressler, 1992, p. 120). Monte Rissell was described by a school principal as always "lost in fantasy" (Ressler, 1992, p. 88). Dodd said, "the more I thought about it, the more exciting the idea of murder sounded. . . . Then I started thinking of torture, castration, and even cannibalism" (Schechter, 2003, p. 237). Kemper, Berkowitz, Rogers, Nance, Rader—the list goes on—and the stories of their fantasies are endless and all-inclusive.

Of course, fantasy is not the private domain of serial killers. It is, however, consistent in much of the most heinous offenders' histories. Even Josef Fritzl, whose crimes included drugging his teenage daughter and then holding her, kidnapped, as a prisoner in the basement of their home while abusing, raping, and impregnating her repeatedly over the course of more than 20 years. Fritzl's criminal personality was described by a Viennese psychotherapist as created between the ages of two and five, and "the sexual fantasies he admits to having about his mother" set the stage for the inner soul created within him (Hall, 2008, pp. 17–18).

Dr. James T. Reinhardt (1992, p. 208) described the role of fantasy:

By fantasy the murderer attempts to wall himself in against the fatal act, while at the same time qualifying the compulsive psychic demands in the development and use of fantasy. These sadistic fantasies seem always to precede the brutal act of lust murder. These fantasies take all sorts of grotesque and cruel forms. The pervert, on this level of degeneracy, may resort to pornographic pictures, grotesque and cruel literary episodes, out of which he weaves fantasies. On these, his imagination dwells until he loses all contact with reality, only to find himself suddenly impelled to carry out his fantasies into the world of actuality. This is done, apparently, by drawing some human objects into the fantasy.

The serial killer has often lost himself in a world of fantasy, a world where fantasy is omnipresent and he cannot discern what fantasy is and what reality is. This psychodynamic makes possible the continued execution of violence, sadism, and murder for personal satisfaction. Fantasy can also be seen as a reason the serial killer can calmly and methodically dehumanize his victims. He then reconnects with the real world (Bundy's live-in girlfriend referred to his "using me to touch base with reality") and carries on immediately after the crime with such seemingly mundane activities as going out for hamburgers (Kendall, 1981, p. 175).

PORNOGRAPHY AND CAUSATION

A logical question, after the subject of fantasy is, what role does pornography play? There are those who feel pornography is a causative precursor in the actions of a serial killer. It's certainly a popular feminist ideal. One FBI study showed that, of the sexual or serial killers surveyed, 81 percent listed pornography as their primary sexual interest. The study also noted that the killers were "characteristically immersed in fantasy," which supports the prior discussion of fantasy but merely suggests the role of pornography. A North Carolina State Police study found that 75 percent of defendants in violent sex crimes "had some kind of hard-core pornographic material" in their homes or vehicles (Mellish, 1989).

Dietz, Harry, and Hazelwood (1986) have suggested that detective magazines contributed to the development of sexual sadism, that they facilitate sadistic fantasies, and that they might serve as training manuals and equipment catalogs for sex criminals. Ted Bundy's claims that he was a victim of pornography, made just before his execution, are well documented. Even Andrei Chikatilo, with pictures of naked women in his holding cell, blamed pornography as the "cause of his troubles."

What of it? Most researchers say that a correlational relationship does not prove anything, much less cause and effect. It would seem reasonable that persons who are so obsessed with sex and fantasy would have pornography in their homes, much as any sports fan would have *Sports Illustrated* or *The Sporting News*. But does pornography or detective magazines incite someone to murder—someone who might not otherwise? Not likely. It should also be noted that Bundy's and Chikatilo's credibility in this matter must be considered suspect and their motives unknown. Durham (1986)—in response to feminist assertions that pornography is harmful, incites violence, and should be regulated—noted that "the use of unsupported assertions, the limited generalizability of the social-psychological experimental research, the inability of the research to measure the magnitude of the effects of pornography and the failure to conduct the discussion in comparative terms severely undermines the persuasiveness of the argument" (p. 101).

The matter of pornography deserves a study of its own. It might be believable that pornographic addiction could relate to a sexual offender. In considering the needs of a pattern murderer, the person who kills, not just sexually assaults, there's a missing link in the argument. It would appear that pornography is to the serial killer as gasoline is to the arsonist. Both are tools of the sexual criminal. Both are immersed in fantasies and have the motivation to fulfill their erotic desires. Magazines and movies definitely help fuel the fire. However, without gasoline, the arsonist still finds a match. Without the pornography, Ted Bundy kills scores of women anyway.

Still, included in this book is a personal series of conversations in 2011 with a serial murderer who had some interesting ideas about pornography—some perspectives I hadn't considered. The subject may need to be revisited. This discussion is found in Chapter 9.

LESSER CRIMES

Obsessive fantasizing, it appears, usually results in a feeling-out period, a time when lesser crimes are committed. Just as in experimentation with fire or animal torture while still a child, the fledgling serial killer usually tries the lesser roles of arson, burglary, theft, sexual deviance, molestation, and assault. Criminal journals are full of Bundys, Dahmers, and DeSalvos who worked their way up the ladder of antisocial acts and behaviors, petty crimes, and control-seizing acts on their way to habitual homicide.

The role of lesser crimes is especially important, as the crimes are usually sexual in nature. These acts—most often arson, breaking and entering, sexual assault, or burglary—represent sexual gratification and control. Although on a smaller scale, these crimes appear to reflect the basic motivations of the serial killer. For example, criminal profiler Diana Sievers (personal communication, 1992) of the Illinois State Police stated that breaking and entering or burglary is an example of the individual gaining the control that he seeks.

Even clearly mentally ill or disorganized offenders such as Richard Chase committed earlier crimes such as breaking and entering, defecating on a child's bed, and urinating on clothing in a drawer—all "signs of classic fetish burglaries" (Ressler, 1992, p. 16).

Russell Williams continued a ritual that included photographing women's bedrooms including "underwear drawers, wall photos, certificates identification and oftentimes would take pictures of the undergarments laid out in painstakingly coordinated arrangements" (Gibb, 2011, p. 217). He'd often take the time to strip down and pose for self-portraits and masturbate in their rooms while wearing the women's underwear.

William Heirens committed his first killings, he says, because the victims walked in on him while he was in the act of committing burglaries described as sexual in nature. Heirens's murders were categorized by Ressler as a "continuation of the burglaries and other crimes he committed earlier in his teenage years" (p. 50), and he continued to commit many more in between the murders. Danny Rolling was serving four life sentences in Florida State Prison for a series of armed robberies and home burglaries committed in Gainesville, Ocala, and Tampa, at the time of his conviction for the murders of five college students (Abdo, 1994).

Heirens's and DeSalvo's countless burglaries, or Berkowitz's arsons (1,488 in New York—he kept a diary—as well as his pulling several hundred false alarms) are lesser crimes with no motivation other than getting a sexual charge and seizing control.

AN ISSUE OF CONTROL

The serial murderer is hard to dissect, even on paper. Factors such as sadism, fear, sexual perversion, emotional maladaptivness, mounting anger, and hostility apply in different degrees to different offenders. The one constant here, however, is control. Control—whether it is sexual, sadistic, revengeful, or any of the other mind-sets held by the killer—seems to be the underlying drive and is the source of the serial killer's motivation and direction to "possess them . . . forever." As Levin and Fox (1985, p. 68) have noted,

> In large part, the pleasure and exhilaration that the serial killer derives from repeated murder stem from absolute control over other human beings. As Roy Norris admitted . . . "the rape wasn't the important part, it was the dominance."

A series of FBI rape typologies used in profiling violent crimes (Holmes & Holmes, 2009, pp. 160–165) includes the definition of the *power assertive* rapist, a psychopath or a sociopath who needs to express personal dominance. This offender type sounds most like the power- and control-seeking rapist involved in many serial killings. However, behaviors also described by *power assurance, anger retaliation,* and *anger excitation (sadistic)* rapists, who often display a compulsive pattern, can also fall into this population.

This link between control, rape, and serial murder was also noted by Egger (1985) and West (1987). It was West who pointed out that "it may take only a small increase in the desperation of the assailant or resisting victim to convert a violent rape into a murder" (p. 19).

MACDONALD TRIAD COMPONENTS AS CONTROL ISSUES

Indeed, from the earliest inklings of the pathology to come, serial murderers seem to deal continuously with issues of control. The elements of the MacDonald triad (enuresis, fire setting, and animal abuse, introduced in Chapter 3) as future predictors of violence are all examples of impulse control issues, whether it be in regard to holding urine, sadism, or pathological sexual expression.

The late enuresis (bed-wetting) in their pasts is a control issue that is hard for them to ignore. Dr. Joseph Michaels, a pioneer in the analysis of the correlation between enuresis and murderous behavior in children, explains "Persistently enuretic individuals are impelled to act. They feel the urgency of the moment psychologically, as at an earlier date they could not hold their urine" (Ewing, 1990, p. 11). The biological implications of lack of impulse control, as previously discussed, plus repeated incidence of such poor impulse control reflect this position.

The prevalence of animal abuse also appears to be a combination of sexual or sadistic urges and control and dominance needs. The literature is again replete with stories such as that of Wayne Nance, who demonstrated his superiority by dropping kittens into an incinerator or skinning them alive. What easier way to act out your control, which is sorely lacking in real life, than by a skinning a cat or mutilating another defenseless creature? The next logical step is to move on to other objects of easy dominance, such as little girls and boys, women, and other potential victims.

Three teenagers arrested for the brutal murder and sexual mutilation of three eight-year-olds had combined ritual and animal abuse as they skinned, cooked, and ate a dog. One of the young killers noted to a priest that he had already committed himself to hell, and he couldn't change that (Castaneda, 1993a, b).

Keith Jesperson, the "Happy Face Killer," killed animals as a child by manual strangulation—a glimpse into the future of how he would kill his human victims.

A 2003 criminology journal article tried to apply a graduation hypothesis connecting animal abuse to serial murder (Wright & Hensley, 2003), but only succeeded in listing case history details of serial murderers commonly known to have a history of animal abuse. However, it seems logical at least that an early offender motivated by sadism and impulse control problems could practice on a vulnerable animal and later progress to human beings.

This control-centered triad of early crimes includes arson, which is also very common in serial killers' pasts. Arson or fire setting has distinct sexual features and represents the actions of taking control of the situation, both in fire setting and in pulling false alarms. Shawcross, Berkowitz, and many other serial killers shared this interest. An additional interesting correlation is the connection of power and control pathology and young fire setters, who often act out of frustration, rage, and a sense of powerlessness. Internal power imbalances caused by organic problems such as ADHD as well as external issues such as family dysfunction and abuse (Kolko, 2002) are commonly related to research regarding fire setting behavior in youth.

PATHOLOGY AND CONTROL

Control seems to be the underlying motivation for the personality types discussed in Chapter 2—the antisocial personality, the psychopath, the sociopath, the borderline personality, the attachment disordered, and the narcissistic. They all crave control, whether it is to build a fragile ego or to demonstrate how weak everyone else is.

Even necrophiles acknowledge the importance of control. In a clinical analysis, when asked what their primary motivation for necrophilia was, the subjects often said "total acceptance of the subject [victim] . . . the completely unconditional positive regard and total acceptance" (Meloy, 1993).

Erich Fromm (1973), in considering necrophilia, postulated that there is a natural development from the anal, control-obsessed personality, to the sadistic character, and finally to the necrophilous character. He felt that this development was determined by an increase in narcissism, unrelatedness, and destructiveness, and that necrophilia can be described as "the malignant form of the anal character" (p. 349). He also said that the relatively small number of necrophiles were severely pathological cases and one "should look for a genetic predisposition" for this (p. 367). Dr. Ashok Bedi, after examining Jeffrey Dahmer, agreed with the connection between necrophilia and control. In regard to Dahmer's necrophilia, he commented:

> His personality disorder, the alcohol addiction, the pedophilia, the necrophilia, his ego and homosexuality, all were layers of his dysfunction. The preoccupation of having sex with the dead person had to do with his feelings at different points in time. A living person could not fill his need. Only a dead person, where he was totally in control and there was no way of retaliation, belittlement, negation or abandonment. It was not so much being sadistic as wanting to be in control. Then it became a question of what he was looking for—nurturing, wanting to be fed, that sort of thing. If there was a need to show anger, then he might use anal sex. It depended on what his needs were in his head at the moment.
>
> (Davis, 1991, p. 264)

When considering the issues of control and sadism, J.A. Apsche (1993, p. 117) noted:

> When, in children, control is substituted for intimacy [as manipulation and control substituted for closeness], the child mistakenly learns that control is a substitute for intimacy. For the sexual sadist, there is a need to take control to demonstrate power and virility. The mode of death selected is one which indicates that the victim had meaning for the killer, and that the intimacy in the murderous act is part of the close bond between the murderer and the victim formed in the killer's fantasies and delusions.

Erich Fromm, in searching for the nature of sadism, stated that there were different forms of sadism, and they were not independent of one other. In observing what he called the common element, he wrote:

> The core of sadism, common to all its manifestations, is the passion to have absolute and unrestricted control over a living being, whether an animal, a child, a man, or a woman. To force someone to endure pain or humiliation without being able to defend himself is one of the manifestations of absolute control, but is by no means the only one. . . .

Complete control over another human being means crippling him, choking him, thwarting him. . . . The person who has complete control over another living being makes this being into his thing, his property, while he becomes the other being's god.

(1973, p. 289)

Edmund Kemper summed it up: "I wanted the girls for myself as possessions. They were going to be mine; they are mine" (Cheney, 1992, p. 171).

THE FIRST KILL

The first kill is often the clumsy, inexperienced, and impulsive act of a virgin to homicide. Reminiscent of the adolescent fumbling in a car's back seat, David Berkowitz made a botched attempt at stabbing his initial victim. It caused him to eventually change to an easier and more efficient method of shooting his prey.

Sometimes the first kill is the result of what began as a rape or assault, but crossed the line as the frenzy of the episode unfolded. The excitement of the moment made the killer cross the threshold separating fantasy from reality. In other instances, a stressful event in the killer's life triggers an escalation of activity, from crimes such as burglary or rape, to murder. Some offenders may even develop a pattern of increased homicides coinciding with peaks of stress in their personal lives, acting out in a manner that provides a pattern that can be observed in a context of life stress looking back.

Occasionally, killers will say that they do not even remember the details of their first kill, while showing extraordinary memory and clarity for subsequent conquests. Their initiation to murder is often followed with guilt, fear, and reflection, similar to the aforementioned adolescent's first time with sex. The shame and acknowledgment that a grave crime has been committed is felt along with the excitement and the rush that comes with the realization of having finally discovered what they truly need. This is also a time to enjoy mental reenactments. As time passes and fear of reprisal fades, these offenders enjoy renewed confidence in their ability to practice their habit undetected. The initial cooling-off period is reinforced within the cycle, and will become part of the dynamics of habits to come.

THE COMPULSION AND RITUAL OF SERIAL MURDER

The completion of the cycle, culminating in the murders, accompanying sexual activity, and post-offense behavior, illustrates the killer's obsessive-compulsive behavior and ritualistic actions.

Albert DeSalvo spoke of the indescribable compulsion that came over him when he strangled (Frank, 1967, p. 378). Increased anxiety about and discomfort with the compelling urge to kill becomes consuming. The eventual killing provides the expected release and satiation, dissipating the tension and introducing momentary relief. Like the addict, the killer will search for the same level of high as experienced during the first kill, but may settle for the release of built-up anxiety. According to the FBI's Robert Hazelwood, "Serial offenders generally commit their crimes as stress is building on them. The stress level reaches a peak, and that's when they make the kill. It's like a weight being lifted off their shoulders" (Coston, 1992, p. 278).

This cycle of anxiety, discomfort, urge, act, and cooling off reflects a similar sequence of emotions and actions cycling within those suffering from OCD or sexual paraphilic obsessions and compulsions, such as exhibitionism. In this case, the urge to kill is obsessive-compulsive.

The times between killings may vary, according to a number of factors. Sometimes there are no victims to meet the killer's criteria, sexually or otherwise. For example, Andrei Chikatilo's killings dropped off in the winter months owing to cold weather. Jeffrey Dahmer reportedly refrained from killing a couple of young victims because he didn't have enough time to go to work. Joel Rifkin went months without killing because apparently "examining trophies—the credit cards, panties and jewelry of previous victims—may have been enough to satisfy him" (Eftimiates, 1993, p. 234). Dennis Rader took years off from killing, only to return to his old compulsion, desiring the attentions of media and law enforcement.

However, the obsession remains and generally does not stay dormant for long. When one of Westley Dodd's young victims asked him, "Why are you doing this to us?" he responded: "Because I have to do it" (King, 1993, p. 288). An example even more illustrative of this compulsion comes from of Ted Bundy:

> I have a sickness . . . a disease like your alcoholism. You can't take another drink and with my sickness. . . . There is something . . . that I just can't be around. . . . I know it now. . . . There is something the matter with me. . . . I just couldn't contain it. I've fought it for a long, long time. . . . It got too strong. I tried, believe me, to suppress it. That's why I didn't do well in school. My time was being used trying to make my life look normal. But it wasn't normal. All the time I could feel the force building in me.
>
> (Kendall, 1981, pp. 174, 176)

Bundy's live-in girlfriend, under her pen name Elizabeth Kendall, appreciated the comparison to her own pattern of alcoholism:

> I didn't pretend to understand or accept Ted's compulsion to kill beautiful, vital young women. But I do understand something of compulsion, and I do understand something of what it feels like to repeat compulsive actions over and over again, even though the intention is to never do it again. In my case it was getting drunk repeatedly when I didn't want to. In Ted's case it was so much worse.
>
> (1981, p. 177)

At this point it would appear that the killer settles into a pattern of cyclical murderous acts, becoming more and more comfortable in his practices, also gaining efficiency and skill in technique and execution. Still, the compulsion and ritual of the kill retains its importance. Wilson and Seaman (1991) observed in regard to Jack the Ripper, "the ritual was of supreme importance to the Ripper. More than that, it was a clamorous, overpowering need, a compulsion, which overruled all other considerations that night—personal safety included" (p. 37). They also noted, regarding an 1809 female killer, Anna Zwanziger, that "as if the need to kill was an addiction, Zwanziger told the judge it would have been impossible for her to cease poisoning others and described the virulent poison as her 'truest friend'" (p. 49).

Ritual was clearly important to Ed Gein, the inspiration for serial killer characters in several movies, who:

robbed corpses and body parts from a number of graves. Gein used these limbs and organs to fashion ornaments, such as a belt of nipples and a hanging human head, as well as decorations for his house, including chairs upholstered with human skin and bed posts crowned with skulls. A shoe box containing nine vulvas was but one part of Gein's collection of female organs. On moonlit evenings he would prance around his farm wearing a real female mask, a vest of skin complete with female breasts, and women's panties filled with vaginas in an attempt to recreate the form and presence of his dead mother.

(Levin & Fox, 1985, p. 4)

Part of the ritual often includes keeping diaries, photo albums, and other visual aids for reenactment of the crimes. Westley Dodd kept a graphic diary of his activities and plans along with a categorically detailed photo album, including descriptions of experiments to perform on the dead (and the living), murder methods, and plans for creating a torture rack.

Trophies were of course as important as the ritual. Immediately after the strangulation of one victim, Russell Williams couldn't resist:

Her killer's first impulse was to run and grab his camera. He took three photographs of her body as it lay on the floor, taking care to pose his murderous flashlight next to her, as though she were a hunter's trophy kill. He then cut the zip tie from around her neck to keep as a souvenir.

(Gibb, 2011, p. 98)

Another example: Robert Berdella, a sadistic rapist and murderer of six, kept skulls, an envelope of teeth, and hundreds of pictures of young men being raped and tortured. He cut up the bodies to be put out with the trash. An excerpt from his diary included this page (Jackman & Cole, 1992, p. 97):

7:30	Bar
Ferris [victim] 9/26 Drug	
9:00	Out
9:05	Shoes + socks off, move arms snoring no rea
9:10	Test need no react [needle] 2 1/2 cp left a "3 cp right a"
9:20	Photo, clothes off, no react
9:40	Turned over, slight arm movement
9:50	Fing F no reac [finger sex] 1 1/2 cc ket arm no rea Front F no react
10:15	BF no reac [anal sex]
10:30	tied arms
10:50–11:00	Carrot F Slight resist 1 1/2 cc cp nk
11:00	2 cc cp vein
11:30–11:45	BF, cub F, slight react Regag
12:00	Fightin

The notes continued for two more pages. The top of the third page was marked "Fri," and the last two entries read:

11:45	Very delayed breathing, snoring
12:00	86

The kills become increasingly intense, lessening the effect of a "fix" for this addict of death. Also experiencing shorter cooling-off periods, the obsessed killer may get sloppy (e.g., Dahmer, Bianchi, Rifkin) or more frenzied (Bundy) as time goes on. Some killers, such as Kemper and DeSalvo, say they reach the point when they could have stopped. This might seem plausible for a Kemper, who finally destroyed the object of his rage (his mother), but it is highly unlikely for seasoned serial killers to walk away from their compulsive patterns. Indeed, frenzy, compulsion, sadism, and ritual were all reflected in the words of one of history's first serial killers, Jack the Ripper:

I left nothing of the bitch, nothing. I placed it all over the room, time was on my hands, like the other whore I cut the bitches nose all of it this time. I left nothing of her face to remember her by. . . . I thought it a joke when I cut her breasts off, kissed them for awhile. The taste of blood was sweet, the pleasure was overwhelming, will have to do it again. It thrilled me so. Left them on the table with some of the other stuff. Thought they belonged there. They wanted a slaughterman so

I stripped what I could, laughed while I was doing so. Like the other bitches she ripped like a ripe peach. . . . One of these days I will take the head with me, I will boil it and serve it up for my supper.

(Harrison & Barrett, 1993, p. 102)

Occasionally, a serial killer's run comes to an end purely by chance, such as with a routine traffic stop, in the case of Ted Bundy. In New York, Joel Rifkin, who was pulled over for running a stop sign, was discovered carrying a woman's decomposing body in the rear of his truck. He quickly confessed to the killing of 17 women ("Man reportedly," 1993).

In the vast majority of the cases, however, serial killers will kill until they are caught, by law enforcement efforts, through their own self-destructive misstep, or when they meet their own death. This cheery observation is tempered, however, by the fact that we can never know how many multiple murderers might have killed, then ceased on their own for whatever reason and were never apprehended. It is rare indeed to have an Edmund Kemper come to the end of the line and turn himself in, but most likely not as rare as a seasoned killer who simply opted to retire from a compulsion that drove him his entire adult life.

Part II

Toward an Examination of a Theory of Violence

5

Theoretical Discussion and Methodology

I will not allow too much time before my next. Indeed, I need to repeat my pleasure as soon as possible.

—Jack the Ripper

PRELIMINARY IMPRESSIONS

In suggesting a pattern for the synthesis of the serial killer, the literature makes reference to many phenomena: the incidence of mental, physical, and sexual abuse; the possibility of organic or biological damage or predisposition; prenatal stress; and the development of mental and attitude maladjustments as well as sexual dysfunctions. With consideration of the potential of variables, the result appears to be an inclusive dynamic: multiple factors acting in concert. The serial murderer's personality develops through a combination of specific variables that feed on themselves, creating a feedback loop for the activity.

Of course, there are many competing varied theories for the most extremely violent criminals. However, most do tend to take a stance favoring heavily on one side or the other of nature versus nurture. Some will lean almost exclusively on nature, which is very difficult to scientifically prove, whereas others put far more weight on the environment. Athens (1992) argued it was a combination of social experiences, including measurable stages (brutalization, belligerency, and violent performance). These stages had to be completed by meeting specific criteria—for example, brutalization had to be experienced by violent subjugation, personal horrification, and violent coaching. While these would be considered common in the creation of many violent criminals, they do not apply consistently to the serial murderer. These features would easily fit a Henry Lee Lucas, but would be very difficult to apply to Jeffrey Dahmer, acknowledging the difficulty in the completeness and accuracy of case histories. The study of the serial murderer still suggests a theory that includes the interaction of the physical and the social.

The concept of an interactional dynamic is not without precedent. Eric W. Hickey (1997) suggested an interactional, socio-developmental model he called *trauma control,* emphasizing the importance of social structure and stressing the influence of a traumatic event, or *triggering mechanism.* The interactional dynamic presented here is similar, but the key element is a biological component, which is at least equal to environmental factors.

THE DIATHESIS–STRESS MODEL

The theory proposed in this book is a *diathesis–stress model,* a systems approach similar to what is currently offered in the psychological literature for conditions such as schizophrenia. There certainly is a social, environmental factor—or trigger; most obviously it is the extreme psychological trauma suffered by the vast majority of serial killers. This alone, however, is not enough. There seems to be an additional component—a physiological, biological ingredient that makes the mix an explosive one. Simply put, the diathesis–stress model combines both nature and nurture. Neither a biological factor nor an environmental situation alone seem to be enough to produce the offender type in question. A biological predisposition acts in concert with a traumatic environmental situation.

The diathesis–stress *(diathesis:* biological; *stress:* environmental pressure) model of schizophrenia was introduced by Meehl in 1962 (cited in Ingram & Price, 2010, p. 26), which "helped to integrate the biological *and* [emphasis added] environmental models of psychopathology." It was further postulated by Gottesman and Shields in 1982. The term refers to a genetic predisposition being a necessary condition, but not sufficient in itself (Lewine, Gulley, Risch, Jewart, & Houpt, 1990). Hans and Marcus (1987) studied a process model for schizophrenia in diathesis–stress terms, underlining the importance of factors such as constitutional vulnerability—that is, biological and genetic risk via family history; early neurobehavioral signs marking a constitutional defect; stressful childhood environment, particularly family environment; and early premorbid childhood signs of poor social adjustment. Their model for etiology "included a constitutional, possibly genetic vulnerability, aggravated by environmental, most likely familial, stresses." It is strikingly similar to the histories of many serial killers and forms a reasonable theoretical position for this particular psychodynamic.

In *Vulnerability to Psychopathology,* Ingram and Price explain that the use of diathesis–stress concept within medical terminology dates back to ancient

Greeks and "was well-lodged in the psychiatric vernacular" by the late 1800s. Furthermore, diathesis:

> Signifies a predisposition to illness and has evolved from its original focus on constitutional, biological factors to presently also encompass psychological variables such as cognitive and interpersonal susceptibilities. . . . Such diatheses are typically considered to be latent and . . . activated in some fashion before psychopathology can occur. . . . Most models also recognize that events perceived as stressful act to trigger vulnerability processes that are linked to the onset of the disordered state. Psychopathology is therefore the interactive effect of the diathesis and events perceived as stressful. Framed within the context of a diathesis-stress conceptualization, stress is integral to virtually all current conceptualizations of vulnerability.
>
> (Ingram & Price, 2010, p. 10)

According to Rowe (2002), "Criminal disposition is one of the more complex traits studied by behavioral geneticists." In *Biology and Crime* (p. 39), he states:

> The source of this predisposition is heterogeneous. In some cases it lies in psychoses. More commonly, it lies in a variety of temperamental and personality traits associated with diagnoses of childhood disorders in psychiatry, or with the presence of psychopathy in adulthood. . . . Evidence suggests criminal disposition is heritable, including studies of psychiatric disorders, crime-linked personality traits and crime itself.

Silverton, Mednick, Schulsinger, Parnas, and Harrington's (1988) study suggested that "genotype may depend on the interaction between genetic factors and environmental trauma. . . . It may be important to consider neuroanatomical sensitivity as an etiological factor . . . in genetically vulnerable persons." Further studies by Walker, Downey, and Bergman (1989) made specific note of the effects of child mistreatment and the incidence of violence. Considering the fact that child mistreatment is more common among psychiatrically disturbed parents (Sloan & Meyer, 1983), a genetic and biological basis could be inferred from later exceptionally violent behavior.

Jaffe, Wolfe, Wilson, and Zak (1986) found that boys exposed to family violence showed adjustment problems comparable to those manifested by abused boys—conditions reminiscent of many serial killers' histories. The Walker et al. study suggested that genetic risk interacted with maltreatment in its effects on aggression and behavior. Over time, the acting-out behavior of high-risk children from maltreating families escalated. It appeared that stressful environments may have acted to trigger externalized behavior in their high-risk (genetically predisposed) subjects.

When examining the histories of children who are severely abused, yet do not develop conditions such as schizophrenia or become serial killers, it would appear logical to assume that the abuse—found so regularly and predictably in the pasts of serial killers—must interact with an unknown factor in a lethal manner.

In these cases, the factor combining with trauma must be a biological predisposition.

Significant Environmental Issues

Given the diathesis–stress model, environmental triggers must be substantial and noteworthy especially when compared to an average upbringing. The factors that consistently surface in reports of these troubled pasts must be recognized as indicators in a progression and become elements of this developmental concept. However, as previously suggested, these stressors or triggers must be perceived as stressful events by the subject and this perception is personal. The discovery of adoption or the abandonment by divorcing parents are events received on a highly personal level.

These prominent elements (or markers, if you will) include antisocial, possibly criminal events in youth; a pervasive sexual dysfunction causing great impact and/or great stress in the person's life; and dissociative episodes or chronic escapes to fantasy.

Antisocial activity is a somewhat broad category representing the lesser crimes most serial killers bring with them to their first murder. These include (but are not limited to) fire setting and animal abuse, along with burglary, breaking and entering, and assault. As discussed in Chapter 4, many of these crimes have control and sexual themes.

The extended discussion of *sexual dysfunction* in Chapter 4 clearly explains the inclusion of this factor in the diathesis–stress developmental theory. It is considered an essential ingredient of the serial killer, and offers insight into some other activities he or she commits peripheral to the murders.

Dissociation and *fantasy* are factors of enormous weight. Time and time again, offenders' stories are colored with dissociative episodes and life in fantasy worlds. Childhood histories are filled with fantasy worlds that were mental practice sessions leading to assaults. Reports of killers experiencing blackouts, dissociative events, and memory loss during and after their crimes have continued over the years.

Theoretical Analysis—Methodology

Case Study Method

This book presents case studies as a means to consider the preliminary impressions gleaned from the clinical and social literature. The case study is the "preferred strategy when 'how' or 'why' questions are being posed, when the investigator has little control over events, and when the focus is on a contemporary phenomenon within some real-life context" (Yin, 1984, p. 13). This describes the analysis of the serial killer and development in society presented here. In the subsequent chapters, case studies will be reviewed in light of two assumptions described in the next section (Observational Direction). The elements of each theory will be considered and discussed.

This case study strategy remains the logical course as this issue is revisited in this book. Yin (2008) further explained this perspective as a "twofold, technical definition of case studies." Yin elaborates noting the boundaries between the contemporary phenomenon (in this case the activities and development of the serial murderer) and its context are not "clearly evident." The case study method would be used "because you wanted to understand a real-life phenomenon in depth, but such understanding encompassed important contextual conditions" (p. 18). The application of analyzing the real-life monster within his context is clearly only done through examination of case study.

The second aspect of this twofold definition exists because "phenomenon and context are not always distinguishable in real-life situations" and require including "data collection and data analysis strategies" as "many more variables of interest other than data points" exist. Yin's explanation underlines that the case study method "also benefits from the prior development of theoretical propositions to guide data collection" as well as stressing "multiple sources of evidence, with data needing to converge in a triangulating fashion" (2008, p. 18).

Yin's 2008 development of the previously chosen model of case study method continues to verify this technique of observing the contemporary serial murder phenomenon in its context. It also provides the collection and analysis of relevant data from the many variables of interest as being the clear choice in developing a theory of the construction of the pattern of the serial killer personality.

OBSERVATIONAL DIRECTION

There are two assumptions considered in this analysis. First, there is a real, recognizable set of behaviors capable of being observed and categorized, much like the antisocial personality described in Chapter 2, who can be called a serial killer. *Serial killer* is a label used quite loosely and without accepted definition at this time. The assumption here is this term can be applied as a reasonably consistent diagnosis using a specific set of parameters.

Second, offenders qualifying for this diagnosis do, for the most part, conform to the theoretical model and its elements discussed herein. The offender suffers a combination of predisposition and life stress much like the schizophrenic, displays a history of early antisocial behavior and obsession with fantasy and/or flights from reality, and endures serious sexual dysfunction.

Clearly, there is no one single cause-and-effect factor issue regarding the serial killer, and a systems-type model must be examined as the sum of its parts. The critical features of this theory, such as biological components and incidences of trauma, can be measured only with a systematic examination of a representative sampling of the literature. This does open the analysis to concern, mainly regarding the correlational nature of such a study and its inherent lack of proof of cause and effect. However, this study does not measure the occurrence of one, peripheral, possibly isolated item such as pornography. The theory postulates a combining, cumulative dynamic—one previously suggested and favorably tested with regard to other mental conditions, such as schizophrenia. This theory simply goes one step further, noting the propensity of violent offenders to have genetic abnormalities and serial killers to have suffered environmental traumas.

Furthermore, although the correlational nature of this study does not necessarily prove causation, a "high correlation occurring would strengthen the credibility of the hypothesis in that it has survived a chance at disconfirmation" (Campbell & Stanley, 1963, p. 64). Given the number of variables within the theory under consideration, high correlation would legitimately indicate the presence of a condition, clinically recognizable as the serial killer, much as it does for the antisocial or the borderline personality.

The case study analysis is an appropriate method of examining this theory, considering the limited population of subjects available. Small numbers of hard data would result in minimal statistical validity, weakening a quantitative analysis. Sproull (1988) noted, "In some research projects it is not feasible or desirable to carry out experiments which often intrude on the natural setting, are perhaps more costly or perhaps [when] subjects are not available in a laboratory situation. The research problem still needs to be explored but under nonexperimental conditions" (p. 149).

Also, much of the available information could be deemed secondhand and occasionally anecdotal. This could cause problems in what Denzin (1978, p. 225) refers to as the *reality distance* problem, leading to errors from translation and interpretation. Indeed, it is this anecdotal dimension that weakens much of the research. Even the actual guilt of some killers could be brought into question—for example, Albert DeSalvo. According to one retired New York policeman, another suspect may have killed as many as 12 of the 13 DeSalvo admitted to murdering ("2nd Boston strangler eyed," 1993).

Other problems include a built-in weakness regarding external validity, in that some information comes from convenience samples of incarcerated individuals or other reactive subjects, such as victim's and offender's families and relations.

Finally, ecological validity might be compromised by the manner in which killers speak after being apprehended as opposed to how they respond while engaged in their crimes and when unconcerned with consequences. Researcher Howard S. Becker observed incarcerated criminals "are no longer operating under normal circumstances; they now respond to vastly different controls, and in particular may think by telling their story in one way or another they can use the researcher to influence the authorities on whom their fate depends. They may tell only 'sad stories,' self-justifying tales of how they got where they are" (Denzin, 1970, p. 87). Clearly, the most challenging aspect of this material is judging credibility and using multiple sources for comparative analysis and interpretation. Errors and biases must be considered and guarded against.

However, this ex post facto qualitative analysis does allow review of a theory that is intuitive in nature and deals with a subject difficult to translate into qualitative data. This naturalistic inquiry allows for simplified understanding of variables (coherence conditions) that may well develop simultaneously with the inquiry, rather than prior to it (Lincoln & Guba, 1985).

Lincoln and Guba also note "the output of naturalism often is a locally grounded theory" and "such theories typically take the form of pattern theories" (p. 49). They quote Reason, a researcher familiar with pattern model theory: "The pattern model involves a number of phenomena all of equal importance, then explaining the connections between them" (p. 49). Lincoln and Guba argue that theories commonly emerging from naturalistic inquiries are of a form (pattern theories) well understood by philosophers of science.

This analysis is a step away from a pure grounded theory, in which a model is developed as a result of continuous evaluation of the literature. It has been, as Egger (1990) put it, "continually shaped and reshaped from analytical interpretations and discoveries" and "shaped intentionally from the data rather than from preconceived, logically deduced theoretical frameworks" (p. 138). The diathesis–stress aspect of the model presented here could be considered grounded theory, yet it is but part of a larger picture.

The theory proposed is appropriately described as intuitive and developed from personal insight, stemming from accumulated study and a review of the research and literature. Glaser and Strauss (1967) said: "An insight, whether borrowed or original, is of no use to the theorist unless he converts it from being simply an anecdote to being an element of theory" (p. 254). This being the case, the preliminary theory presented here must be considered by analysis measuring the elements of the model and through examination of the case histories.

ELEMENTAL ANALYSIS

The assumptions outlined earlier and the correlational approach described provides the basic structure for analysis of the case studies. These studies must be viewed from a consistent vantage point, considering the existence of the aforementioned elements of the theory.

There is essentially an inductive thematic content analysis performed in this study. The themes comprising the eventual elements observed are a result of a review of the literature (or data)—they are noted as a pattern of behavior and are considered to be measurable. Berg (1995) noted, "researchers must first decide at what level they plan to sample and what units of analysis will be counted" (p. 178). The categories (or elements) emerged from a thorough review of the literature and case studies and essentially chose themselves.

First, is there evidence of physiological anomalies in the subject's history? Analysis will apply the biological component of the theory to see if there is evidence of distinct physiological differences, whether congenital, hereditary, or induced by trauma.

Secondly, is there evidence of severe environmental trauma in the subject's history? This consideration will pertain to abuse, either emotional or physical, but severe enough to markedly disturb the individual or affect personality development.

Has the subject evidenced clinically antisocial behavior from an early age and/or committed lesser crimes prior to his first murder? This question looks for activities such as the MacDonald triad, as well as other antisocial behaviors that might mark the subject as different, possibly dangerous, from an early age. It also seeks incidences of criminality prior to the subjects' first murder.

Has the subject ever evidenced problematic sexual deviance? As mentioned earlier, this is an element viewed with varied importance among researchers. However, it is a critical aspect of this book's theoretical basis. The analysis simply regards the history of violent sexuality, problematic homosexuality, or other sexual paraphilic motivations or desires that might be tied to later predatory behavior.

Next, has the subject shown evidence of dissociative episodes? The examination will look for a historical propensity to live in a fantasy state or to be lost from reality for noticeable periods of time, most often by more than one observer.

Since the analysis of the initial four case studies in the original work, I have added four additional case studies, and introduced a level of diversity by including an African American offender as well as a woman. Clearly, the sample size reduces any general inference to be made across these groups, but it does provide additional dimensions to consider.

As well, the additional four cases along with the original ones consider the presence of personality disorders that can tell us quite a bit about the subject's personality and potential mental illness.

Finally, has the subject committed predatory murders of a serial nature? This question simply asks if the individual falls within the strict parameters of this analysis. It could be said this reduces the serial killer to what Gibbons (1987) called an *offender typology*. Gibbons was concerned that this caused an "oversimplified characterization of the real world of criminality" (p. 219). However, the serial killer diagnosis is reasonably clear and explicit enough to be able to assign the offender to a distinct typological category, which can be explored and substantiated through research efforts and not be considered oversimplified. The serial killer label is also narrowly focused within the context of this book.

Andrei Chikatilo. (© Georges de Keerle/Sygma/Corbis.)

Arthur Shawcross. (© Bettmann/CORBIS.)

Jeffrey Dahmer. (© Reuters/CORBIS.)

Anthony Sowell. (© Mark Duncan/AP/Corbis.)

Edmund Kemper. (© Bettmann/CORBIS.)

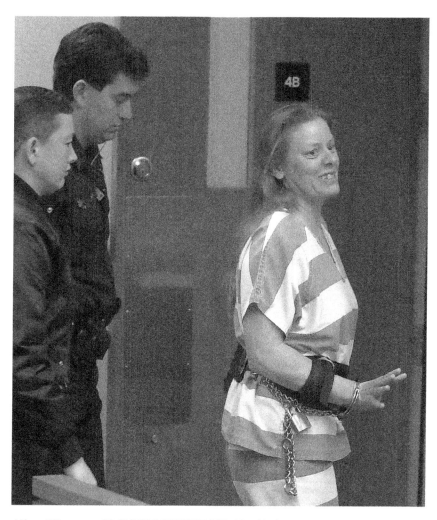

Aileen Wuornos. (© DOUG ENGLE/AP/Corbis.)

Dennis Rader. (© Handout/Sedgwick County Sheriff's Office/Reuters/Corbis.)

Rodney Alcala. (© Nick Ut/AP/Corbis.)

6

Case Studies

I feel like I'm—kind of like I'm a star right now.

—Dennis Rader

SELECTION OF CASES

A total of four case studies were originally reviewed for this study. These cases were selected mainly for their ease of availability and completeness of material. Their names and span of killing include:

Name	Span of Killing
1. Andrei Chikatilo	1978–1990
2. Arthur Shawcross	1972–1989
3. Jeffrey Dahmer	1978–1991
4. Edmund Kemper	1964–1973

Originally, the temptation to include Aileen Wuornos in the group was resisted, because changing the homogeneity of the subject population would confound the issues being studied. The population sample for female killers is limited, therefore can be an unreliable basis for drawing any conclusions.

These cases are well documented and reasonably complete. They also represent a time period ranging from the 1960s through the 1990s. The sample was limited to four to allow proper examination of each case; four has been a workable number of cases for comparable studies (Egger, 1985).

These subjects have all proved to be receptive to interview. Interviews of the subjects as well as of family and friends are an integral step in assembling a complete historical picture; indeed, these subjects' interviews offer a depth of information. At the time of the original analysis, all of the subjects were still alive and all had freely admitted their crimes, paving the way for personal introspection of their motivations and outside observation of their personality development.

Since the time of this study, additional cases were the logical next step. This time, I did include Aileen Wuornos, for the exact opposite reason I did not include her the first time. Another dimension of the latest look at this subject should include a representative sample of (1) a woman and (2) an African American. Clearly in terms of scientific method there are issues of small sample size, but in a case-study approach, inclusion of race and gender do offer a larger picture. Further discussion of differing elements from the first study is found in Chapter 7.

In addition to Wuornos are case studies of Anthony Sowell, an African American male from Cleveland; Dennis Rader, the Kansas BTK strangler; and Rodney Alcala, the Dating Game Killer from California.

Additional Cases

5. Anthony Sowell	2007–2009
6. Aileen Wuornos	1989–1990
7. Dennis Rader	1974–1991
8. Rodney Alcala	1971–1979

The only other significant change to this analysis was the addition of related personality disorders to the examination of dissociative process, in the first four cases, and in the later ones as well. Most serial killers have a litany of personality disorders, usually antisocial or borderline at a minimum, but in some cases the disorders are actually related to the fantasy or dissociative process.

SUMMARIES OF CASES

CASE 1: ANDREI CHIKATILO

Andrei Chikatilo has been labeled by some as the most prolific serial killer of modern times. The Russian accumulated at least 53 murders to his credit, while the ferocity and pure sexual sadism he inflicted on his victims was hard to imagine.

Chikatilo, born in 1936, was raised during the squalor and famine of the Stalin regime. He and his sister, Tatyana, were told a horrific tale of the fate of their brother, Stepan: that he had been captured and eaten. His father had been captured by the Nazis during the war, and placed in a work camp, which for Chikatilo proved to be a source of shame and rejection by those around him.

Chikatilo retreated to the safety of his own mind, all the while suffering the continual taunts of schoolmates for his ineptness, often the result of terribly poor and uncorrected eyesight. Dressed in rags, he had no friends, and often clung to his mother's side, another trait that usually exacerbated the torment from other children.

Chikatilo married and had two children, a wonder in itself considering his aversion to normal sexual activity. It took a great deal of effort and patience for his wife, Fayina, to lead Chikatilo through the traditional sexual acts, as his interests were of a different kind. He soon embarked on a long career of molesting young children, losing jobs, and moving around as a result. He also had an interest in prostitutes, who helped him practice his more hard-core proclivities, but it was the children—along with the torture, capture, and fear he could inflict on them—that excited him.

Chikatilo committed his first murder in 1978, stabbing to death a 9-year-old girl after an unsuccessful attempt at rape. This murder resulted in the forced conviction of an erroneous suspect, who, sadly for him, had a past that included the murder of a teenage girl and whose semen type matched the specimen found at the Chikatilo murder scene. The suspect was executed five years later.

Another change of jobs required Chikatilo to travel, and suddenly his interest in predation fitted nicely with his daily habits, offering a convenient excuse for travel and stays away from home. He would meet victims at bus stops, earn their trust, and take an eventual walk in the woods—always with the same result—violent death and carnage. He killed males and females of different ages, the important point being that they were powerless and easy prey. His need for inflicting fear and pain painted his attacks, as he dismembered, cannibalized, stabbed with frenzy, raped, and masturbated at the scenes of his slaughter.

Finally, in November 1990, Citizen X, as he came to be known, was apprehended, ending a reign of terror the Russian society had never experienced. Chikatilo attempted many defenses, ranging from claims that he was influenced by dirty pictures and videos to assertions of insanity, complete with examples of proper bizarre behaviors to support his charade. After a six-month trial he was found sane and guilty and was sentenced to death. He was executed in 1994.

PHYSIOLOGICAL FACTORS

Chikatilo's background information at times mentions head trauma, although this is unproven. Interviews commonly include stories of beatings of the head, but these reports are spotty and unspecific. In 1984 he received treatment for dystonia, a neurological movement disorder where sustained muscle contractions cause twisting and repetitive movements or abnormal postures. Potential causes include physical trauma, heredity, and infection.

Chikatilo reported a history of severe headaches, although these also are unsubstantiated. His mother supposedly had a history of the same problems.

His blood type of AB was originally mistakenly analyzed as A because the B antigen was not clearly defined in his blood; it was contained in his saliva, sweat, and hair. This condition greatly confused the authorities during the investigation, as his odd sperm and blood type are found in only 1 in 20,000 people. This condition was not even considered until a medical team from abroad published findings regarding this rare anomaly in late 1988 (Krivich & Ol'gin, 1993).

Andrei Tikachenko of the Serbski Institute in Moscow, who analyzed Chikatilo for two months, noted various physiological problems. He observed impotence and attributed certain urges to prenatal brain damage. He also noted a familiar trait—bed-wetting until age 12 (Solotaroff, 1993).

Evidence regarding other biological issues, especially chemical details and genetics, is incomplete. The fact that the killer was in Russia, and these types of studies were not routinely considered, left much unexplored. However, the biological considerations cannot be overlooked, whether they are predispositions or developed after birth. The fact is that other members of his family, as well as neighbors, who shared his background, did not grow up to be serial killers. This observation is, of course, intuitive and is based on weakly substantiated correlations.

ENVIRONMENTAL TRAUMA

Chikatilo's background of trauma, witnessing "blown-apart children" and "gathering the corpses . . . in pieces" (Krivich & Ol'gin, 1993, p. 113), as well as the sheer squalor and poverty of his youth, would certainly justify his experiencing symptoms of posttraumatic stress syndrome. He would clearly qualify as one who experienced an exceptionally damaging upbringing.

The experience that appears to have had the greatest impact was hearing the harrowing tale of his older brother, who was said to have been kidnapped and eaten. Instances of such happenings were true in this area during that time. The story is unconfirmed, but even if Chikatilo only believed it to be true, it still would have had a devastating effect. In fact, his psychiatrist, Aleksandr Bukhanovsky, felt that his story of cannibalism, real or imagined, was the main factor that led him to his crimes as a cannibal killer.

Another significant factor stemmed from the muscular condition suffered by his younger sister, which "caused her rectum to fall out of her anus." Chikatilo "spent his prepubescent years haunted by the sight of her and their mother stuffing it back in" (Solotaroff, 1993, p. 96).

His childhood was seriously flawed. He was relentlessly mocked and ridiculed by his peers for his shortcomings in school and the embarrassments of his family. His young life was spent friendless. Chikatilo's own rationale was that he, before he became a criminal, "was first a victim" (Krivich & Ol'gin, 1993, p. 143).

EARLY ANTISOCIAL BEHAVIOR AND PRIOR CRIMES

Chikatilo's early crimes of child molestation (his pink period), during which time he discovered his preference for sadism, was the very beginning of his developing pathology. His sexual deviance culminated in his committing the largest number of confirmed kills by any serial killer to date. This statistical distinction is likely the result of law enforcement agencies' inability to catch him, however, rather than any particular skill or psychological aspect of his personality.

His early crimes included fondling and injuring a girl in a boarding school where he worked, costing him his job. This was all it cost him, unfortunately, as he eventually ended up in a teaching position and repeatedly made advances to young students. He also accosted his own six-year-old niece. He knew from the outset that young children excited him. However, he was yet to learn the sexual thrill of eliciting cries of help and inflicting pain. Only after his rape and first murder of a little girl in 1978 did he "understand how to satisfy his own lust" (Krivich & Ol'gin, 1993, p. 173).

PROBLEMATIC SEXUAL DEVIANCE

Chikatilo's sexual problems began with his inability to sustain an erection during normal sex and the discovery that orgasm could be reached only after infliction of sadistic pain, coupled with the act of coitus while the victim was in the process of dying. It is hard to determine whether his sadism was driven by rage over the inability to consummate a normal sexual act, or his ineptness was caused by a lack of interest in nonviolent sex. His only conventional sexual relationship with a woman other than his wife was with a mistress he took while married, a former wife of his brother-in-law.

His interests before developing a taste for sadism focused on children; he was "irresistibly drawn to children." He wanted to "see their naked bodies, their sexual organs" (Krivich & Ol'gin, 1993, p. 77). However, after his first murder, he realized that blood aroused him and that nothing else would satisfy him sexually. He was excited by inflicting pain and often had orgasms while the victims were in the final spasms of death. His actions were clearly sexually deviant:

> Chikatilo boiled and ate sawn-off testicles or nipples of his victims, or carved slits in some corpses to use for his own brand of necrophilic sex, often not bothering to kill his trussed teen-age victims before the butchery started. . . . The cutting or biting off of male genitals and the excision of a female uterus was followed by a chewing of the organs. Uteruses, he said later, "were so beautiful and elastic."
>
> (Martingale, 1993, pp. 135, 140)

He was actually described not just as a sadist but also as a necrosadist. "He needed to see his victims die to achieve sexual satisfaction," wrote

Dr. Aleksandr Bukhanovsky. "His killings were an analogue to sexual inter-course" (Cullen, 1993, p. 126).

PERSONALITY DISORDERS OR DISSOCIATIVE EPISODES

Chikatilo had often been described as detached and removed, which could suggest a dissociative process. It would seem closer to doubling, given his remarkable memory for detail in the majority of the murders. His ferocious sadism during the crimes would resemble Grotstein's description regarding doubling in Chapter 2: that Chikatilo displayed "evil, sadism, destructive-ness and even demoniacal possession" while wearing the mask of sanity as husband, father, and grandfather. Also, comments from Chikatilo himself, such as "I'm alone in my fantasies, my daydreams" (Krivich & Ol'gin, 1993, p. 115) and "I fantasized my whole life and sometimes couldn't tell my fanta-sies from reality" (Lourie, 1993, p. 230), reveal a preference to remain within himself.

Others in his life agreed. Fellow employees stated that "his head was in the clouds" and "he was not all there." During meetings in the director's of-fice, he sat in silence, staring off into space, or yawning (Krivich and Ol'gin, 1993, pp. 187–188). Even when he taught school, students and colleagues alike noted his listless, detached manner, snapping out of daydreams saying, "What was I talking about?" He could "stand silently, for almost an entire class session, rocking slightly to and fro with his hands clasped behind his back" (p. 162).

SERIAL MURDER

Chikatilo's well-documented history of 53 murders committed in a preda-tory, methodical manner easily qualifies him as a serial killer within the pa-rameters established for this study. All his killings appeared to be driven by a desire to commit the act and relieve the accompanying pressure and sexual tension. The acts continued for years and it appears would have done so in-definitely, if not for his eventual capture.

OTHER OBSERVATIONS

Chikatilo's history reflects the clinical observations of serial killers. Ob-viously, his murderous activities over the course of 13 years would suggest obsessive compulsiveness, along with his rituals after each crime. Also, his signature wound inflictions (eye and genital mutilation) are quite consistent with FBI profiles of serial killers. He escalated in frenzy and sadism:

Not only had he tormented the boy with knife pricks on the throat and chest, not only had he inflicted wounds after death . . . not only had he taken the genitals and wounded the eyes, this time he had opened the body and ripped out the heart with his bare hands.

(Lourie, 1993, p. 179)

Chikatilo most definitely suffered from a defective mental capacity; however, the trial court's decision in finding him sane and responsible for his actions appears correct. This is evidenced most clearly by his ability to hold back his killing for a two-year period while he knew they were looking for him. He could not claim being unable to control his actions, as he managed to refrain from killing as frequently in cold months, when it was more difficult and uncomfortable.

In further testimony to his planned behavior, he always carried his knives with him when he traveled, an obvious predatory behavior. He did display some suggestion of paranoia, but it is hard to discern the true pathology needed for an insanity defense at this point.

His skill level reflects that of prior killers, as his first crimes were committed "cautiously, nervously and ineptly," whereas later ones were "handled with more finesse and resolve" (Krivich & Ol'gin, 1993, p. 190). The crimes increased in their ferocity, and as discussed previously, did not appear to have an end in sight at the time of his capture.

CASE 2: ARTHUR SHAWCROSS

Arthur Shawcross, dubbed the "Genesee River Killer," terrorized the city of Rochester, New York, with a series of 11 killings over a two-year span beginning in February 1988. He was finally captured as he was observed revisiting a corpse at the site of one of his murders. He was convicted and sentenced to 250 years in prison without parole. He died of cardiac arrest in prison in 2008.

His history includes grisly stories of violence and cannibalism while serving in Vietnam. His erratic, abusive relationships with his mother and family, along with personal sexual problems, clouded and affected his development throughout his early and adult life.

Shawcross committed two child-sex murders and was in prison for 17 years. Regrettably, and against the protests of his parole officers and other prison officials who had examined him, he was released, only to continue his habits of rape and murder. He then practiced against powerless adults and added cannibalism to his crimes.

His case is an interesting study in the consistent nature of a serial killer. He was profiled by the FBI during his New York rampage, and the profile fit almost perfectly—with one flaw. The FBI estimated his age at mid- to late 20s; Shawcross was 43. The difference was the 17 years of prison. When he was released, he picked right up where he had left off in his late 20s.

PHYSIOLOGICAL FACTORS

From a biological standpoint, Shawcross may be the best researched serial killer. The research conducted by Richard Kraus, cited in previous chapters, is extensive and conclusive in its position that Shawcross had a different biological makeup from most men. The discovery of his genetic (XYY) coding, elevated kryptopyrrole reading (10 times the normal amount), abnormal

EEG readings, and head traumas all have clear links to violence and impulse control.

Kraus also noted that Shawcross's kryptopyrrole level correlated to:

> partial disorientation, abnormal EEG's, general nervousness, depression, episodes of dizziness, chest and abdominal pains, progressive loss of ambition, poor social performance and decreased sexual potency all found in the history of Arthur Shawcross. Other correlates were "marked irritability, rages, terrible problems with stress and anger control, mood swings, poor memory, violence and antisocial behavior."

> (Norris, 1992, p. 306)

While in prison Shawcross displayed severe scars on his arms, caused by apparent regular self-mutilation, something often found in borderline personality cases. He was also diagnosed with a prostate ailment.

As a child he experienced many head traumas, including being hit in the head with a stone, an injury that caused periodic bouts of childhood paralysis. He was hit in the head by a discus while in high school, and also by a sledgehammer in a work accident. Several injuries also occurred as a result of beatings in his home. Radiological studies revealed lesions on his brain and a cyst as a result of childhood injuries. His mother felt that "maybe because he had been knocked unconscious a few times it distorted his thinking"—a bit of an understatement.

Shawcross's case history contains a plethora of biological and physical research that would be considered ideal in most studies, but rarely is made available. Kraus's work, along with details discussed by Dorothy Otnow-Lewis, a defense expert witness, included chromosome analysis of his cells revealing an XYY condition, a brain magnetic resonance imaging (MRI) exposing a cyst in a temporal lobe, scars and lesions in both frontal lobes, and a history of seizures (Otnow-Lewis, 1998, pp. 273, 275, 281).

ENVIRONMENTAL TRAUMA

Shawcross's history of trauma also fits the standard profile. He was seen as visibly unnerved in the presence of his mother. Once, during a visit by his parents while in prison, he just hung his head and spoke in baby talk. He always required mothering and nurturing from women, presumably, to replace what he lacked from his mother.

His mother continuously berated him and disapproved of his actions. He never could please her or win her love in any way, nor could he develop any sense of esteem or intimacy. She constantly withheld physical and emotional love from Shawcross, according to several reports, and treated him differently from the normal children. She beat him regularly with a variety of instruments, yet she denied any deficiency in their relationship. It's unlikely Shawcross developed any degree of normal attachment.

He spoke of an incident of oral sex with his sister, but reports of this incident remain inconsistent and are unsubstantiated. His experiences in Vietnam were also unsubstantiated, but appear to have had a profound effect on his life. He told stories of incredible violence in a misspelled, hand-written account:

> I shot one woman [and] tied her up. . . . I cut that first girl's throat. Then took off her head and placed it on a pole. . . . That girl at the tree peed, then fainted. . . . I gave her oral sex . . . then retied her to two other small trees. . . . I cut her slightly from neck to crotch. She screamed and shit herself. I took my M16, pulled on a nipple then put the gun to her forehead and pulled the triger. Cut off her head and placed it on a pole. . . . I killed 39 people in Viet Nam. Scared alot and wounded more! When I left Viet Nam, I wasn't ready for the states.

(Olsen, 1993, pp. 190–191)

EARLY ANTISOCIAL BEHAVIOR AND PRIOR CRIMES

Along with his first murders and war crimes, Shawcross had a history of antisocial and illegal activity. He had a past filled with arson, theft, and breaking and entering, much of which he explained away as not knowing what he was doing. He often blamed his actions on stressors such as his divorce or alcohol.

However, his antisocial behaviors started at an early age. Shawcross wet the bed and repeatedly ran away from home. A teacher reported that he brought an iron bar on the school bus and hit other children with it. He constantly was involved in fights and was ferociously brutal, as he never knew when to stop. He accompanied each blow with a sound effect from a comic book (Bang!-Zap!-Pow!). One school report stated, "there is a general feeling one can't tell what he will do" (Olsen, 1993, p. 169).

Further evaluations noted that he had no playmates, was negative toward everything at home, and directed hostility against defenseless objects and younger children. He would often talk baby talk and fake a cry to get attention. His scores in school were below normal, and he clearly demonstrated he did not care.

He still wet the bed in his teens and set fires, a behavior he began as a young child. He would often talk to himself in public, as others kept their distance. He also tortured animals regularly, and his cousin reported that he liked to watch them suffer and see how long it took them to die. Friends reported that this included skinning live fish, snaring rabbits and snapping their necks, placing bats inside parked cars to watch the drivers panic, tying cats together and drowning them, pounding squirrels and chipmunks flat, shooting darts at frogs nailed to his dart board, running a stick completely through a snapping turtle and scraping the feathers from baby birds.

His misbehavior continued, usually following his main interests of thievery, fire, and sex. Numerous scrapes with the law followed him straight to his draft into the army.

PROBLEMATIC SEXUAL DEVIANCE

Shawcross's sexual problems are also not hard to illustrate. In a statement he tried to explain how he was introduced to sex:

> After I was first introduced to sex by my Aunt Tina, I became obsessed with sex . . . [he would constantly masturbate and have touching sessions and oral sex with another boy his age, about 9]. Then I started to have oral sex with my sister. . . . One time Mike [his friend] and I started playing with sheep. We didn't know that sheeps had organs like a woman. . . . When I was 14 a man stopped to give me a lift, then he grabbed me by the throat and told me to take my pants down! He held onto my balls and sucked me off. . . . After that when I masturbated I could not cum until I inserted a finger in my ass. Why I don't know. One day I did it to a chicken. It died. Then a cow, a dog and a horse. I didn't know where this was leading up to.
>
> (Olsen, 1993, p. 184)

An army psychiatrist also warned Shawcross's wife to keep him away from fire, because arson provided him with sexual enjoyment. While in Green Haven, the maximum-security correctional facility in Stormville, York, where Shawcross was imprisoned, he was often examined by psychiatrists and counselors. One diagnosis stated that he was a dangerous schizophrenic pedophile and had an oral erotic fixation with a need for maternal protection. Another referred to his psychosexual conflicts.

When his parole office referred Shawcross to the Genesee Mental Health Center, he was diagnosed as suffering from inhibited sexual excitement, inhibited orgasm, secondary impotence, sexual sadism, and a prostate ailment. He admitted to numerous (85–100) dates with prostitutes in Rochester, in an attempt to find out why he couldn't keep an erection or have an orgasm.

He killed some prostitutes after they mocked his sexual inadequacies. He also enjoyed having hookers act dead during sex, exciting him from necrophilic standpoint of the total control and acceptance. He finally committed acts of cannibalism:

> He returned to the site [of a prior murder where he buried the body in the snow] and with a small handsaw, scraped off the snow and cut out her vagina. "After I sawed it out, I pulled out the hairs and wrapped it in a bar towel. Went back to the car and . . . sat playing with myself and the vagina. Then I put it in my mouth and ate it. I had no control at all. Why did I do this?"
>
> (Norris, 1992, p. 47)

PERSONALITY DISORDERS OR DISSOCIATIVE EPISODES

Shawcross reportedly showed periods of fantasy states and dissociation throughout his life. He commonly would "retreat into himself, mute and immobile for hours," according to his wife. Others spoke of his going for walks and blacking out, often not remembering where he'd been or what he'd done.

Diagnostic reports observed his hearing voices when depressed and the fact that he was engaged in fantasy as a source of satisfaction. They also noted his inappropriate or lack of affect. A girlfriend also reported that he heard taunts in his head when he hid in the woods.

His childhood was colored with the same stories. A cousin noted that "Artie" always had a blank look, evident in baby pictures, looking straight ahead with no expression. At 7, he created imaginary friends out of loneliness. He carried on conversations at length, apparently talking to himself.

A teacher's evaluation said that he "appears to be indulging in a considerable amount of fantasy in which he perceives himself as a new person with respect and dignity" (Olsen, 1993, p. 170). Dr. Richard Kraus noted that Shawcross retreated to a fantasy world as a child, and 35 years and 13 murders later was still involved in the same fantasies, "denying his failures and masculine inadequacy" (Olsen, 1993, p. 490).

Defense witness Dr. Otnow-Lewis also noted a childhood history including "hysterical paralysis, a psychiatric disorder induced by trauma and consistent with his later dissociative states" (1998, p. 275) and stated Shawcross fell into a "deep, postseizure sleep" and awakened after the murders with a "hazy and distorted" memory of his crimes (p. 272).

SERIAL MURDER

Shawcross meets the criteria for a serial killer. He, like many others, felt nothing toward his victims other than using them as sources of sexual satisfaction and stress relief. He killed children for sex and pleasure, spent 17 years in prison, obtained his freedom, and promptly continued killing for his own gratification. He escalated as time went by, getting more careless and stepping up to cannibalism. He killed 11 more people and was stopped only through apprehension by law enforcement authorities.

OTHER OBSERVATIONS

Shawcross exhibited the impulse-control difficulties shown by many serial killers; he used anger to deal with stress. He also was seen to develop elaborate and somewhat dysfunctional defenses in managing his feelings.

His past was filled with dysfunctional features, such as borderline personality disorder, schizophrenia, posttraumatic stress, antisocial personality disorder, narcissism, sadism, and psychopathic behavior. It also included long-term obsessive-compulsive behavior, prompting observations of Shawcross as someone evidencing an external attempt to control inner chaos. Also, returning to a scene and urinating over a recent victim in broad daylight is a classic way for the lust murderer to demonstrate control. It was during this important phase of behavior that he was observed and apprehended.

CASE 3: JEFFREY DAHMER

On Tuesday, July 23, 1991, Tracey Edwards, still wearing handcuffs, flagged down Milwaukee police and took them to Apartment 213, North 25th Street, where he said he had been the near victim of a homicide.

Here, police discovered photographs of the mutilation of human bodies and the secret of Jeffrey L. Dahmer was uncovered. Edwards, who later at trial said Dahmer had told him he would "eat his heart" ("Witness," 1992), led police to where Dahmer had killed, dismembered, defiled, and even cannibalized a series of young men. This brought an end to a grisly pattern of death that had, for years, gone on seemingly unnoticed.

Dahmer's legacy began in 1978, when the then 18-year-old picked up a male hitchhiker and brought him to his grandmother's house for drinking and sex. When he attempted to leave, Dahmer hit him with a barbell, killing him. He then used a sledgehammer to smash the body into pieces and disposed of the evidence in nearby woods.

From that first murder until the time of his arrest, Dahmer admitted luring 15 to 17 men from various locations, including shopping malls, bus stops, and gay bars. He took them to his grandmother's house in West Allis, Wisconsin, and later to his apartment in Milwaukee, drugging and killing them.

He would offer his guests a concoction of alcohol or coffee, spiked with a sleeping potion suspected of either a benzodiazepine such as Lorazepam (a tranquilizing medication he received while under treatment), menzodiazepine, or another undetected drug. Police also discovered chloroform in his closet (Davis, 1991, p. 275).

Dahmer admitted to taking pornographic and postmortem Polaroids of victims in various stages of mutilation, killing by strangulation, stabbing and battery, eviscerating the flesh, and dismembering the bodies. He told of cutting up the pieces with knives and an electric saw so they were small enough to be thrown in the trash or flushed down the toilet. He also melted down the torsos of victims in a 57-gallon drum of acid he kept in his apartment. He kept trophies, boiling the heads to keep the skulls, and even painting them to make them appear artificial and more acceptable for display. He also kept body parts, such as skeletons, hands, and penises, for gratification and masturbation (Milwaukee Police Department, 1991).

He subsequently admitted performing crude brain surgery on victims in hopes of creating zombies as sexual slaves. He told police that he ate one victim's heart, a bicep, and a thigh, and planned to eat body parts stored in his refrigerator ("Juror," 1992). He also had oral and anal sex with the bodies (Dvorchak & Holewa, 1991, p. 273). This necrophilia was introduced as evidence of an uncontrollable influence in his life by his defense, a cornerstone of his unsuccessful plea of insanity.

He was eventually found sane and guilty of 15 counts of murder receiving 15 consecutive life sentences, totaling 962 years, before he would become eligible for parole. In his first public statement since the slayings, he told the judge he was not seeking freedom by pleading insanity, only understanding. "This has never been a case of trying to get free," he said (Holewa, 1992). His prison stay was short, however, as he was beaten to death at Wisconsin's Columbia Correctional Center by another inmate in November 1994.

PHYSIOLOGICAL FACTORS

The majority of evidence regarding Dahmer's physiological abnormalities concerns his family history—mainly his father's childhood and his mother's condition prior to delivery. As a child, Dahmer developed various infections that required injections. He also had a birth defect diagnosed as a double hernia. However, no other biological abnormalities were noted or, more specifically, measured in Dahmer himself. The significant biological factors regarding Dahmer appear inherited.

His mother, Joyce, experienced a litany of problems during her pregnancy, ranging from excessive nausea, extreme nervousness, severe depression, and hypersensitivity to noises and odors. She suffered from lack of sleep and developed uncontrollable muscle spasms. About two months prior to Jeffrey's birth, she developed a form of rigidity, which her doctors could never precisely diagnose. She also suffered uncontrollable seizures:

> At times, her legs would lock tightly in place, and her whole body would begin to tremble. Her jaw would jerk and take on a similarly frightening rigidity. During these strange seizures, her eyes would bulge like a frightened animal, and would begin to salivate, literally frothing at the mouth.
>
> (Dahmer, 1994, pp. 33–34)

Joyce received a host of medications for her physical and emotional problems, including barbiturates, morphine, and phenobarbital. Eventually, in the waning months of her pregnancy she was taking as many as 26 pills a day.

Dahmer's father, Lionel, had a childhood obsession with fires, one to almost burning down a neighbor's garage. Later, he began making bombs, once blowing a boy off a bicycle. He also noted a deep-rooted bond between himself and his son, in the sharing of recurring violent fantasies:

> There were areas of my son's mind, tendencies and perversities which I had held within myself all my life. Jeff had multiplied these tendencies exponentially, his sexual perversion generating acts that were beyond my understanding. . . . Nonetheless, I could see their distant origins within myself, and slowly, over time, I began to see him truly as my son in far deeper ways than I had previously imagined.
>
> (Dahmer, 1994, p. 212)

Lionel Dahmer related observations of Jeffrey's violent thoughts and fantasies as a teenager, dreaming repeatedly of murder. He himself had shared the same fantasies and dreams from the age of 8 to his early 20s. He also recalled a desire as a child to hypnotize and control others, much like Jeffrey's later cravings for sex zombies.

ENVIRONMENTAL TRAUMA

Dahmer's home life, while apparently not featuring physical abuse, was filled with upheaval and discontent. His parents' divorce was ugly, angry, and upsetting, and their bouts were legendary, including Joyce's threatening Lionel with a knife.

Dahmer would flee the house during these brawls and slap at trees. An eventual custody battle ensued over his younger brother, David. His mother eventually abandoned Dahmer, alone in the house with little food, and left with David. He was 18 at the time, but not emotionally prepared for the situation. Dahmer was found shell-shocked and alone like a lost little boy (Dahmer, 1994, p. 94). Also found in the house was a pentagram drawn in chalk on an old coffee table. He admitted he was conducting a séance, trying to contact the dead.

Details of specific trauma are sketchy. After returning from prison (for child sexual assault) in 1990, he "had no light in his eyes. Jeff lost his soul in there. He said he'd never go back to prison," his stepmother Shari said. "Something happened to him in prison that he would never talk about. We all know what can happen to a child molester in prison" (Dvorchak & Holewa, 1991, p. 96).

An episode of the *Geraldo Rivera* TV show included a guest described as a former family acquaintance who called Shari "the epitome of the evil stepmother." This accusation does not have much support from other accounts and is denied by family members, however.

Other accusations arose from that program. A man identified as Nick, claiming to have had an extended homosexual relationship with Dahmer, said Dahmer told him his father had sexually abused him. This was repeated on the *Phil Donahue* TV show, with the claim that the abuse lasted until Dahmer was 16. Dahmer immediately filed a legal affidavit denying he had ever been abused or molested by his father. His father also vehemently denied this. There were also vague reports about Dahmer being molested as a child by some other individual in the neighborhood, but again details are unsubstantiated and unclear.

EARLY ANTISOCIAL BEHAVIOR AND PRIOR CRIMES

Dahmer was observed as never being able to converse with other children or relate to anyone. He almost invariably remained alone. His foolish acts in school had earned the label for anyone acting silly as doing a Dahmer.

His first expression of violence was reported to have been an act of revenge. He gave a teaching assistant, for whom he developed a rare attachment, a bowl of tadpoles as a gift. She eventually gave the tadpoles to another child. Enraged, Dahmer snuck into the garage where they were kept and poured motor oil in the bowl, killing them.

At age 10, Dahmer was "experimenting" with dead animals, decapitating rodents, bleaching chicken and other animal bones with acid, nailing a dog's carcass to a tree and mounting its severed head on a stake (Newton, 1992, p. 103). He accumulated a vast collection of bodies in his animal cemetery and would impale the skulls of chipmunks and squirrels on crosses. His friends also noted that when they would go fishing, instead of tossing the catch back in the water, Dahmer would cut it open, saying, "I want to see what it looks like inside" (Dvorchak & Holewa, 1991, pp. 40–41).

A pattern of antisocial and irresponsible behavior continued. He was caught with a friend stealing jewelry from his stepmother. In an attempt to get Dahmer on the right course, his father enrolled him in a vocational school, only to find out from Dahmer's grandmother that he had never attended the school.

His brushes with the law included public drunkenness, fights, an arrest for indecent exposure at a state fair, and for masturbating in public, witnessed by two 12-year-old boys. Later there was an arrest for drugging and sexually abusing a Laotian boy, who ended up being the brother of a future victim.

PROBLEMATIC SEXUAL DEVIANCE

Dahmer never had a meaningful sexual relationship with a woman. His homosexuality troubled him, becoming a problem as noted in the *DSM-IV* for a sexual disorder when one's sexual orientation leads to persistent and marked distress. It was the homosexuality factor that Dahmer saw in his victims.

His first killing apparently stemmed from an interlude with a male hitchhiker whose company he enjoyed. When the hitchhiker wanted to leave, Dahmer panicked. He crushed his skull and dismembered the body. He learned to associate violence with his need for intimacy with another man in order to avoid the thing he dreaded most—abandonment.

Dahmer claimed that he had interludes with more than 200 men he met cruising the gay bars and bathhouses of Milwaukee. The relationships were shallow, purely for sex, and devoid of meaningful aspects. His victims were male homosexuals, selected for their attractiveness and chosen to be his sex partners of unconditional acceptance. In other words, he wanted a hostage who could be directed to act as instructed, a warm torso where he could listen to body sounds, and eventually a corpse he could use for any form of personal gratification he chose.

When Dahmer spoke of fantasizing about attacking a jogger, it was in order to lay with him. Dahmer's entire sexual motivation had developed into violence and ultimate demonstrations of control. Incredible thoughts of death and dismemberment had become sexually charged, driven, and satisfied. Dahmer also engaged in cannibalism, which was claimed to be a directly sexual act. Judith Becker, a defense expert witness, stated that "he would periodically take portions [of victims' remains] out of the freezer and cook them.

When he ate them he would become sexually aroused" ("Expert," 1992, p. 3). There was no food in his apartment, only condiments. Inside the freezer were packed lungs, intestines, a kidney, a liver, and a heart, he said, "to eat later" (Chin & Tamarkin, 1991).

PERSONALITY DISORDERS OR DISSOCIATIVE EPISODES

Dahmer's body language suggested dissociation and his lack of affect was noted by family members as early as his childhood. "It was in his motionless face, his dull eyes, in the hard rigidity of his body, in the way his arms did not sway back and forth when he walked, even in the expressionless way he muttered 'sorry'" (Dahmer, 1994, p. 186). His stepmother, Shari, stated, "he couldn't embrace. He couldn't touch. His eyes were dead. This child has no heart left within him. He was a walking zombie" (Dvorchak & Holewa, 1991, p. 32). His father continually referred to Dahmer's demeanor as a "dull, unmoving mask" and noted he had "drifted into a nightmare world of unimaginable fantasies" and his "increasing inwardness and disconnection" (Dahmer, 1994, p. 81).

Dahmer would also drink himself into a numbed state, developing the alcoholism that eventually caused his discharge from the army.

Dahmer was also noted with borderline personality disorder in at least one evaluation.

SERIAL MURDER

Dahmer's acts of predatorily killing at least 15 men and performing sexual acts with the corpses qualify him as a serial killer. He clearly understood the wrongness of his actions, but continued to fulfill the perverted desire to kill and defile the remains. His acts of cannibalism, trophy collection, ritual, and obsession with control are hallmarks of this diagnosis. He also went to great lengths to avoid detection.

OTHER OBSERVATIONS

Some mental health professionals note that during Dahmer's killing career, he had a killing frenzy that represented reconnection with his estranged mother. There had been no contact with her for five years, then after a telephone call from her there was a cluster of seven or eight murders. Dr. Ashok Bedi noted that the bulk of Dahmer's aggression took place after his mother's call. "It was almost as if he had finally managed to secure his mother's attention and he didn't want to lose it again. By doing what he has done, he has irreversibly connected their fates" (Davis, 1991, p. 262).

CASE 4: EDMUND KEMPER

Edmund Kemper set a chilling example for those who would attempt the risky practice of predicting dangerousness. He was incarcerated for the double homicide of his grandparents at age 15. He was "deemed cured in 1969, and the California Youth Authority, responsible for juvenile offenders, took charge of him for the next three years. He was freed in 1972" (Ellroy, 1991,

p. 165). Similar to Arthur Shawcross, Kemper proceeded to commit the grisly murders of eight women, soon after his ill-fated release, decapitating and cannibalizing some of them and performing sexual acts with the corpses.

He was raised by a "shrilly belittling university administrator (and her succession of husbands, none of whom could measure up to her fierce social ambitions) who locked him in a cellar and endlessly berated him for his social failures" (Leyton, 1986, p. 25).

Kemper, who displayed repeated incidences of sadistic behavior as a child, was sent to live with his grandparents. After an argument with his grandmother in August of 1964, he shot her in the back of the head with a rifle, then stabbed her repeatedly after she was dead. He then shot his grandfather and subsequently called the sheriff to confess. He reportedly said during the confession, "I just wondered how it would feel to shoot Grandma" (Cheney, 1992, p. 22).

The doctors recommended, after five years at Atascadero State Hospital, above all that he never be returned to live with his mother. The Youth Authority kept him for three months, then promptly returned him to his mother. Kemper's difficult relationship with his mother only worsened, escalating into furious fights as she ridiculed and embarrassed him. He soon began rehearsing his plans for murder while picking up an estimated 150 hitchhikers in 1970–1971, then finally committed the first of his serial murders.

He killed two coed hitchhikers in May 1972, took the corpses home, and cut them up while his mother was out. He buried the remains in the mountains. He continued killing hitchhikers, carving them up, and performing sexual acts with the cadavers. Once his mother was at home, causing him to have to wait until the next day to dissect and have sex with two of the bodies. Another time, he sliced flesh from the legs of at least two bodies and ate it in a macaroni casserole as a way of possessing his victims.

Eventually, Kemper realized the most prominent of his murderous fantasies. As a child, he would periodically slip into his mother's room with a hammer and knife and fantasize about killing her. Now, faced with the impending discovery of evidence that might tie him to one of the murders, he decided it was time to kill his mother:

Once she had fallen asleep, at five in the morning, Kemper took a claw hammer from the kitchen and, as he had done so often in his imagination, went into her bedroom while she slept. This time, he actually brought the hammer down with considerable force on her right temple, then slashed her throat with his pocketknife. Blood was still gushing as he decided to sever the head as he had done with his other victims. Another slice removed her larynx, and he threw this part into the disposal unit in the kitchen sink. When the disposal was unable to digest the larynx and spewed it back out, Kemper thought this was poetic justice. He wrapped the body in bloody sheets and stashed it in the closet.

(Ressler, 1992, pp. 257–258)

Kemper raped the headless corpse of his mother and propped the head on the mantle for use as a dart board. Not yet satisfied, he invited a friend of his mother over for a surprise dinner in his mother's honor. He bludgeoned and strangled her, decapitated the corpse, and left the headless body in his bed.

After a brief flight, he called authorities and confessed to eight murders. When asked what he thought his punishment should be, he replied, "death by torture." He received life in prison with the possibility of parole.

PHYSIOLOGICAL FACTORS

Physiological research regarding Kemper is incomplete. During some interviews, it has been reported that he would have fits, wobbling his head while never changing the position of his arms, and fixing a gaze on the interviewer. His face would become flushed, his breath came quickly, and he would begin to stutter (Cheney, 1992, p. 195). Kemper also reported experiencing hallucinations and referred to losing control of his body during the killing of his grandparents. His episodes of mental involuntary seizures were what he called his "little zapples."

No organic brain disease was reported during the trial phase. It is not clear what sort of testing, and to what extent, was administered. Kemper, after sentencing, also requested psychosurgery to control his violence and to become productive again. Psychiatrist David Lunde dismissed any application of the XYY theory to Kemper, although he noted that Kemper fit the description of the XYY—unusually tall, above-average intelligence, and unusually violent (Leyton, 1986, p. 59). However, it is unclear what type of testing was done or, more importantly, was not done.

Finally, consideration must be given to Kemper's unusual and enormous size, "in 1969, a 21-year-old behemoth grown to six-foot-nine and some 300 pounds" (Newton, 1990, p. 180).

ENVIRONMENTAL TRAUMA

Kemper's environment was the most obvious dimension of his development. The product of a broken and abusive home, he was belittled by a shrewish mother, who occasionally locked him in the basement when he failed to meet her standards of behavior. He grew up timid and resentful, nursing a perception of his own inadequacy that gave rise to morbid fantasies of death and mutilation (Newton, 1990, p. 179). He was eventually banished to the basement, as his enormous size made his sisters uncomfortable, and his mother considered him a sexual threat to them.

His hellish relationship with his mother destroyed any possible sense of esteem, and ended in her murder. His home was replete with "an alcoholic and overbearing mother, an absent father, favored sisters and a grandmother who was in many ways a worse nurturer than the mother" (Ressler, 1992, p. 249). His mother continuously belittled and embarrassed him, and told him he was the source of her problems. She remarried and divorced twice more between the time Kemper was 10 and 14. Each time, when the marriage was going badly, he would be sent to live with his grandparents on their farm. He hated that and eventually killed them both.

His mother continued to blame her dating problems on Kemper. She once told him, "because of you, my murderous son, I haven't had sex with a man for five years, because no one wants to be with me out of fear of you." She never stopped abusing him mentally (Ressler, 1992, p. 250). He said that their relationship was filled with continuous verbal warfare, so vicious that they would have resulted in fistfights had they not involved his mother. He felt she insisted on these battles, usually over insignificant topics such as having his teeth cleaned (Cheney, 1992, pp. 37–38).

Although the mental health professionals at Atascadaro recognized the incredibly negative effect she had on his obviously fragile psyche, and despite the fact they that strenuously objected to releasing him in her custody, the courts did just that.

EARLY, ANTISOCIAL BEHAVIOR, AND PRIOR CRIMES

Kemper's violent nature was evident from the beginning. As a child, he often played a game in which his sisters took the part of executioners, with Kemper as their victim, writhing in imaginary death throes when they "threw the switch." Preoccupied with visions of decapitation and dismemberment, he cut off the head and hands of his sister's doll—a modus operandi he would repeat as an adult with humans (Newton, 1990, p. 179).

Before the age of 10, he killed his first cat—to make it his—by burying it alive in the yard. When it was dead, he brought it into the house and cut off its head, which he stuck on a spindle and kept in his room. He prayed over it (Cheney, 1992, p. 9).

He later shot to death a pet dog belonging to another boy in the neighborhood. At 13, he was sharpening his father's machete while sitting in the same room with the family's Siamese cat. The pet sometimes seemed to ignore him and appeared to prefer his sisters (much like his mother). Suddenly,

> without even feeling angry toward the cat, he picked it up by the nape of the neck, seized the machete, and slashed off the top of the cat's skull, noting with surgical interest that he had thus exposed the brain. The cat went into convulsions. Edmund, splattered with blood, seized a knife and, holding the cat by one of the forelegs, proceeded to stab it repeatedly in the chest and abdomen. . . . Fearing his mother would call the police and have him jailed, he picked up the dead animal, buried it in the backyard, and cleaned up the mess in his room. Parts of the cat, for reasons that he did not fully understand, he decided to hide in his closet.

> (Cheney, 1992, p. 15)

PROBLEMATIC SEXUAL DEVIANCE

Kemper's assessment of his sexual past was that it was poor, although the particular stories vary. He reported he had a normal sexual relationship only once, but also said that on other occasions he never did and again that he frequently attempted intercourse but never reached climax. He admittedly was constantly consumed with thoughts of sex. In any case, his sexual history was clearly abnormal.

One afternoon, at 7 years of age, he was discussing a childish crush on a teacher. His sister asked why he didn't just kiss her. His deadly serious response was, "If I kiss her, I would have to kill her first." His entire childhood was full of violent fantasy attached to sexual urges. Identified by mental health professionals as a classic sadist, his entire sexual orientation was based on carnage and necrophilia, as well as on the sexual implications of his cannibalism.

His sexual drive conflicted with his incapacities. His earliest sexual fantasies were of women, but the key area was not orgasm but the fact the woman was dead. He felt inadequate sexually, and therefore sexual fantasies were primarily dissatisfying. He said, "I couldn't follow through on the male end of the responsibility, so . . . if I killed them, they couldn't reject me as a man. It was more or less making a doll out of human being" (Leyton, 1986, p. 41).

He had repeated sexual fantasies about his mother and sisters, also complete with violence. He once stood outside a teacher's house one night and imagined what it would be like to kill her and make love to her. He also imagined what it would be like to kill his neighbors and have sex with the corpses (Martingale, 1993, pp. 86–87).

Kemper's need for violence was clear in his having very little sexual contact until after he killed. Moreover, the only act he found sexually exciting was decapitation:

> I remember there was actually a sexual thrill, he said, for he loved to hear the "pop" when the head was separated from the body. You hear that little pop and pull their heads off and hold their heads up by the hair. Whipping their heads off, their body sitting there. That'd get me off.
>
> (Leyton, 1986, p. 42)

PERSONALITY DISORDERS OR DISSOCIATIVE EPISODES

Kemper's fantasies have been previously discussed at length. Escaping from his terrible family life and left with no playmates or friends, he escaped to his mind, filled with violent and sexual fantasy. This was his place of comfort.

In his fantasies, the person was depersonalized, made into an object. "I'm sorry to sound so cold about this," Kemper said, "but what I needed to have was a particular experience with a person, and to possess them in the way I wanted to; I had to evict them from their human bodies." In other words, Kemper was saying that in order to have his sexual fantasies fulfilled, he had to kill his partner (Ressler, 1992, p. 97).

He often sat and stared at people until he made them uncomfortable, in dissociative-like states. In a statement sounding like someone experiencing a mental state resembling dissociation, he once stated, "I believe . . . that there are two people inside me." At times it seemed to him the killings were "horrendous," yet at other times he said "those feelings don't enter my mind" (Cheney, 1992, p. 171).

SERIAL MURDER

Kemper killed a total of 10 people; however, not including the killing of his grandparents at age 15, only the 8 committed after his release from Atascadaro are considered serial by some theorists. I disagree. He did stalk and kill the victims in an obsessive fashion, and he cannibalized and sexually defiled them. He kept trophies and escalated into frenzy toward the end of his rampage. He fits the criteria of a serial killer from the beginning.

OTHER OBSERVATIONS

It is interesting to note a psychiatrist's observation of Kemper, who during the trial, seemed to get great satisfaction and enjoyment from his new-found status as a highly publicized killer. It was suggested that this was the recognition sorely lacking and so craved in his childhood (Cheney, 1992, p. 181). This, of course, is not uncommon among serial killers and is consistent with their narcissistic and overcompensating nature.

He also displayed the obsessive-compulsive pattern of escalation reminiscent of many serial murderers. Kemper mentioned that late in his homicidal career, the urge to kill again struck him as often as a week or two after his last murder. He said the urge was powerful and "the longer I let it go, the stronger it got, to where I was taking risks to go out and kill people" (Cheney, 1992, p. 140).

CASE 5: ANTHONY SOWELL

Anthony Sowell, the only African American serial killer profiled in this chapter, is an offender with a long criminal history who lived in East Cleveland, Ohio. In 1985 he pleaded guilty to attempted rape and served 15 years in prison. He was released in 2005. In 2009, the bodies of 11 women were discovered in his home in a run-down neighborhood. Most of the victims had been strangled in what was being referred to as the "Imperial Avenue Murders," and he was later nicknamed the "Cleveland Strangler." He was charged with 85 counts of aggravated murder, kidnapping, abusing a human corpse, and tampering with evidence (Galbincea, 2010). He considered pleading insanity. Sowell was convicted of 11 counts of murder in July, 2011 and was sentenced to death in August.

Sowell served in the United States Marines for seven years in Okinawa and North Carolina (*Prisoners and Detainees of Ohio*, 2010), earning a few medals and serving without incident. He was known to drink too much at the time, which increased upon his discharge.

According to a court-ordered evaluation of Sowell for a sexual predator hearing in 2005, he stated that he had never received mental health care, participated in counseling, or experienced significant psychiatric symptoms of a mood or thought disorder. "Mr. Sowell stated that he has never experienced prolonged periods of depression," the report said. "He denied current difficulty with sleep, appetite, energy, mood, memory or concentration. He described his general mood as 'good'" (Farkas, 2010).

PHYSIOLOGICAL FACTORS

A public defender stated Sowell had medical problems including a heart condition and required medication (Friedman, 2009). Opening remarks made by Sowell's defense team at trial in 2011 included statements claiming after suffering a heart attack in 2007, Sowell's behavior changed. The theory that Sowell's behavior was markedly different after the heart attack continued throughout the trial. Sowell's attorney claimed after the 2007 heart attack, Sowell's life fell apart. He reportedly could not work, his sexual compulsions got the better of him, and shortly after, women began to disappear (Atassi, 2011b).

A neuropsychologist, Dr. Dale Watson, testified for the defense that he determined Sowell's IQ was 86 and that he had blackouts and heard voices in his head. Watson stated he "processed information more slowly than other people" and concluded Sowell "had a moderate degree of dysfunction and impairment" to his brain (Palmer, 2011).

It was noted at trial by the prosecution that MRIs or other tests were not performed to determine theories regarding brain defects Sowell may have had.

During his 2005 sexual predator evaluation, Sowell admitted to being hit on the head by a light pole at age 16 and had amnesia for about two days (Court Psychiatric Clinic, 2005). A former fellow inmate of Sowell's testified he frequently fell and hit his head on the concrete floor in prison basketball games (Sheeran, 2011b).

ENVIRONMENTAL TRAUMA

Sowell reportedly grew up in a fatherless household with his half-sister and seven cousins who came to live there after the death of their mother. His missing father was never spoken about, and he reportedly didn't get along with his father. He observed a great deal of violence growing up. He reportedly witnessed two cousins stripped, tied with ligatures including extension cords (a method later used by Sowell himself), and beaten. His niece testified to the beatings of Sowell and her at the hands of Sowell's mother and grandmother, while stripped naked and tied to banisters and poles ("Serial killer Sowell's mother," 2011).

Sowell's mother had five children by the age of 18, and according to a social worker, there were rampant mental illnesses, physical problems, and drug abuse on both sides of his family. Reportedly his siblings all acted out in various ways including sexual dysfunction, obsession, overeating, seizures, and lack of ability to care. Social worker Lori Towne also said Sowell reported sexual abuse against him as a child ("Serial killer Anthony Sowell," 2011).

This conflicted with previous statements by Sowell as, according to Sowell, his home was crowded but described his parents in positive terms. He reported being teased and bullied by other children, as a child. He denied all forms of abuse and neglect and left home at 18 to join the Marines. He did not receive a high school diploma (Court Psychiatric Clinic, 2005).

Prosecutors at trial noted that all reports of abuse in the Sowell home environment came from Sowell himself to doctors and social workers who did not witness or verify the stories, nor was there any documented evidence of abuse.

EARLY ANTISOCIAL BEHAVIOR AND PRIOR CRIMES

A cousin reported that Sowell raped her on a regular basis in their pre-teen years (Brown, 2010). He was arrested for public intoxication and domestic abuse in the 1980s, and increased his alcohol abuse and drug use.

Sowell was knocked down from sergeant to corporal after "an alcohol-related incident with a military police officer" while in the Marines in the 70s (Scott, 2011a).

Sowell was investigated in connection with an aggravated battery case in 1989 but was released. At that time, he stated he was arrested and adjudicated as a juvenile for breaking and entering at age 16. Later, he was reportedly convicted of domestic violence (Court Psychiatric Clinic, 2005).

The most significant prior criminal offense in Sowell's history was a rape of a woman who was three months pregnant and came to his home for a drink. She was bound, gagged, and raped. Sowell eventually pleaded guilty to attempted rape and went to prison until 2005. He was a registered sex offender upon his release.

PROBLEMATIC SEXUAL DEVIANCE

Sowell belonged to an online bondage website, where he advertised himself as a potential "Master" and was looking for a "sub" (submissive) for his use. He joined *alt.com,* an online "adult personals, alternative lifestyle, BDSM, Leather & Fetish Community." There he took on the role of master and advertised for slaves willing to receive his sexual training and discipline (Martinez, 2009).

This conflicted with prior statements by Sowell (Court Psychiatric Clinic, 2005) stating he never used a telephone or computer for sexual purposes. He also denied any sexual fantasies regarding violence, children, or his sexual offense. During his murder trial, he was also found to be a violent sexual predator.

Dr. George Woods, a defense mental health expert, testified he suffered from sexual compulsions and mimicked sex with a toy doll and spreading feces on it as a young boy (Barr & Sheeran, 2011). Dr. Woods also pointed out that many serial murder cases "have a strong sexual component to them" and said Sowell had sexual encounters with at least 50 different people in his life, starting as a child with relatives, through his contact with his victims. He described Sowell as "sexually confused," witnessing relatives having sex with each other and being abused by his mother three times. He also described Sowell's "aggressive sexual tendencies" (Scott, 2011b).

Tragically, Sowell's 1995 sexual predator evaluation psychological report included a conclusion that his chance of committing another sex offense after 15 years in prison was low, specifically approximating a 6 in 100 chance for offenders with histories similar to Sowell's (Baird, 2009).

PERSONALITY DISORDERS OR DISSOCIATIVE EPISODES

Sowell reportedly made statements to investigators that he heard voices telling him not to enter the room with the bodies, that he had episodes of blacking out, and later coming to and not remembering what happened. The voices reportedly called him "Artie."

His lawyers also claimed that Sowell related stories of breakdowns, confusing dreams with reality, suffering from depression, and that he remembered meeting some of the women but waking up in a fog later after they were gone (Farkas, 2010). He said, "it was like everything's cool, she was spending the night or something. . . . And I'd be like, 'Damn, where'd you go?'" (Sheeran, 2011a).

Sowell admitted to significant problems with alcohol, including experiencing "loss of control" and drinking blackouts (Court Psychiatric Clinic, 2005). A 2005 evaluation included a diagnostic impression of alcohol dependence but did not note enough symptoms for other disorders.

Defense expert Woods noted Sowell suffered several mental illnesses, including OCD and posttraumatic stress disorder, and observed unspecified psychoses and a cognitive disorder (Barr & Sheeran, 2011). Sowell demonstrated OCD behaviors by counting the number of inmates and staff members when incarcerated and would be "impossible to calm down" when he couldn't find a personal belonging.

Dr. Woods also stated Sowell displayed dissociation and stated "dissociative amnesia" can become so severe that someone might not remember what he's done (Scott, 2011b).

Sowell made a statement in court referring to a lack of nurturing by his mother and the fact he could not hug his sisters or hold hands, suggesting an attachment issue.

At trial in July 2011, a video of his interrogation taped during the discovery of the bodies in his home was played. Sowell described episodes of blackouts and nightmares in which he would hurt women with his hands. He told detectives that a voice in his head told him not to go into a bedroom where bodies were found. He also said he began losing control of his temper around the same time the women began to disappear (Sheeran, 2011a).

SERIAL MURDER

In September 2009, a woman who was invited to Sowell's home reported that he beat, choked, and raped her. Police returned with a warrant and two bodies were actually found on his living room floor. Additional bodies and a skull were discovered upon a subsequent search. Neighbors commented on the stench emanating from his home. A total of 11 women were found in Sowell's home. Some women were found buried in the yard. Reportedly, they were all led to Sowell's home and went there of their own accord. Most had been strangled and raped.

The victims of Sowell seemed to fit Steven Egger's description of less dead, in that they could have been seen as throwaway members of society who would not be missed or searched for very quickly. It is not clear if Sowell chose these women for this reason or if it was just that these were the women he met within his social sphere.

Sowell's victims were all African American. Their ages ranged mostly from the 30s to the 50s. One woman was unable to use one arm. At least three of the women were known to have gone missing in the past and were not reported missing right away. Most had criminal histories including drug charges and theft. Many of the bodies discovered in his home were found still bound at the wrists and with ligatures around their necks. A head was found in a bucket. Sowell's pattern of offenses and conceal-ment of bodies in his home certainly includes him within the descriptor of a serial murderer.

When questioned about the bodies found by detectives at his home, Sowell said, "I guess I did that . . . it had to be me . . . Cause nobody else could've did it" (Sheeran, 2011a). Sowell explained he punished the women for being crackheads and abandoning their children, like a former girlfriend of Sowell's (Atassi, 2011a).

OTHER OBSERVATIONS

Sowell's case has brought a great deal of attention to the cost of a pub-lic defender's case. The defense cost is a shade under $150,000. It would become the most expensive publicly funded criminal defense in Cuyahoga County history.

Among the highest expenditures is $24,985 for a mitigation expert—a social researcher whose job is to humanize Sowell, evoke jurors' sympathy, and ultimately save him from the death penalty. Much of the funding Sow-ell's attorneys, John Parker and Rufus Sims, requested was for psychological evaluations and mitigation services—preparation for the monumental task of portraying Sowell as anything but a ruthless killer worthy of death row. Parker and Sims asked the court in June 2010 for more than $62,000 for a mitiga-tion expert, arguing that the effort requires extensive record collection and interviews with nearly 200 people who once knew Sowell in Ohio and at least four other states (Atassi, 2010).

Sowell's case also bears an interesting resemblance to the case of Dahmer, who both had bodies littered at their homes and preyed on vulnerable, less dead victims in a bad neighborhood who were not missed from society right away. Sowell's similarities to Dahmer's issues with alcohol, attachment, and a near dissociative affect were noticeable as well.

CASE 6: AILEEN WUORNOS

Aileen ("Lee") Wuornos was one of the most famous female serial killers, the subject of at least two movies and countless media coverage. She murdered seven men over a two-year period in 1989 and 1990 while working as a prostitute in Florida. She robbed the men and used the money and belongings in support of her lesbian lover. Wuornos confessed to the killings shortly after being arrested as a result of pressure exerted on her to protect her lover and was eventually executed in 2002.

Peter Vronsky (2007) noted that Wuornos "unleashed the female serial killer from the cult of feminine domesticity" (p. 138) and that she "thrived in the very territory where other women feared to go and where so many women were themselves killed," referring of course to the dark highways where Wuornos turned tricks.

Her murders were varied examples of a similar theme. She killed Richard Mallory in November 1989 after turning a trick with him. She stole his Cadillac and later claimed he tried to rape her, actually claiming after her arrest that she realized he was "going to" rape her. At home that evening, she spontaneously blurted out, "I killed a guy today" to her lover Ty.

Her next murder was six months later. She killed David Spears and stole about $700, tools, and his pickup truck. Wuornos accused the man of attempting to rape her. Two weeks later, she killed Charles Carskaddon and explained she discovered a .45 handgun in his car after killing him, which meant he planned to kill her. She was so enraged she reloaded her .22 revolver and pumped several more shots into his body (Vronsky, 2007, p. 155). This murder resulted in another Cadillac.

Wuornos met 65-year-old preacher Peter Siems seven days later in a coffee shop. According to Wuornos they were about to have sex when she again realized the man she was with was about to rape her. She shot him, stole his belongings and car. Troy Burress, a truck driver, was killed next, complete with the requisite story of his plan to rape her.

Dick Humphreys was shot seven times including one to the back of his head. Humphreys was a former police chief and was employed as a child abuse investigator. In November of 1990, Wuornos's final murder was a 60-year-old trucker Walter Antonio. According to Wuornos, Antonio, a member of the reserve police, flashed a badge at her and tried to force her to have sex with him for free. After a struggle, she said, she shot him in the back and again, execution style as with Humphreys, in the back of the head (Vronsky, 2007, p. 157).

PHYSIOLOGICAL FACTORS

Wuornos suffered facial burns while setting fires at age six. She also could have suffered physical effects from rape and life as a prostitute. The fact that her father, whom she never met, was a child molester and attempted murderer long before she followed in his footsteps suggests a pattern within her genes.

Wuornos's mother Diane talked about when she was a baby: "She was real late. . . . It was an unusual birth. Breach. Bottom first. She was possibly conceived at the time of a horrible beating. It's the day I left him" (Reynolds, 1992, p. 252). The 15-year-old mother was terrified that the abusive father would reenter their lives. She lived in a state of panic and fear, both for their safety and her inability to provide for herself and two children. She continued:

> The thing that keeps coming in my mind is that she was a very unhappy baby. Both Keith and Aileen were unhappy, crying babies. I believe they were both feeling the stress. . . . Keith . . . just cried all the time. All the time. It was like colicky and sick and crying and then Aileen was of the same disposition and I was under so much stress coming out of a battered relationship and then arguing with my parents.

> (Reynolds, 1992, p. 253)

During a trial, she was described by a defense neuropsychologist, Elizabeth McMahon, as an alcoholic, suffering hearing difficulties since elementary school, and stated she suffered from a "mild degree of cortical dysfunction" (Reynolds, 1992, p. 282).

ENVIRONMENTAL TRAUMA

Wuornos's upbringing was, in fact, impossible. Her mother was a 15-year-old girl, filing for divorce from her father while he was in prison. He hung himself there. Her mother abandoned her and her brother; they were taken in by their grandparents. However, they did not feel welcome there, with Wuornos's uncle Barry stating the adoption was "always a sore spot in the family" (Reynolds, 1992, p. 255). Wuornos's grandmother died, leaving the children as wards of the court. Her grandfather finally threw her out of the house at 15, forcing her to live in the streets and turn to prostitution and drugs to survive. Wuornos had already brought shame on the house by getting pregnant at 15, just like her mother.

Wuornos said her grandfather sexually abused her. "He'd do stuff to me and give me pocket change to shut up. He'd finger me. I lost my virginity to his fuckin' finger when I was about seven. He'd beat the shit outa me, ya know? But he'd strip me naked beforehand . . . that's fuckin' wrong . . . you understand? He made me what I am" (Berry-Dee, 2002, p. 227).

The same grandparents singled her out for the cruelest punishments as a child. Her grandmother did not allow her to receive Christmas presents. She was forced to eat a baked potato she did not finish out of the garbage. On another occasion, her grandfather forced her to watch him drown a kitten she was not allowed to keep (Vronsky, 2007, p. 141).

Berry-Dee observed that throughout Wuornos's formative years, she was "humiliated, sexually abused, beaten and rejected and her world was filled with pain, rage and alcoholism" and suffered behind closed doors (Vronsky,

2007, p. 228). After discovering her parents were not her real parents, she completely rebelled and rejected their authority. "The foundations of her antisocial behavior were implanted by the family surroundings in which she was reared" (p. 229).

EARLY ANTISOCIAL BEHAVIOR AND PRIOR CRIMES

Wuornos had a long history of problems with the law related to drinking, disturbing the peace, and violence. She married a much older man for a short period and assaulted him as well. Wuornos was arrested in 1981 for robbing a convenience store. Later, there were incidences of passing bad checks, theft, a stolen firearm, stealing a car, and obstructing justice. Incidences of assault and explanations of others attacking her continued up until the start of the murders, including an attempted armed robbery of a man in a car.

Wuornos compiled a list of criminal convictions throughout the 1970s and 1980s, including assault and battery, armed robbery, theft, prohibited possession of a firearm, drunk and disorderly, and drinking under the influence (Vronsky, 2007, p. 146). Male friends commented that she liked to fantasize about being like the violent Bonnie and Clyde, and was fascinated with outlaws and bikers and their violent subculture.

PROBLEMATIC SEXUAL DEVIANCE

Wuornos never had any sort of normal sexualization. She was known to have multiple sex partners from a very early age. Accusations of rape continued through her early life, from unnamed men to her own grandfather. She reportedly stated she had sex with her own brother (Newton, 2000, p. 242). Wuornos became pregnant at the age of 15. She became a prostitute for survival at a young age and likely never had any inkling of a normal sexual relationship at any time, nor had she been exposed to one in her home life.

Her short-lived marriage with an elderly man was a farce, and her only significant relationship otherwise was with her lesbian lover Tyria Moore.

PERSONALITY DISORDERS OR DISSOCIATIVE EPISODES

Wuornos was diagnosed as having borderline personality disorder while in custody. She was also described as diagnosed with antisocial personality disorder as well (Berry-Dee, 2002, p. 227). A defense neuropsychologist at trial stated she was a classic borderline, reviewing a battery of tests she performed as well as a review of tests on Wuornos from her school days. "She meets all eight criteria as established by the *DSM-III*" (Reynolds, 1992, p. 282).

Wuornos's case clearly marked an example of severe attachment disorder. Like Ted Bundy, who discovered his father was actually his grandfather and his mother was his sister, she found out around age 11 the people she believed were her parents were actually her grandparents and her siblings were actually her aunt and uncle (Vronsky, 2007, p. 140).

Reports of dissociative episodes are slight, although she alluded to blackouts in her confession when it was convenient. In interviews, Wuornos herself stated she became a different person when she was drunk, which mirrors a similar dissociative state described by Dahmer and Bundy when drunk (Berry-Dee, 2002, p. 225). She said, "but when I get drunk, I just don't know. It's just . . . when I'm drunk it's don't mess the fuck with me. Ya know? That's the truth. I've got nothing to lose. That's the truth."

Wuornos echoed her pedophile father's weak excuses that he couldn't remember offenses he committed, that it was pills he took, or the whisky, or that he wasn't even there. Her confession repeated "the same lame denial, the same excuses" (Reynolds, 1992, p. 257). "I don't remember. . . . I was drunk . . . drunk royal."

Vronsky noted a psychiatrist's remark at trial that Wuornos's marked gap between her functional IQ and her verbal IQ, gauged at a low score of 80, represented sand in the fuel line of an otherwise working engine. It was observed that this could have been related to her uncontrollable behavioral episodes and hair-trigger temper (2007, p. 142).

SERIAL MURDER

Wuornos's murders started in 1989 with the shooting death of Richard Mallory. Mallory was later found to have an assaultive past, and he may have attacked Wuornos to precipitate the event. However, Wuornos's history of violence and assault with a firearm made the claims of self-defense against seven different older men, johns she accused of trying to rape her, shot multiple times, and robbed, ring hollow.

Wuornos's relationship with Tyria Moore and the pressure to provide for her likely contributed to her need to turn up the intensity in attacking men for their possessions. The long-held anger for men and against society in general likely made her pattern of murders easier to follow. She meets the criteria of a serial killer, murdering men in a predatory, calculated fashion.

OTHER OBSERVATIONS

Wuornos did seem to have a pattern of killing that more closely resembled a male killer as opposed to many female serial killers. Her activities invariably resulted after entering a motor vehicle with a man, either as a prostitute or a hitchhiker. Her behavior seemed consistent and planned, and had a predatory purpose. Her continual simmering anger was key, but the personal violence and eventual establishment of final control appears paramount. Her behavior patterns sound like the "Tornado Effect" described by Schurman-Kauflin (2000) in describing female multiple murderers.

Biographer Sue Russell (cited in Ramsland, 2006, p.74) noted that Wuornos's killing days were preceded by personal stressors, so the killings may have restored a sense of power. While this scenario is not uncommon, the free-floating rage, past sexual abuse, mental illness, horrendous life history, alcohol and drug addictions, and out-of-control relationship with a need for material acquisitions all make it very difficult to assign one reason for Wuornos's murderous ways.

Case 7: Dennis Rader

Dennis Rader, or as he is more commonly known, "the BTK (bind, torture, and kill) Killer," murdered 10 people in Kansas between the years 1974 and 1991. Rader's favored method was strangulation, after stalking his victims carefully and attacking them in their homes. He loved the psychological rush of entering their homes and he tortured and sexually assaulted them prior to and after the murders. He also took trophies from the crime scenes and relived the killings in his mind later, as many serial murderers do.

Rader is known for his continuous contact with police and media, taunting them with details and attempting to evoke response. Rader often took offense to not getting enough attention. It would seem that this personality flaw led him to resume sending letters in 2004, allowing modern detection techniques to be used, which eventually led to his capture. He was sentenced to 175 years.

Wenzl, Potter, Kelly, and Laviana (2007) referenced a letter sent by Rader to *Wichita Eagle* columnist Don Granger complaining that "the three dude(s) you have in custody are just talking to get publicity" (p. 32). He went on to describe in detail how he murdered Joseph, Julie, Josephine, and Joseph Otero II of the Otero family without help, and provided the particulars of the positioning of bodies, manner of death, clothing, and other items only the killer would have known about. He went on to say:

> I'm sorry this happen to the society. They are the ones who suffer the most. It is hard to control myself. You probably call me "psychotic with sexual perversion hang-up." Where this monster enter my brain I will never know. . . . I can't stop it, so the monster goes on.

The letter was classic Rader, complete with obsession with detail, insight to his desires, and complete annoyance with the idea that someone else might be getting credit for his work.

Rader went on to kill six more people, Kathryn Bright, Shirley Vian, Nancy Fox, Marine Hedge, Vicki Wegerle, and Dolores Davis between 1974 and January 1991.

Physiological Factors

After his capture, Rader said he couldn't control himself. He blamed his behavior on demons and Factor X. He also claimed to have been dropped on his head as a child (Ono, 2005). There were no other reports of physiological issues with Rader.

Detectives researching his background and interviewing his family found "no broken home in his past, no evidence of abuse in his childhood, none of the clichéd explanations for his deviant behavior" (Wenzl et al., 2007, p. 359).

Environmental Trauma

Rader stated in his 33-hour interrogation that "there was nothing in his family or his past that made him what he was" (Wenzl et al., 2007, p. 359).

He said Factor X, a demon within, a monster that controlled him, was the only explanation that made sense. While some listeners scoffed at this as an excuse, psychologist Tony Ruark opined that it was not an excuse, just a method of putting a label on the compulsion that churned inside him to kill, something Rader could not otherwise explain. I agree with this observation.

Ruark noted, "something really did happen to Rader early in life to make him the way he is. I wish I could be the one to find it." He added, "I do believe the detectives when they say that there was no child abuse in his past, no broken home, no sexual abuse" (p. 361). He explained further:

Eventually we would find something that happened to him, probably early in childhood. . . . Whatever it was, it doesn't necessarily need to be something big or traumatic—or even relevant to the rest of us. . . . it would be something that happened not from outside but within Rader's own mind. Somehow, very early on, Rader encountered an event where he immediately linked sexual pleasure with watching a living creature suffer and die.

(Wenzl et al., 2007, p. 363)

It might have been when Rader experienced "curious, enjoyable sensations, vaguely sexual," when he watched his grandmother twist the heads off chickens, the headless fowl dancing, "blood spurting from the empty socket at the top of their neck" (Douglas & Dodd, 2008, p. 131). Douglas observed that this dizzying feeling could have been an early time of development, of associating death and sexual arousal. Rader reportedly also felt a similar odd arousal when being spanked by his mother Dorothea, described as a woman with a movie star quality by his friends.

EARLY ANTISOCIAL BEHAVIOR AND PRIOR CRIMES

Rader by his own admission tortured animals as a child. He insisted he did not kill any animals as a child, going as far as to refer to "that homicidal triangle" (Douglas & Dodd, 2008, p. 311). However, he admitted to tying a few up in the safety of a barn, and masturbating next to them (p. 312). Rader's sexual compulsions were always driven by the stalking and control of others, which gave him sexual gratification.

During an interview with John Douglas, Rader mentioned that over the years, he'd broken into many homes and stolen watches, jewelry, and underwear. He said the "burglaries were almost as satisfying as the killing" (Douglas & Dodd, 2008, p. 307). The burglaries, described as fetish or sexual burglaries by some theorists, provided the control rush Rader always craved.

PROBLEMATIC SEXUAL DEVIANCE

Rader's fetishes manifested when he stole and wore women's underwear. He was known to check into a hotel, dress up in women's clothing, tie himself up with rope and handcuffs, and then photograph himself in various poses with a remote camera. Psychologist Tony Ruark (Wenzl et al., 2007, p. 362) noted, "I've treated people with sexual fetishes before, but I've never seen anyone like this guy, where there were so many fetishes, where they so dominated his life."

Jack Levin of Northeastern University in Boston feels Rader's method of killing was typical of a control-oriented psychopathic sexually oriented serial murderer. "The last thing they would want to do is distance themselves. So they typically, like Rader, use up-close-and-personal methods to kill—whether strangulation, stabbing, or bludgeoning," he says. "The killing is a mere footnote. The text has to do with the torture of the victim, hearing her scream. Pleading and begging for mercy makes the killer feel good" (Mann, 2005).

Rader admitted during his court confession that he had sexual fantasies about an 11-year-old female child he hung in her family's basement. He also masturbated on the scene after strangling a 25-year-old woman with a belt, after explaining to her he had "a sexual problem" (Rader's testimony, 2007). He also took bondage-posed pictures of a woman he killed and stripped after death.

Personality Disorders or Dissociative Episodes

Rader, like most serial killers, carried the fantasy of killing long before his first kill. "The fantasy became an obsession that demanded fulfillment. The planning and execution of this seminal event took over his conscious thought. Just once, he told himself, and then he would be free of this overwhelming need. It wouldn't be necessary to ever risk doing it again" (Bardsley, Bell, & Lohr, 2010).

While reviewing Rader's journals, John Douglas noted that as a child, Rader longed to drive to California and abduct Annette Funicello, tie her up, take her to an abandoned house, and do sexual things to her. By eighth grade he hid in the back of the classroom, "losing himself in the increasingly dark world that festered inside his head" (Douglas & Dodd, 2008, pp. 136–137). He dreamed about tying the hands and legs of female classmates and binding them to train tracks.

Rader also told Douglas in interviews that the fantasy was better than the crime because everything was always under control (p. 307).

Rader also displayed evidence of obsessive compulsiveness, for example, he used to cut advertisements out of the *Wichita Eagle,* picturing women in underwear and modeling outfits. His collection numbered in the hundreds (Wenzl et al., 2007, p. 175). He would paste many on index cards while writing notes about the fantasies he enjoyed.

MSNBC analyst and former FBI profiler Clint Van Zandt describes Rader as, "someone who has no conscience, no guilt, someone who takes no responsibility for his actions." These are the characteristics of antisocial personality disorder or the more severe psychopathic personality disorder (Ono, 2005).

Detective Clint Snyder (Wenzl et al., 2007, pp. 360–361) stated Rader was the closest thing he's seen to a human being without a soul. "You don't see that very often, even among murderers," said Snyder.

An excerpt from Rader's confession in court specifically referred to his sexual fantasies:

JUDGE WALLER: At this particular location, did you know these people?

RADER: No, that was part of what . . . I guess what you call my fantasy. These people were selected.

WALLER: So you were engaged in some kind of fantasy during this period of time?

RADER: Yes, sir.

WALLER: Now, when you use the term fantasy, is this something you were doing for your personal pleasure?

RADER: Sexual fantasy, sir.

[*Rader provides graphic explanations of all 10 killings, in great detail, by various methods*]

WALLER: So, all of these incidents, these 10 counts occurred because you wanted to satisfy sexual fantasies. Is that correct?

RADER: Yes. Um hum.

(Rader's testimony, 2007)

SERIAL MURDER

Rader methodically stalked his victims. He carefully planned the killings in a predatory manner, strangling each one. He took trophies from the crime scenes, another classic serial killer trait. Between his sexual assaults and the obsessive need for control and dominance, he clearly fits the profile of a serial murderer.

Rader apparently had planned to kill again when he was captured, and at one point bitterly complained about failing to kill a victim he stalked and waited for in her home for hours. His pathological need for attention and fame and desire for his old ways caused him to recontact the police and media years after his last crime, and led to his arrest.

OTHER OBSERVATIONS

Rader seems more motivated by power and control than most serial killers. His underlying behavior in his personal life as well as his killing activity seemed to express a pathological need for control. His need for recognition was at a pathological level as well. Ramsland (2006) noted that Rader "obviously relished the attention" when he went to court to confess as part of a plea deal. He clearly indicated he wanted "complete credit for his crimes" (p. 47).

Rader, after his confession of 10 murders in front of a judge, sat in front of a camera and said, "I feel pretty good. . . . I feel like I'm—kind of like I'm a star right now" (Wenzl et al., 2007, p. 362).

CASE 8: RODNEY ALCALA

Rodney Alcala was convicted and sentenced to death in California in 2010 for five murders committed between 1977 and 1979. He was also indicted for two more murders in New York, one of a stewardess as early as 1971, under the alias John Berger, and is suspected of many more. Alcala is also a convicted rapist whose main claim to fame is being known as the serial killer who was once a winner on an episode of the TV show *The Dating Game* in 1978. The bachelorette eventually refused to go out with him, whereas another bachelor on the show said, "he was a standout creepy guy in my life" (Miller, 2010).

Alcala was found to possess hundreds of photographs he took of women and girls, leading to speculation that many more unsolved crimes could be attributed to him. He was known to commit acts of torture on his victims, strangling them to unconsciousness, and then reviving them repeatedly before finally killing them. He would then pose them for graphic nude photographs (Ayers, 2010).

Alcala was tried, convicted, and sentenced to death for the 1979 murder of 12-year-old Robin Samsoe, who disappeared on the way to ballet class. Her earrings were found in a Seattle locker rented by Alcala. Incredibly, the conviction was overturned because the jury had been allowed to hear about his previous rape convictions. He was convicted once again in 1986, sentenced to death once again, but the conviction was thrown out by the Ninth Circuit Court of Appeals because an expert witness was not allowed to support his contention that the female park ranger who found Samsoe's animal-ravaged body had been "hypnotized by police investigators" (Pelisek, 2010). The ranger supposedly was so traumatized after finding the body, she failed to report it, gave erratic testimony at trial, and suffered such trauma that was unable to testify at all at the second trial because of "some kind of amnesia, a post-trauma condition" (Lasseter, 2004, p. 281).

In 2003, Alcala's next trial included new evidence of DNA matching semen as well as blood and fingerprints left at the rape-murder scenes of four additional California women. More earrings found at his storage locker matched one of the victims. The additional four murders were added to the previous charges for Samsoe's death and trial of Alcala in 2006. The new trial with all charges began in 2009. He was sentenced to death for a third time after found guilty of all five counts.

PHYSIOLOGICAL FACTORS

I have not found evidence or information of physical or biological issues related to Alcala. There are no reports of such testing in his case. Alcala acted as his own defense attorney, and under the premise of innocence, offered no insight to his past—physical, mental, or environmental. As this book goes to print, the availability of information related to physical factors in Alcala's history is nonexistent.

ENVIRONMENTAL TRAUMA

Rodney Alcala, born Rodrigo Jacques Alcala-Buquor, was born in San Antonio, Texas, and lived with his two sisters, one brother, mother, father, and maternal grandmother until approximately age 8. When his maternal grandmother became ill, she told her daughter she wanted to spend her final years in Mexico. While living in Mexico, "two key events took place in young Alcala's life" (Sands, 2011, p. 17). His beloved grandmother died and his father walked away from the family and moved back to the United States.

Alcala and his siblings were raised by his mother in Los Angeles after moving from Mexico following his father's abandonment of the family and the death of his grandmother. The impact of this rejection is unclear, although it does raise a comparison to the background of Ted Bundy, to whom Alcala is most often compared. Bundy never seemed to get over his adoption issues. Killer Jeffrey Dahmer also suffered extreme anguish and fears of abandonment after his parents' horrendous divorce.

There was no other information regarding Alcala's upbringing in relation to possible trauma.

EARLY ANTISOCIAL BEHAVIOR AND PRIOR CRIMES

Alcala went AWOL while in the Army in 1963 and was unable to perform his required duties. He was hospitalized and told he was in need of psychological care. He was discharged several months later (Sands, 2011, p. 19). He committed his first known sexual assault in 1968 in California and fled to New York.

After his murders, approximately 1,000 photos belonging to Alcala were found in a storage locker, hundreds of which were of underage girls. Alcala used his interest in photography in luring many women. The pictures were released to the public in the event other victims of Alcala were not identified (Knowles, 2010).

Some photos show women or young girls in the nude and engaged in sex acts. Some show women or young girls who appear to be unconscious. Others show women posing, staring into the lens of a camera held by a man who was a serial killer, in remote settings—similar to the locale where Robin Samsoe's body was found in 1979. A few are of young men in sexually suggestive poses (Welborn, 2010b).

PROBLEMATIC SEXUAL DEVIANCE

Alcala was a registered sex offender and a convicted child molester when he was hired as a typesetter with the *LA Times*. In 1968, he raped and nearly beat to death an 8-year-old girl named Tali Shapiro. He pleaded to a lesser charge and was paroled after 34 months. Less than two months later, he violated parole after offering marijuana to a 13-year-old girl who claimed she was kidnapped and assaulted. Four months before he murdered Samsoe, he raped, sodomized, and beat a 15-year-old victim who was hitchhiking in Sierra Madre.

Alcala's history included a pattern of both sexual assault and violence towards women and very young girls, tainting any idea he could have enjoyed normal sexual relationships with women.

Personality Disorders or Dissociative Episodes

A defense psychiatrist testified during the trial penalty phase that Alcala suffers from a borderline personality disorder that could lead to psychotic episodes. Alcala has claimed he doesn't remember some of his actions ("Relatives' joy," 2010). During the last trial, Defense expert Dr. Richard Rappaport testified that Alcala asked him for insight into his psychiatric condition in light of his contention that he has amnesia about the sadistic killings of the four women in Los Angeles between November 1977 and June 1979 (Welborn, 2010a). The psychiatrist told the jury that Alcala had a borderline personality disorder that may have occasionally been jolted into psychotic episodes by stress, which could explain his alleged lack of memory. Rappaport said a person suffering from a borderline personality disorder might be horrified with what happened during a psychotic episode, and then block it out of his memory as a coping mechanism.

While in the Army, he suffered a nervous breakdown and was discharged in 1964 after a military psychiatrist diagnosed him as an "anti-social personality, chronic, severe". At the time his mother stated she'd never seen her son so anxious and upset, and he was unable to articulate his feelings regarding what was bothering him (Sands, 2011, p. 19). She was convinced her son had some serious emotional problems.

According to Sands (2011, p. 44), Detective Steve Hodel, when picking up Alcala in 1971 to extradite to Los Angeles for the rape and assault of Tali Shapiro, asked him why he committed the crime. Alcala, seemly speaking about another person, stated, "I don't want to talk about Rod Alcala or what he did."

The very close of Alcala's case, during the penalty phase determining a potential death sentence, exposed a unique glimpse into his mind. He played a clip of a 1967 song by Arlo Guthrie, Alice's Restaurant, where:

> the narrator tries to avoid being drafted for the Vietnam War by trying to convince a psychiatrist that he's unfit for the military because of his supposed extreme desire to kill. 'I wanna see blood and gore and guts and veins in my teeth,' the song's narrator sings. 'Eat dead burnt bodies. I mean: kill, kill, kill, kill.'

> ("Relatives' joy," 2010)

The point of this tactic is unclear. It's almost an insanity defense. Or, as suspected by one victim's relative, a look at who Alcala really is. Either way, the reflection of the off-the-charts vicious psychopath or hopelessly insane killer remains a clinical specimen.

SERIAL MURDER

Alcala's murders included kidnapping, torture, sexual trauma, rape, bludgeoning with a hammer, and strangulation. He easily fits the description of a serial murderer, who stalked and lured his victims like a sociopathic predator. He kept trophies and keepsakes from the victims as well as photos, all packed away in a storage locker. His reported near-genius IQ, charming manipulativeness, and even his acting as his own defense attorney is reminiscent of a Ted Bundy.

In his self-penned book, *You, the Jury* (1994), Alcala meticulously lays out detail after detail, aiming to bring reasonable doubt to the Samsoe case. He offered his own responses to points made throughout by others, practicing the moment on the stand that was denied him until he was able to act as his own attorney. His complete denial of guilt never wavered, stating:

> An innocent man agonizes on California's Death Row, convicted of Robin Samsoe's murder. He also has been victimized—not by an unknown assailant, but by the seeming conspiracy of the trial judge, the district attorney, the defense attorneys, and now the California Supreme Court. Each pursued their own agenda, unfettered by conscience, justice or truth. Each contributed in denying the man his Constitutional right to a fair trial. I am that man.
>
> (Alcala, 1994, p. 4)

Again, it's hard to determine if this is a state of mind Alcala convinced himself to believe, or the typically remorseless rejection of guilty by a predatory psychopath. It's hard to tell. His defense strategy evolved in the 2010 trial, taking on a combined flirtation with celebrity and a touch of diminished capacity. In a short letter to this author, Alcala admitted that his defense perspective as displayed in his book is different from that in his 2010 trial.

His indictment in New York (Weber, 2011) was for killing two women in 1971 and 1977 after he fled there following his 1968 sexual assault. His uncontrollable pattern is clearly that of a serial predator. He is also suspected in many other murders in various states. Authorities believe the numbers could be extremely high.

OTHER OBSERVATIONS

It is interesting that Alcala's crimes occurred mostly while the Los Angeles area was engrossed in the activities of the Hillside Strangler murders and Alcala was considered a suspect. Alcala could have actually set type while working at the *LA Times* for stories about the horrific serial killings in California in which he was suspected.

It's also of note that it could be opined that some of Alcala's acting out could have happened as a result of his rejection by the female *Dating Game* contestant. "One wonders what that did in his mind," criminal profiler Pat Brown said in an interview with the CNN. "That is something he would not take too well. They don't understand the rejection" (Miller, 2010).

Reflecting on Case Studies

7

I wasn't going to rob her, or touch her, or rape her. I just wanted to kill her.

—David Berkowitz

METHODOLOGY

THE ORIGINAL FOUR CASE STUDIES

When this study was first completed in 1996, these cases were selected mainly for their relative completeness and the fact that they covered a workable time span. This is not to say the information on the subjects is truly complete, especially in the older cases, but every effort was made to maximize the scope of information.

Information sources included books, newspapers, magazines and journals, film, television, police reports, interviews, personal communication, and other case materials. It would have been best to offer a true triangulation of data by complementing the written data with personal interviews of case study subjects, but unfortunately, requests for interviews were denied by Dahmer before his murder in prison, Chikatilo has been executed, and Shawcross has also passed away. An interview with the lone surviving subject, Kemper, is unlikely at this time.

In accumulating the data, a system of recording the measurable elements was applied; these elements generated by the significant factors discussed in Chapters 2, 3, and 4 include evidence of biological conditions, environmental trauma, early crimes, dissociation, and sexual dysfunction.

Examination of the case histories of Chikatilo, Shawcross, Dahmer, and Kemper reveals details of their pasts that are truly relevant to this analysis and suggest certain patterns, discussed here. Overall interpretation and discussion is held until Chapters 8 and 10.

Adding Four More Cases

This text includes the case studies of an additional four subjects: Aileen Wuornos, Anthony Sowell, Dennis Rader, and Rodney Alcala. The choices of these individuals were for many reasons. Wuornos was originally excluded because she was a woman. In this work, I chose her for that reason. The same is true for Sowell; I wanted to include an African American killer. Dennis Rader, the BTK Killer spanned a long time frame, had a great deal of media involvement, and stretched into a more recent time, as did Rodney Alcala and Sowell. While these choices had their plusses, they also proved to create difficulties.

One significant difference is the availability of much more information in the way of Internet sources. While one has to be wary and critical of all sources, the availability to search periodicals and other references online is an advantage, and the last four cases have far more online references than the previous four, which are heavier in newspaper and book items, mostly produced around the time of those crimes.

A downside was that in all four cases, the backgrounds and childhood information did not seem as fully developed as the previous four. Although it would have been convenient (and easy) to cherry-pick four more cases that had more available background information as well as cases that could be more supportive of my original hypothesis, these cases were selected for reasons of inclusion and representation as opposed to convenience, and let the chips fall as they may.

An additional issue with the new cases is the fact that two of them, Sowell and Alcala, had cases render verdicts very recently—Alcala, Spring 2010, and Sowell, found guilty in Summer of 2011. Alcala was then indicted for additional killings in New York in 2011, and more may follow. Sowell's case will likely generate appeals, as will Alcala's New York trial. Cases this recent tend to offer a lingering attempt at denial of guilt, and therefore offer less history and insight as regarding the development of a pathological killer's psyche. Such details usually arise in not only defense and prosecution cases presented, but also in the consideration of mitigating factors in court. Unfortunately, some backgrounds seemed incomplete in the cases of Sowell and Alcala. Testimony regarding Sowell's history improved at the sentencing phase after his conviction, but Alcala, acting as his own attorney, demonstrated no desire to offer insight into his own development. My feeling is that it's much easier for an offender to reflect more insightfully and, if possible, honestly after a case has been fully adjudicated and the pressure and consequences of trial are several years old.

Regarding interviews, requests made to Rader and Sowell went unanswered. Alcala refused. Wuornos is deceased.

It is also noted that with the inclusion of a woman (Wuornos) and an African American (Sowell), it is plain this is not a representative sample that could allow one to infer across entire populations, and these two cases are certainly a small sample size, as are the entire population examined in this book (Chapter 8). Observations made about race and gender must be considered in that limited context.

EVIDENCE OF PHYSIOLOGICAL FACTORS

The appearance of physical abnormalities in these case studies was consistent, although difficult to measure. Andrei Chikatilo's youth revealed different instances of head trauma. There was also a diagnosis of dystonia, a neurological movement disorder. During the murder investigation, it was revealed he had a rare combination of blood and semen type. There were reports of severe headaches throughout his history, an affliction his mother reportedly shared.

Arthur Shawcross's case history contained the most solid evidence of various physiological anomalies. The extensive evidence of abnormalities included elevated kryptopyrrole levels, abnormal EEGs, and XYY genetic coding. Reports also included stories of repeated head injuries and other physical traumas.

Points of interest within Jeffrey Dahmer's physical history most often concerned his parents. There was familial evidence of excessive prenatal medication by his mother, plus she experienced seizures. Also, there was reported paternal obsession with fire and violence from early ages.

Edmund Kemper's physical history and background were the least complete of the original group. Very little formal analysis was done, as compared to the Shawcross case. There were reported fits and seizures by Kemper, but no organic brain disease was noted. Kemper's enormous size was his most glaring physical feature, and the suggestion of the presence of XYY is understandable.

The biological aspects of this study are the most incomplete. It is not customary to run a complete battery of physiological tests on convicted murderers as was done in the case of Shawcross, therefore many potential results are not available.

Some evidence of personal biological abnormality is clear for Shawcross, or found in the family in Dahmer's case, but physical histories are not as complete for the other two subjects. This is especially true of Chikatilo, as these analyses were unheard of in Russia at the time.

Information being limited for Chikatilo and Kemper, however, does not mean that biological abnormalities were not present. It simply means the possibility of including such data does not exist. This weakness continued in the later case studies as well. Sowell had little background of medical issues, outside of a heart condition. There was also a report of head trauma at age 16. Wuornos likely had a litany of physical issues. She was born to a 15-year-old mother who left her and a father she never knew, who killed himself while in prison for molestation charges. She had injuries to her face from a fire and suffered beatings throughout her life. She was also observed as experiencing cortical dysfunction.

Rader, like Sowell, had little history of biological issues or events. He was reportedly dropped on his head as a child but his history did not contain nor inspect physical factors further. Rodney Alcala as well had no inspection into this dimension of his background.

Measuring biological issues without the scientific workups of an Arthur Shawcross unfortunately results in the interpretations of details in the case histories that do leave conclusions open for criticism. The biological prong of this study is still credible, but is the most loosely supported by concrete data.

EVIDENCE OF ENVIRONMENTAL TRAUMA

The history of Andrei Chikatilo is highlighted by extensive poverty and famine, as well as exposure to grotesque physical injuries. He also believed a story regarding his brother's capture and cannibalization, although this is difficult to confirm. He had no father or friends as a child, and was socially ostracized by those in his village when he was a youth.

Various physical and mental abuses filled Arthur Shawcross's childhood. His tortuous relationship with his mother was damaging and lifelong, while his father played a weak role. He also had no friends as a child, owing to his extremely low socioeconomic status and frightening personality. There were also reports of possible sexual abuse.

Jeffrey Dahmer's chaotic and disturbing home life was intensified by his parents' bitter divorce, which came at a time when he appeared most vulnerable emotionally. He was abandoned by his mother at a time when he found loneliness to be devastating. He also did not enjoy the company of friends as a child. Again, there were reports of possible sexual abuse.

Edmund Kemper's alcoholic and mentally abusive mother rivaled Shawcross's in pure dysfunction. His grandmother was not any better, he did not have a father, and his sisters were physically afraid of him. His history includes tales of physical abuse. As were the other subjects, he was rejected by siblings and peers.

Rodney Alcala's home life could have been the most affected by his father's rejection of the family. The resulting fatherless childhood could possibly affect someone in a profound way, much like Dahmer's abandonment issues crept into his psyche. Could this be the source of Alcala's anger and control issues?

Dennis Rader's environment is another that did not seem to contain obvious abuse and trauma, but the violent imagery Rader witnessed as a child could have affected him at a developing stage. This is also true of Sowell, who did not report specific traumatic events, but lived in a social situation that could have been difficult for a child to thrive. His childhood included the observation of violence that, after time, appeared ordinary.

Aileen Wuornos's childhood was one of the most obvious disasters. Abandoned by her 15-year-old mother; taken in by grandparents and a family who did not love nor want them; the death of her brother; reportedly raped and assaulted all through childhood; prostitution, drugs, fights, injuries, living on the street, and her own pregnancy at 16, Wuornos had no chance in her environment.

A dysfunctional environment is a trait shared by all the killers in the study. Problems ranging from chaotic home lives to physical and mental abuse existed. All the subjects had childhoods that could be viewed, at the very least, as excessively difficult, and most likely damaging and traumatic.

All subjects clearly had serious obstacles in their ability to develop a reasonable sense of self, normal attachments, or strong positive role models, as well as little chance to understand intimacy or sexuality.

OBSERVATION OF PRIOR CRIMINALITY

Prior criminality is one of the easier items to identify in these case studies. Andrei Chikatilo built an extensive career as a child molester and sadist, seeking employment to facilitate exposure to children and potential victims. His past also suggests the possibility of incidences of burglary.

Arthur Shawcross's records reveal occasions of arson, burglary, and extreme violence toward others, beginning at a very early age. He suffered from late bed-wetting and engaged in continued torture of animals. He enjoyed an extensive history of sexual misconduct and child molestation.

Jeffrey Dahmer's past was full of early antisocial behavior and problems in school. He, too, engaged in continued animal abuse. Later on, he experienced employment difficulties and repeated bouts with alcoholism. He had scrapes with the law involving child molestation as well as burglary.

Edmund Kemper displayed an early obsession with violence, death, and sadism, disturbing everyone who viewed it. He practiced extreme animal abuse and had a long pattern of sexual misconduct. He was institutionalized for the double homicide of his grandparents at age 15.

Alcala demonstrated a history of sexual crimes throughout his known history. Aileen Wuornos again had a long history of all sorts of crimes, including drugs, prostitution, theft, fraud, and so forth. An argument could be made that much of Aileen's early crimes were a function of her abandonment and near poverty, as opposed to early acting-out and mental disorders.

Sowell is another offender with crimes in his history similar to Wuornos's, and could be viewed within the prism of poverty, desperation, and environment as opposed to inner desires. Also, like Wuornos, he had charges against him for domestic violence and other offenses related to substance abuse. He did, however, have a history of sexual crimes. Finally, Dennis Rader, like Alcala and Sowell, had a clear history of sex-related crimes as well as a long history of abusing animals.

All eight subjects share a degree of early criminality and antisocial behavior, ranging from burglary to extreme violence and sexual offenses. These individuals displayed markedly noticeable antisocial behaviors that should have alerted the people close to them. They were clearly not just immature, working through the typical personality problems of development.

The evidence of crimes involving assaults, fire setting, and extreme animal abuse suggests that biological factors include lack of impulse control and a predisposition to violence. Other crimes, such as burglary, may involve a seizing of control, possibly on a sexual level.

INCIDENCE OF SEXUAL DYSFUNCTION

Sexual dysfunction is a factor that is not difficult to observe. Much of all eight of the subjects' backgrounds involving prior crimes included dimensions of sexual issues. Andrei Chikatilo was an extreme sexual sadist, pedophile, and child molester. He continuously struggled to attain erection and orgasm, later developing a penchant for necrophilia and cannibalism.

Arthur Shawcross's entire life revolved around various sexual dysfunctions and perversions. He was sexually charged by arson and violence. Similar to the other subjects, he encountered erection and orgasmic difficulties. Bestiality, sexual sadism, necrophilia, child molestation, and cannibalism were in his paraphilic portfolio.

Jeffrey Dahmer dealt with a long-term conflict within himself concerning his homosexuality. He had no normal sexual relationships in his personal history, neither heterosexual nor homosexual. He engaged in exhibitionism, child molestation, and necrophilia as well as cannibalism. One of Dahmer's motives was described as a way to "punish and deny" a hated part of himself, as a form of displaced aggression (Merz-Perez & Heide, 2004, p. 63).

Edmund Kemper's personality was dominated by his extreme sexual sadism and interest in masochism. He was also obsessed with necrophilia and, as found in the other three subjects, cannibalism.

The more recent four case studies were no less obvious. Dennis Rader was obsessed with sexually charged thoughts of control, dominance, and assault. Aileen Wuornos, though a female who did not commit sexual acts when killing her victims, struck usually after she was paid for prostitution. She exhibited a lifetime of impossible relationships with men, owing to the rapes, abuse, and assault, perpetrated against her from an early age.

Anthony Sowell's past was marked by serial sexual assaults and antisocial behavior. And Rodney Alcala started rape and attempted murder of children as far back as 1968, with a long, repetitive history of rapes, kidnapping, child molestation, and sexual crimes.

The subjects' various extreme sexual dysfunctions are the most obvious aspect of this study. None of these case histories show any normal (or at least not dysfunctional) sexual patterns or relationships. Conversely, not only did they share problematic feelings of inferiority and difficulty or anxiety regarding performance (as does much of the population), but they also engaged in extremely dangerous and threatening sexual activity. Violence and death were pervasive themes. It is also interesting to note that many subjects were reported to have engaged in necrophilia and cannibalism, suggesting ultimate issues of power and control fused with sexuality.

OBSERVATION OF FANTASY AND DISSOCIATION

Andrei Chikatilo was often observed in a continued fantasy state. There were repeated public incidences of emotional detachment. Arthur Shaw-cross's family and acquaintances reported that he engaged in fantasy-obsessed behavior throughout his life, and was often observed in lengthy periods of dissociation.

Jeffrey Dahmer, too, displayed a lifelong lack of affect and was observed in deep fantasy states. Everyone in his immediate family reported his appearance of dissociation. Edmund Kemper's history as well revealed a pattern of deep fantasy states and that he had trancelike episodes.

Wuornos's dissociative states seemed related to alcoholic blackouts as opposed to fantasy issues or mental disorders, although repeated rapes could suggest otherwise. Again, Sowell's experience with alcoholic blackouts could mirror Wuornos's, but he did mention voices and "coming out of a fog" to discover crimes.

It may be intuition, but it's hard to imagine a person with literally thousands of photos of young, attractive subjects hidden in a storage locker by a person with a history of sexual assault, not being engrossed in a fantasy state for much of his history. I'll make the leap and include Rodney Alcala in this group.

Dennis Rader's history has the most clear references to fantasy and dissociation out of the later four case studies. He was referred to as losing himself in his own dark world as early as the eighth grade, and his longstanding violent sexual fantasies fueled and generated his later acts.

All of the case histories show how the subjects spent extended periods of time in fantasy or dissociative states. These episodes would often be observed in public, including at work or in school, not only while the subject could be considered alone with his thoughts.

The subjects displayed these traits from a very early age, possibly compensating for a lack of social contact and withdrawing to a safe place within their own minds.

An additional consideration to the dissociative process has been a look at related personality disorders. For example, a defense expert suggested Rodney Alcala suffered from dissociative episodes possibly caused by his borderline personality disorder. Anthony Sowell reported blackouts related to depression. While these suggestions may be a stretch or possibly just defense strategies, it raises the thought of dissociative process as connected to or as a result of other mental distress.

All eight subjects have a string of personality disorders easily attached to their backgrounds. Narcissism, borderline, and antisocial are just the beginning of this observation. Attachment disorder is another issue, while not always considered, which had to have a huge effect on all of these offenders.

RACE AND GENDER

An obvious question is: What did the inclusion of a woman and an African American man do for this analysis? First, it must be reiterated that the sample size is so small it cannot be considered statistically significant. Any results in considering these cases simply come from intuition and opinion.

Still, consider the basic motivations of Anthony Sowell and Aileen Wuornos. Sowell routinely lured women who were down on their luck, invisible, vulnerable members of his immediate society. They were easy prey for control, sexual assault, and serial murder. They were not missed and easily overlooked, glittering examples of Steven Egger's "less dead" theory. Sowell was interested in sexual control, and he was interested in repetitive killing. A race element is not seen in his crimes at all. He fell into a profile of killing within his race, and killing those he pursued for sex, as many serial killers do. Race did not seem a factor in victimology (outside of personal preference) or motive. His general behavior, luring home targets while living in a bad neighborhood, was very comparable to Jeffrey Dahmer's or another African American killer, Lonnie David Franklin, Los Angeles's "Grim Sleeper" killer. Franklin had as much in common with Dahmer and Alcala, who also collected an enormous cache of photographs of various women (Effron, Sher, & Karlinsky, 2010), as he did with Sowell. While there have been black mass killers where race appeared to play a specific role (e.g., subway killer Colin Ferguson), there have been others that seemed to have no racial component at all, such as spree killer John Mohammed, one of the DC Snipers.

Another African American high-profile serial killer is Wayne Williams, from Atlanta. Williams's case, where he lured young men and killed them within his rough neighborhood, again seemed devoid of a racial component. Like in Dahmer's case, there was a period of inaccurate assumptions because the victims were mostly black, wondering publically if they were targeted for their race in a type of hate crime. The fact the victims in both cases were simply sexual targets of preference, regardless of the race of the offender, seems to support a position that states there does not seem to be a racial component in the serial murder offender, regardless of his or her race. The limited literature available supports this opinion. Yet another black serial murderer, Walter Ellis of Milwaukee pleaded guilty to the murders of seven women in 2011. They were mostly black and also seemed to be selected according to convenience over a 21-year period as opposed to some other method of choosing victims that would suggest a difference in killers according to their race and the race of their victims. When sentenced to seven life terms, the judge remarked that although everyone would have liked to know why Ellis killed the women, "Mr. Ellis has the right not to tell us" ("Wisconsin serial killer," 2011).

Regarding female murderers, an enormous amount of additional research needs to be done on these offenders. At this point, most research lands on the main differences between male and female offenders, in that women kill differently, more often for money than men, and are often observed to be more obviously mentally ill. This component is subjective and could reflect the social bias of the observer. An exception to the stereotypical female killer is in fact Aileen Wuornos.

Wuornos's terrible upbringing and history has been discussed at length. It should be noted that her upbringing is similar to that of many male killers. She does seem to represent a male killer more closely in her behavior, most notably in her marked predatory nature. Now, she and some apologists attempted to play the "I was raped" card and may continue to do so, but a woman who has spent the majority of her life with countless johns as a hooker, has a hard time convincing most people that she was just completing another evening at work when she was shocked by an attempted rape and beating. Wuornos's cluster of several kills, with the men placed in similar powerless positions in remote areas and executed pretty much in the same manner and relieved of their valuables, do not reflect a woman reacting in self-defense. It also lines up with the pressures Wuornos was experiencing at that time, in trying to provide for her lover and the desperation she felt in potentially losing her.

Peter Vronsky (2007) states Wuornos's "rages, parasitical behavior, inability to form attachments, and grand narcissisms rise like monsters in the nights from her dysfunctional childhood" (p. 164). Clearly, Wuornos is a poster child for attachment disorder applied to the highest degree of pathology. However, it is still not clear in any study of Wuornos that her history and crimes are gender-specific.

Wuornos's crimes actually fit nicely in the eight case studies discussed here. She killed in a predatory, repetitive manner. She executed her victims, took trophies, and carefully avoided detection. She had a horrific background and extreme sexual dysfunction. She seemed to hate her victims, who were systematically chosen and resulted as targets of her general anger and violent, homicidal impulses.

Still, Wuornos's murders cannot be considered an anomaly as a predatory female killer. One example: A 15-year-old Missouri teenager, Alyssa Bustamante, admitted luring a nine-year-old neighbor girl to the woods, where she stabbed and strangled her, and slit her throat, to see "what it felt like." She prepared by digging a shallow grave ahead of time. At her sentencing hearing in February 2012, the words she wrote in her journal were read:

> I just fucking killed someone. I strangled them and slit their throat and now they're dead. I don't know how to feel atm. It was ahmazing. As soon as you get over the "ohmygawd I can't do this" feeling, it's pretty enjoyable. I'm kinda nervous and shaky though right now. Kay, I gotta go to church now . . . lol.

> (Lieb, 2012a)

Bustamante's case also recalls Wuornos's as her childhood included teenage, drug-using parents, a father in prison, and being abandoned by her mother, finally taken in by her grandmother (Lieb, 2012b).

Wuornos's crimes are not any different than the other cases, much less related to gender. Aileen Wuornos did not hate men any less than Shawcross hated women. Both killed the opposite sex. All the offenders, Sowell and Wuornos included, had consistent issues of pathological power and control, buried in a deranged need to commit homicide.

SERIAL MURDERER: AN APPROPRIATE DIAGNOSIS?

It is clear from this analysis that there is a consistent pattern for this criminal. All killed in a predatory manner, deriving satisfaction (or relief) from the very act of killing. They continued their activities regardless of the obvious wrongfulness and potential consequences, while remaining aware to avoid detection. They killed in an obsessive, cyclical fashion, exhibiting a period of anxiety before killing and displaying a time break between victims, commonly referred to as a *cooling-off period* (Ressler, Burgess, D'Agostino, & Douglas, 1984).

This pattern constitutes a set of consistent activities that can be diagnosed and categorized, as noted by Apsche (1993). The behaviors and etiology are found across the board, and are discussed at length in Chapters 8 and 10.

SUMMARY: POSITIVE AND NEGATIVE ASSUMPTIONS

The negative observations in this limited study simply do not exist. The weakest factors are the biological ones and even they do offer some support for the theory proposed here. Again, this weakness is due to the lack of available testing results, perhaps showing an apparent bias by researchers against biological factors. This issue continues with the more recent case studies offered, as biological analysis is not a measure commonly made in a serial killer personality assessment. Still, the ongoing increase of biological-based theory and scientific study regarding behavior, especially criminality and violence is strengthened as time passes.

Are there gender or race issues in the serial killer personality? More information is needed. The limited subjects in this analysis suggest that they operate in a manner similar to the prototype white male serial killer, in that power, control, dominance, sexual violence, and sadism are the common motivators. Issues related to women and minorities, namely extreme anger to specific personal history and experiences, are possible factors that may set them apart, but are not clear or significant enough in my opinion to separate women and different races within the serial killer population yet.

The behavior of Sowell seems more typical of a racial minority serial killer than Wuornos seems typical of women, and therefore would suggest that classification of killer (African American) probably operates in a manner similar to white serial murderers. However, Wuornos seems to behave more like a typical male serial killer than like other female serial murderers, suggesting additional case study comparisons of females to males would be helpful in drawing comparative conclusions to male killers.

Regarding the other factors in this study—namely, was there environmental trauma? Were there prior crimes? Was there sexual dysfunction? Were there dissociative episodes? Is there a recognizable syndrome called a serial murderer?—the answers must be a resounding yes. There is no question that these factors and patterns were present, and they cannot be explained away by differences in interpretation. It's unnecessary to recount the litany of examples both in the case studies and the vast literature review of other cases to prove the presence of significant environmental trauma, other crimes at an early age, pervasive sexual deviance and dysfunction, and a history of dissociative episodes exist. As far as a syndrome of serial murder, the upcoming chapters will hopefully present the existence of just that.

8

Theoretical Analysis and Development

I think I got more of a high out of killing than molesting.

—Westley Allan Dodd

Any reflection on these case histories makes revision of initial impressions a necessity. The analysis, in conjunction with the patterns found in the literature review, drive the following conclusions and result in a comprehensive theory regarding the personal and psychological development of the serial murderer.

In this chapter, the resulting theory is broken down into three separate stages: (1) the foundation, or primal basis of the pathology; (2) the path of the stressors, which combine with predisposition as they develop to the first murder; and (3) the obsessive-compulsive and ritualistic cycle of serial murder. Each component of each stage is briefly reviewed here, as they have been discussed at length in earlier chapters.

STAGE 1: FOUNDATION OF PATHOLOGY

Figure 8.1 shows the basic ingredients and combination of factors that lead to the development of the serial killer.

BIOLOGICAL PREDISPOSITION

A biological predisposition, as examined in the literature review, remains a critical point of this theory. Biological abnormality appears consistently in the case histories discussed, and although its presence remains basically intuitive and correlational, it combines with environmental trauma to produce

Figure 8.1 Foundation of Pathology—Diathesis–Stress Model

```
┌─────────────────┐                    ┌─────────────────┐
│   Biological    │ - - - - - -        │  Environmental  │
│ Predisposition  │                    │ Trauma/Stressors│
└─────────────────┘                    └─────────────────┘
            │           Diathesis-              │
            └───────────  Stress  ──────────────┘
                         Syndrome
                            │
                            ▼
┌─────────────────┐                    ┌─────────────────┐
│  Development of │ - - - - - -        │     Sexual      │
│ Esteem/Control  │                    │   Dysfunction   │
│    Problems     │                    │                 │
└─────────────────┘                    └─────────────────┘
```

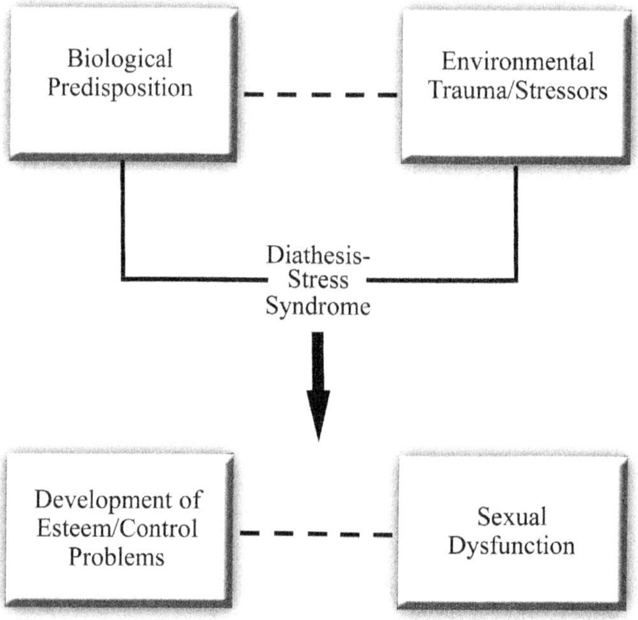

the dynamic for the diathesis–stress model. Environment alone does not appear to produce the serial killer, so it seems the biological factor is a key to the mix.

ENVIRONMENTAL TRAUMA AND STRESSORS

The catalyst of the diathesis–stress model is the environmental trauma shared by all the subjects of these case histories, as well as the vast majority of other serial killers. Clearly, there is no dispute regarding the trauma these killers sustained, for both the cases reviewed here and those outside the scope of this analysis. A history of environmental trauma is shared by all so this factor constitutes the second half of the diathesis–stress theory.

DEVELOPMENT OF ESTEEM AND CONTROL PROBLEMS

The case histories reveal the direct result of traumas experienced in childhood that resulted in a disastrous loss of self-esteem, a lack of sense of self, and thwarted development of a sense of intimacy. The personality problems of Chikatilo, Shawcross, Dahmer, and Kemper all progressed to greater degrees as they grew older.

Socioeconomic factors combined with familial failures to rob these subjects of a fair chance at personality development. This feature was found in all the case histories, usually interacting with their traumatic backgrounds and decidedly damaging their personalities during critical stages of formation.

SEXUAL DYSFUNCTION

Sexual problems go hand in hand with personality problems and serve as a springboard for life in a fantasy world, obsessive behavior, criminal activity, and sexually dysfunctional preferences and motivations.

Sexual difficulties are a prevalent aspect of these offenders' lives and serve as a bridge, taking the killers from early stages of inadequacy, anger, and frustration to lives of seeking out deviant sex featuring control, dominance, and dangerous paraphilia.

STAGE 2: PATH OF STRESSORS AND DEVELOPMENT TO FIRST MURDER

DEVELOPMENT OF MALADAPTIVE COPING SKILLS

The problematic personality traits (low self-esteem and lack of sense of self) and poor coping skills demonstrated by these subjects resulted in their maladaptive reactions to society. All of the subjects withdrew into private worlds and expressed their frustrations by committing crimes even before their serial murder careers began.

These individuals, both the subjects of the case histories and other killers mentioned in the literature, never learned to truly relate to others in their families or society, providing a basis for troubles to come. These maladaptive coping mechanisms determined how the subjects dealt with family, friends, potential lovers, and anyone else with whom they interacted. Difficulties with sex, personal relationships, and friendships of any quality, as well as problems with day-to-day interactions with people were inevitable.

RETREAT INTO FANTASY WORLD

A consistent maladaptive coping process among these subjects was their total withdrawal into fantasy worlds. Not only could they escape to these private worlds and enjoy their unacceptable sexual preferences, but they could also change their surroundings entirely. They found acceptance, status, and other missing parts of their lives in these fantasy worlds.

Retreat into fantasy, as discussed in previous chapters, is endlessly attractive. Eliminating other people and their impossible standards eradicates the enormous stress and certain failure these killers anticipate in their interactions with others. This is not to say that fantasy in itself can drive homicidal patterns of behavior; fantasy is enjoyed by a large segment of the population without dire consequences. It is just that a combination of a maladaptive personality and a fantasy life allows deviant sexual themes and violent ideas to become reality for the developing serial killer personality.

LESSER CRIMES

The manifestations of poor coping skills are often criminal behaviors, in both an antisocial disregard for authority and attempts to secure control and status. As shown in Figure 8.2, the maladaptive coping skills progress to criminality and disregard for others.

Some behaviors manifested in the case histories were fetish burglaries or other sexually charged attempts at seizing control. Sexual misconduct with children or other powerless subjects also demonstrates a consistent goal of achieving the control and acceptance missing from these subjects' lives.

Histories also include drug and alcohol abuse, possibly a form of self-medication or an intentional technique to reduce inhibitions. Some early crimes reflect a need to continue an exaggerated need for arousal as well as control, such as pulling false fire alarms and arson.

Disastrously developed sexual dysfunctions, such as pedophilia, necrophilia, and sexual sadism as evidenced in the case studies, also result in criminal activity and forced violence.

DISSOCIATIVE PROCESS

The dissociative process, which appears to be a higher state of fantasy, is the next level to which the fledgling serial killers move, by drawing real people into their dark fantasy worlds. As analysis of the case studies shows, there is a key difference between fantasy and dissociation.

It is one thing to be continuously lost in a dream world of fantasies, consciously creating an arena of unconditional love and acceptance, as well as sexual satisfaction. However, in a dissociative state, the subject takes this mental orientation to its moral and legal limits and advances toward a physical realization of his spiritual cravings.

The developing killer is often lost in a fantasy state, and returns there to enjoy the crimes again and again. However, the dissociative process begins when a Chikatilo becomes a wild beast, a Shawcross sees someone else kill, a serene Dahmer's face becomes a mask of evil, and a Kemper lives out his childhood rehearsal for murder. Dennis Rader was consumed by his sexual fantasies. Anthony Sowell awakens from a fog or blackout. It is a doubling process that allows the individual to fulfill his or her deadly compulsion with a minimum of responsibility.

FIRST KILL

Eventually the offender loses control of a situation—during a child rape (Chikatilo, Shawcross, and Alcala), when he feels panic or fear of another rejection (Dahmer), or in an explosive rage (Kemper and Wuornos). The trigger may have been a significant stressful event. Whatever the situation, it is perceived of and reacted to in a way far different from that of an average citizen. The killer reaches a breaking point and, at last, commits his first homicide. The act is inevitable, and it introduces the killer to an obsessive cycle from which one can never escape.

Figure 8.2 Path of Stressors Leading to First Murder

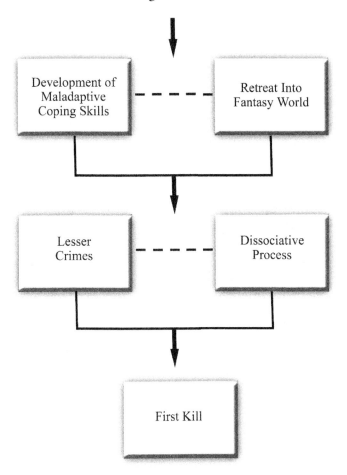

STAGE 3: OBSESSIVE-COMPULSIVE AND RITUALISTIC CYCLE

RENEWED URGE TO KILL

The killer has begun the cycle (Figure 8.3). Chikatilo now knows what he needs for sexual gratification. Dahmer now understands he must continually murder for men to lay with, men who won't leave. Kemper knows he will kill his mother again and again until he gets it right, reveling in the sheer sadism of his action. Shawcross knows he must cruise for prostitutes until one strikes him just right, who might play dead, one who will pay for his rejection by and hatred for women. Sowell has practiced what he must do after he lures another target to his Cleveland home. Rader's needs to sexually terrify and control his victims cannot be ignored.

Figure 8.3   Obsessive-Compulsive Ritualistic Cycle

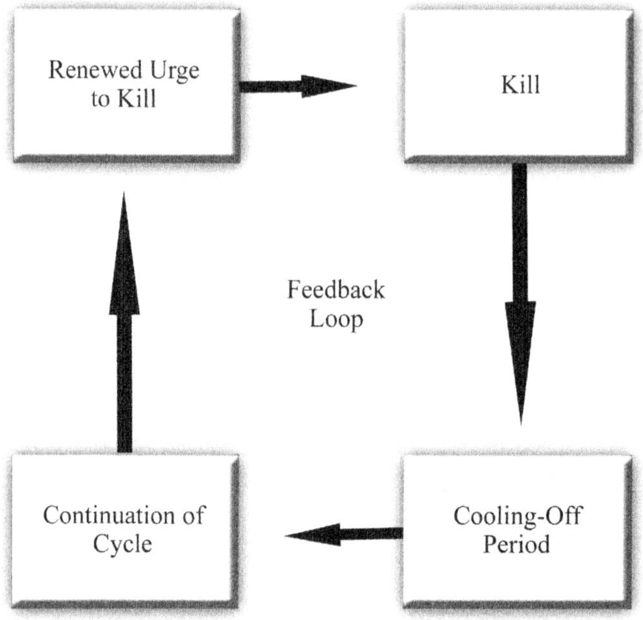

The killer has experienced the act that will now become his addiction. He has a taste for blood that cannot be satisfied by anything less. In the words of a killer, "there's a need to feed."

COOLING-OFF PERIOD

A central portion of the cycle is the cooling off, or the period between murders. There may be shame, guilt, or fear of detection and reprisal. However, Chikatilo waited until the weather and the time was right to again satisfy his thirst. Wuornos continued her cycle of anger and revenge once she gained a taste for it, but collected valuables and trophies for herself and her girlfriend along the way.

Kemper and Shawcross tried to control themselves, but failed. Dahmer allowed potential victims to leave because they were not his type or he didn't have enough time before work, but eventually he caved in to his compulsion. Alcala took more photographs, until . . .

Another aspect of this cooling-off period is the reliving of the crime. The mental rush and sexual thrill is renewed when these deeds are replayed, the mental repetition reinforces the behavior and ensures the inevitable reoccurrence of the crime. Items that seemed like cheap trophies are in fact tangible gateways to the killer "rolling in the dirt" as John Douglas once said. Sowell, like Dahmer, operated in an area comfortable with disappearing victims who were shadows in society. Cooling-off seemed like an integral part of the process for Rader, but eventually had to strike again, even many years later. Sex criminals like Alcala seemed to have less time and patience between assaults.

CONTINUATION OF CYCLE

The cycle repeats itself. In all the case studies considered here: Andrei Chikatilo, Arthur Shawcross, Jeffrey Dahmer, Edmund Kemper, Aileen Wuornos, Anthony Sowell, Dennis Rader, and Rodney Alcala, the killers were doomed to cyclical patterns of murder, cooling off, renewed urge, and murder. They became ritualistic, addicted to their compulsive patterns of death and achieving orgasm, collecting trophies, and avoiding detection. The tension before the act and the relief afterward cements the pattern. The cycle escalates until an eventual careless overkill, a gap in security, a relentless investigation, or just dumb luck dooms the killer to discovery.

These wretched souls, as well as countless others, have joined the ranks of serial murderers, a pathological, destructive obsession that possibly only the most extreme alcoholics, child molesters, or drug addicts might understand.

9

A Conversation with a Monster?

There's nothing grand about being in prison for what I am.

—Unnamed serial killer, death row

Over the course of completing this book and researching this subject over the years, I've had the occasion to have some limited conversation with offenders. The majority of these have taken place by correspondence and the commentary has often been, well, interesting.

I've received a lot of commentary that's obviously been meant for maximum impact. I resisted the temptation to print any of it in this book, as I've always taken them as cheap attempts at attention. Comments that seem designed for maximum reaction ring hollow to me.

Another grouping of comments is the obvious attempts at exposure or publicity. I've had offenders try very hard to be featured in the pages of this work and I have to say that's never been particularly interesting to me. I've had killers point me to their websites, refer me to people who appear to be acting as spokespeople or agents, and talk up their various previous exposures to the public. I've quickly dismissed these interactions. Contrary to their desires, I have not used their names.

I did appreciate one bit of salesmanship. I received a prompt response from Rodney Alcala after requesting a correspondence conversation. I also asked for information on his book, *You, the Jury,* which I'd had quite a bit of difficulty in obtaining. Alcala responded quickly, and I mistakenly thought there was a glimmer of hope for a conversation with someone I felt could be a fascinating study. Unfortunately, Alcala was quick to point me in the direction of where I could buy his book, but promptly refused further discussion. He did acknowledge and agree with my statement that it seemed his book was of a different take than his recent trial defense, but did not elaborate. I appreciated the book, anyway. To be fair, as I was working on Alcala's case study, his criminal case continued to be prosecuted by additional jurisdictions, so a complete refusal to discuss anything related to his crimes was not unexpected.

There's been quite a bit of bragging going on as you might imagine. Many are very comfortable with their notoriety and do not shy from it. Several are also quite comfortable with their status as study subjects for the students of the field. Functioning as a research subject seems to give some personalities just the attention that makes them the happiest. And, I really haven't been all that interested in some of the resulting obligatory excuses and deferrals of guilt.

I sent out feelers to a number of individuals, both the notorious and very obscure. This was intentional, just to see if such status mattered. Again, it did not, and results were mixed. I believe through this exercise that anyone wanting to write a true crime book and obtain some flashy, graphic comments to quote should have no problem doing so. Of course, it was the last thing I was looking for.

AN INTERESTING SUBJECT

However, I did make a contact that proved to be interesting. I spoke to a man, incarcerated on his state's death row, who politely, promptly answered my correspondence. He was straightforward and did not appear to respond in a manner that was designed for anything other than to communicate clearly. His initial response was actually friendly but reserved and guarded, and stated he had concerns about a conversation like I was suggesting. He actually at one point suggested another offender by name, who he described as "articulate and very interested in telling his story." He felt this individual would be a fine subject for my discussion. I had in fact heard of this offender and felt he would not be who I was looking for in this case. I politely continued to express interest in my correspondent's story, and he responded with another letter.

At this point he acknowledged my persistent nature and honestly listed some of his personal concerns. He first mentioned the issue of exploitation, and it seemed he might have had a problem with this before, or had at least been exposed to it.

He also talked about murderabilia—the practice of collecting true-crime artifacts such as letters, signatures, art, and so forth, as well as selling them. He was appreciative that I admitted to owning a few pieces and understood that I liked to display them while teaching university classes. I did make it clear I had no interest in obtaining any sort of such items from him. He was most concerned about someone making money based on his acts.

He stated, "I haven't even given any interviews dealing with my cases," which, I believe to be true. I had not seen any published commentary by him in regard to his crimes. I did see a very superficial exchange between him and someone that must have sent him a questionnaire once online; it was hard to determine if it was legitimate, or possibly something he was embarrassed about. Still, my opinion would be an offender could speak very differently to different people in different circumstances.

Later, I obtained some more insight as to the online interview (loosely termed) and it was more of a light conversation with a female and I determined it to be an actual exchange. I also found some letters written by this subject that had found their way to online crime artifacts auctions and sales, which may have been the source of his distrust in my intentions. I did not find any reference to case details in anything I found connected to this person, although the material gave me another small glimpse to the man's personality.

He asked me to drop the formalities of "Sir" and "Mr." and was glad I was straightforward in style. It did feel like we had no need to play games of any kind.

We discussed other true-crime authors. He was familiar with some I've dealt with and not some others. I sent him a copy of my first book but was unsuccessful in it being delivered, which was unfortunate. Prison can be a difficult place to receive personal items. He said most books on this subject that he'd read, "seemed to be selling 'how to get away with crime' books in order to cash in." I agreed.

GROUND RULES AND A PSEUDONYM

We came to some agreements early. He stated he was not interested in any sort of exposure or fame. "I don't want notoriety or exposure," he said. To be honest, this attitude was one of the reasons I found him such an interesting subject. He sincerely wasn't interested in having his name printed anywhere. He said, "I . . . wouldn't want any credit."

We agreed this would be the case. As stated previously, I understand the allure of dropping names in a work such as this, but I just wanted a conversation with a person who might give me a special insight. He suggested I just refer to him as "a white male, 40's, who's convicted of multiple murders [and] once expressed in an interview." For the remainder of this book, I will call him "Rick." Rick was a resident of death row when we first spoke, and his location is irrelevant. Rick by his own description is a convicted murderer of more than 10 women, in a series of sexual assault-related cases.

Early in our talk, Rick made it clear that while he does consider himself narcissistic, he did not consider his crimes to award him some lofty status. He also did not speak with a haughtiness that a movie psychopath might take. He related options thoughtfully, carefully, and clearly. One of the things I liked most about Rick as a person to share these ideas with, was that he truly did not seem to find a need to say things for effect, for impact. Most references to the crimes and details were muted, and referred to for a logical reason.

In one of our first discussions Rick made a statement I found especially significant:

"I do not have delusions of grandeur. There's nothing grand about being in prison for what I am. It's more embarrassing than anything else. That takes out graphic case details and headline-grabbing terms or talk."

I appreciated his sincerity and humbleness, which I didn't expect.

Opinions That Sound Familiar

We talked at length about my previous book's theory, about nature versus nurture, about the idea of biological bases for behavior. Rick agreed that he didn't see the choice of nature or nurture, but a combination of the two. I of course agreed, offering that my book's diathesis–stress theory sounds a lot like that. He said, "it has to be."

Regarding the way different people react to the same stimuli, I asked what he thought about biology. He simply said, "we're not all wired the same." I did notice a comment made by one of his defense attorneys in court echoing a similar thought: "he's just wired differently."

Rick demonstrated an insight that surprised me. He said he had some conversations with another teacher or author, but from what he said that person's input didn't sound like anything Rick was offering, nor did I agree with as well. Supposedly, the other person Rick spoke to felt all (yes, all) offenders who commit serial sexual crimes hate women or possibly their mothers. While I'd say there's a certain percentage of sexual assault cases that would fall under Hazelwood's typology of the anger retaliation rapist, that still leaves quite a few out. Rick adamantly agreed.

He felt that yes, some offenders did hate women and used their victims as "surrogates," and for revenge and to "kill personal demons." He did say some offenders hate women "for good reasons." However, he felt more men involved in sex crimes usually liked women too much as opposed to hating them. He said there was a "certain something they get out of violence, ultra-arousal that is personally gratifying and exciting." He described the process as it "goes from a controlled obsession to a criminal obsession when the trigger is tripped. You can only put in so much of the fantasy world before something escapes into reality."

Rick's prior conversations may have helped him organize his thoughts, but it seems his conclusions that run parallel to the opinions of this book were his.

Rick explained the nurture part, the stress half of the dichotomy, as something that happens at a very young age, sometimes a traumatic event, but definitely not always. Just as often he felt it was a personal event of some kind that interacted with something else. He used the words "coping mechanism," addiction, and "a negative," but repeated that "there is something. 'It' starts at a young age."

His nurture explanation was even more clear:

> there's a whole other belief I have dealing with these crimes in general. There's a part of our brain that is believed to be linked to our own primitive beginnings. More violent and criminalistic. I have a theory that something happens in a person where they tap into this and it causes the "conscious override effect" which in turn lets violent acts take over. There can be a need to feed once blood has been so-called spilled. Now a predator is loose and when a person presents themselves or triggers the prey radar it's a done deal.

This does sound a lot like the biological principles discussed in earlier chapters. The idea about "it" happening as a child, whatever "it" is, especially given his belief that "it" might not seem so devastating on the surface at the time of occurrence, again, sounds like ideas found on these pages. As I mentioned, I did send Rick a copy of my first book that he said he'd never heard of (he didn't know me either), but the book was held up in prison publication review, which typically took months. He did not get a chance to read it before we spoke. It was eventually decided by prison officials to be a subject matter that was not appropriate or approved.

GETTING FROM POINT A TO POINT B

Rick and I, through these conversations, came to refer to the development of an offender's psychopathology as getting from point A to point B. He had a self-awareness that demonstrated he'd given a lot of thought and time to some self-analysis, and he was truly interested in a certain self-actualization that our exchange could help crystallize.

I had a number of opinions related to the pattern of creating a violent serial predator and so did Rick. He didn't have much use for typologies or clinical psychological labels. He felt people could have many antisocial traits but not fit into any category. He was less convinced that the pattern for killers I described was consistent across offenders. He used himself as an example:

> I don't believe I fall into any accepted pattern. My behavior as a child wasn't perfect but I didn't start fires, kill animals or hate my Mother or women. . . . I don't think my personal development was much different or less typical than other kids . . . the one thing that was different was I was more adventurous than most. If I didn't think a limit or rule was based on a practical reason, I tested it.
>
> I was addicted to horror movies before I was ten. At 13 I was renting any VHS movie I wanted. Soon it was porn. Some porn had horror. . . . Over the years I can see that maybe that's it?

Here was an interesting point. First, if the reader remembers my personal comments about growing up being obsessed with horror movies at a young age (Preface), they will note the irony of that statement. Furthermore, Rick's searching for "it," that factor in his childhood that possibly combined with his primitive brain to bring out the predator that laid just below the surface, took him to the point of horror movies, porn, and violent pornography.

This obviously relates to my prior reference to Ted Bundy and his insistence that violent pornography was critical in his turn to violence. He insisted the night before his execution that it (porn) helped crystallize his dangerous desires and helped take him from the fantasy to the action. From a person like Bundy, it's easy to dismiss. Hearing it again from another offender who seems to be legitimately in search for an answer, it might be an idea to reconsider.

He insisted his childhood was unremarkable and ordinary. He didn't pretend it was perfect, but said he had plenty of friends and girlfriends, and didn't act out in a noticeable manner. He described himself as a popular jock and said people have a hard time believing his crimes when they find out about them.

Rick sincerely sounded like he's been searching for a certain stressor or combination of them that caused that significant negative reaction. He said he had not been able to identify them in himself but had no doubt they existed. This factor or factors, along with their connection to that deep part of his brain that brought him to where he is today, is the journey of point A to point B. We have not positively identified the landmarks just yet.

Rick at one point referred to his "WHY" search. He noted things he'd read about Bundy included statements that referred to "the killer, but not in the first person." I also asked if he had inconsistent childhood discipline (as suggested in FBI organized offender literature), as roundabout way of wondering about his need for control. He admitted his childhood discipline was inconsistent in fact, but adamantly denied any need for control. He said "I don't try and control others. The reality is, I don't care enough to try."

Pornography, Revisited

As I said, Rick's perspectives regarding pornography made me take a step back. Bundy's statements to a person with a very high-profile public bias against pornography can easily be doubted. But when speaking with Rick, it does seem most presentations of his history come with a minimum of filter. During his period of introspection, it sounds like he's given not only a lot of thought to the subject, but has also decided there could be something to it. He explained:

> Here's what I believe about porn in general. It's not the single cause of sex crimes or killings. What it does is aid in furthering the growth of objectification. It might also aid in the person being able to dehumanize another. A lot of the worst crimes done to people are by those who [don't] see their victims as human anymore. Only objects. . .

He went on to explain that he felt that "horror movies that have naked or sexy women being killed or raped are a whole lot more damaging" than nonviolent porn. He acknowledged the difference in rape or torture pornography in Bundy and how it might have "started to open the primitive door" for his crimes. He remained baffled by Bundy's interest in necrophilia, especially with a body in late stages of decomposition, and said he "can't begin to try and understand that" and decided there was "a lot more going on in his mind."

He felt a child who had access to pornographic movies, especially the B-movie sex-and-violence kind, could at a stage of early sexual development potentially head down the wrong path. He wondered if the combination of objectification and sexual violence as material for "a kid's first sexual experience . . . there was no negative consequence [and] . . . the action is just repeated over and over. . . . Maybe that's the pattern?"

Still, Rick said the porn fusing with sex and violence "opens the primitive door more than anything else." He thought a person who is vulnerable to such things could have the primitive part of their brains affected by hard-core violent pornography.

Interestingly, Rick ended his comments by saying, "I, however, didn't watch or ever see violent hardcore violent porn or read the mags." He referred to himself as a "mainstream porn type."

A Conversation in Person

In addition to many letters I shared with Rick, I had the occasion to have a face-to-face conversation with him in prison. On a dreary, stark November day, I arrived at the prison not really knowing what to expect. I didn't seem all that significant to Corrections personnel, which was fine by me. The cold, gray atmosphere was timeless and unsettling, and set a physical backdrop to the experience that I didn't anticipate.

After the obligatory layers of background and security, I finally made my way past the various physical obstacles. As a high security risk, Rick was behind a glass barrier. Oddly, I felt like the barrier and the physical separation didn't exist very long. It was an easy conversation, with all of the stops and starts you might expect in a session lasting a few hours. But, I felt that Rick tried to answer most questions as honestly as he could, and of course there's quite a bit not included in these pages.

Rick is convicted in the murders of more than 10 women. He's often been referred to as a sexual sadist. He made no attempts to deflect, dispute, or otherwise minimize his guilt. Conversations that seemed to go down the road of how bad things are for him now generally included a comment like, "but I'm responsible for where I am." Recounting our discussions in these pages does not include an analysis of truth nor a prism of morality; they are taken at face value and are simply reported.

He was very versed on the subject of various serial murderers. Among many others, we discussed Dahmer, Kemper, Bundy, Brudos, Alcala, Richard Ramirez, BTK, and additional offenders like sexual sadist Paul Bernardo and other cases not found in the news very often. He said prison was the place for learning about how to be a better criminal. He reiterated his distaste for books that seemed to offer a "how to get away with it" function for active criminals and wondered if people like John Douglas understood how they instruct offenders to alter their methods.

Along with Douglas, we discussed the work of people like Robert Ressler and various experts in the field on both the defense and prosecution sides. He described Park Dietz as a narcissist, a label he also used for Douglas and himself. He stressed that I, as a writer and theorist, should be wary of the overuse of typologies and blanket assumptions. It's very important to understand that every case, every offender is unique in some way, and there's a danger in painting all serial killers with too broad a brushstroke. This was one of many lessons I took home with me.

THOUGHTS ABOUT THE INSANITY DEFENSE

Like many serial murderers, Rick's defense in court was centered around an insanity claim. His attorneys proposed the logic that he could not control his sadistic impulses and he could not learn from the consequences. He told me he didn't particularly care for this strategy, that he didn't agree with it, but also agreed there wasn't a better option. What else could he say?

He said he spoke to various experts, was interviewed by the expected doctors, and found their general position was to make him fit into a certain mold, either as a convenience for the defense angle or to agree with their particular theory or orientation. Rick said most doctors were not prepared for truth or answers.

I asked if he'd been hit on the head as a child, an obvious question. He said the doctors pushed him toward this as well, and he struggled to remember falling off a swing in the first grade and losing consciousness. It was what they wanted to hear, but he didn't find it significant.

He also mentioned doctors searching for "frontal lobe" issues. He said "he'd had every test." We mentioned CAT scans and MRIs. He said they had found absolutely nothing, much to his dismay.

I noted his defense described his childhood as including a brain disorder and a history of impulse control issues, which some might say could describe a number of children. Rick simply couldn't support either concept at all, did not feel there was a brain disorder, and again chalked this up to strategy. He noted his general attitude about his childhood made him appear like he was in denial while in therapy, but he said he was just speaking the truth.

He said he did not have anyone in his family he knew of with a history of mental illness or significant criminal behavior.

Rick of course did not take the stand in his own defense. I asked if he felt cheated out of a chance to say something that might help him, but he did not. He saw no positive in testifying. He recognized that opposing attorneys would make him look bad no matter what he said and there was no point. He was again, more embarrassed to be in the courtroom than anything anyway, and wasn't interested in being attacked on the stand.

A KILLER'S IDEAS ABOUT WHY

We did spend a lot of time recounting his childhood and what red flags might have been there. We discussed the things he'd talked about in his letters: that he was adventurous, not willing to take no for an answer, and enjoyed the status a child has when he tried or accomplished things other children did not. He described the place of respect he enjoyed as a child when he hit a big home run or tried something no one in the group would dare.

He came back to a couple of key issues. He said there was a combination of factors that seemed to lead him down the wrong path. First there was a unique freedom that allowed him to rent sex and violence movies, ones that most children would never be allowed to walk out of a store possessing. He understood that not all children might be affected in the same way, but it seemed to him he was wired to be deeply affected by the synthesis of sex and extreme violence, and it stayed with him to fantasize and think about this for years to come.

We spoke again about his mind going to a primitive place, and mentioned most people go there at some point. He said many people find themselves in a dark, primitive place in their personalities when faced with certain situations. I agreed, and mentioned the stories I'd been told by therapists of high-risk children literally reverting to their primal nature under severe episodes of trauma or horrifying upbringings with zero human attachment. Therapist Cathy Clevenger had described children actually pawing the ground and growling in some instances. Rick said he understood this completely.

This combined with an extraordinary success rate in sexual conquests, according to Rick. He said he religiously read the *Penthouse Letters* and thought, these must all be true. He said he always tried whatever attempt at sexual relations he could find, thinking there was no reason not to. This resulted in an inordinate amount of trysts with women of all ages, friends' mothers, girl-friends, and wives of his own friends—a string of fodder for the *Letters* section of his own making. It seemed at a very early age his appetite for new, different, extreme, and ultimately satisfying sexual experiences became insatiable.

I've often theorized that most killers' first kill was an accident, and then the offender discovers what ultimately satisfies him. Not so in Rick's case. I asked if the first kill was an accident, and he said, "no, absolutely not. I'd been thinking about that for a long time."

Intrigued by this assertion, I went on to ask if there were triggers that caused him to act out in committing murders. He felt there were triggers or stressors that caused him to develop the feelings he carried within him, but no, there were no clear incidences of acting out in his crimes. I noted this was a pretty common occurrence and offered examples, but he said it didn't apply to him.

This took me to another question: he had a series of kills in a very short time, a cluster of murders. I said some people might argue that it was a spree as opposed to a serial murder pattern. I again mentioned the idea of acting out or escalation.

He said escalation was one of the concepts the doctors examining him tried to pigeon-hole him into. He said there was absolutely no significance to the admitted clustering of murders, psychologically. We discussed the general difference between a serial killer and a spree killer, and we agreed he didn't fall under the heading of a spree. He said the pattern was simply explained: "opportunity."

Instead of assuming there was a psychological significance to the kill frequency, I needed to understand his thought process. He told me he was "always ready" to commit a murder, and that he "always had what he needed with him." He explained the details of his job at the time, and that there were periods where those particulars made it impossible to find a victim during work hours. Then the particulars of his job duties changed where he could actually approach strangers and find victims and have time, unlike before. He said when these parameters were all just right, he continued to kill as everything fell into place. He insisted that this was not a psychological cycle, that he was not escalating or building up a need to kill again. He said it was simply a case of all the details falling into place and making the hunt easy. He said the opportunity was irresistible.

He described himself at that time as being able to wear a "mask of sanity" and was able to "hide in plain sight." I wasn't sure if he was familiar with Cleckley's 1941 work of the same name, but it was interesting nonetheless. He said some criminals wear masks, whereas others hide in their normalcy.

He did not blame victims, but did criticize them a bit. He felt given his normal looks and personality that people too easily let their guards down. He said, "whether it was greed or laziness or just carelessness," they should be more aware of the threats around them.

THE SEMANTICS OF PSYCHOPATHOLOGY

Rick had an interesting take on his status or classification as a psychopath. He said they had the "Psychopathy Checklist" in the prison and that inmates often filled it out and discussed it. He felt it was terribly arbitrary to consider someone who scored a 30 as a psychopath but someone with a 29 as not. This came back to his general opinion of typing everyone the same, but he took it personally.

This led to a fascinating discussion of what Rick referred to as objectification. Rick thought if he felt emotions like any other person watching teary movies or appreciating the sadness of a person's loss of a pet for instance, then he shouldn't be considered a psychopath. He further clarified that a killer who actively objectifies a victim is no longer committing a crime against a human, a living person, so the killer is not showing a callous disregard for human life. This, in his mind, is what exemplified the psychopath.

I have to say this concept took me back a little and I had to think about it. My opinion landed on the following facts: (1) The fact a person can feel a sad emotion or appreciate that someone might feel badly would not necessarily exclude them from psychopathy. (2) A person's ability to actively objectify a victim is a *technique* a person would use to override the values, morals, fear of consequences, and other inhibitors that might block a different type of person from committing such crimes. (3) It is pure semantics that we label this offender a psychopath, sociopath, or whatever else we choose as a descriptor. The point is there are those who might have some antisocial, violent thoughts or impulses, but there is a different sort of individual who is capable of compartmentalizing those thoughts, using the objectification technique and then puts aside any other issues to enable the actual carrying out of those crimes.

Rick's ideas about active objectification reflect his earlier statements about the "conscious override effect," which allows someone who has reached that primitive place in his mind, to use a technique to get past "normal" morality, values, fear of consequences, and other internal controls to obtain what he desperately wants and needs at a given moment in time.

Rick listened carefully to this opinion. It was clear it was food for thought. I also offered the ideas written about by Robert Jay Lifton (*The Nazi Doctors*, 2000) when he suggests the concept of *doubling*, describing how some people can compartmentalize certain feelings and beliefs and commit actions (or unspeakable crimes) that seem entirely out of character for that individual.

It was at this point in the conversation I realized Rick was getting as much out of this exchange of ideas as I was.

IT'S AN ADDICTION, BUT IT'S ABOUT EXPOSURE

Rick explained to me, without hesitation, that he would likely commit these crimes again if released and resume his life routine. I thought of the crimes as a cycle, one of building stress and desire to kill after a certain time period elapsed. Rick did not see it that way.

He said he has many interests in life. He used fishing as an example. He said he could move to a remote region of Canada, fish every day, and be happy forever. He insisted he would not feel those old impulses to go hunting for victims, like Jeffrey Dahmer described. Instead, he agreed the behavior or need was an addiction, but not one that included a "withdrawal" process. He thought it was an "exposure" issue.

Rick said when he found himself exposed to the circumstances ideal for completing an assault with a minimum of risk, this was the situation he would find irresistible. This was an impulse control problem. Exposure equaled opportunity.

He stressed the sexual assault was the main draw, and that the victim was insignificant. She had been thoroughly objectified. I asked, "like a doll?" He agreed. "Exactly." He tried to explain the murder as a logical step in the progression of the crimes, that it simply made perfect sense after the sexual attack, even if it seemed like an escalation to an even worse level. He explained, it's like a stolen car . . . at the end, you get rid of the car."

I asked why he continued the crimes, other than the exposure to impossible-to-resist situations. Did it fulfill a need? He said it was a case of expecting something, of searching for something that never really happened. It sounded something like an extreme drug habit where a person tries to reach that next level, which never happens, but they never stop trying to find it. Rick sounded rather disappointed in this failure.

MORE CLARIFICATION

We discussed a number of issues beyond what I've recounted so far, some adding to the series of topics I looked at differently after our time together. One was the term, "trophies."

I've commonly used the expression trophies in describing serial murderer behavior; the taking of mementos from a crime scene to keep as a physical connection later. Once during a *Fox News* segment, I was asked by an interviewer if the jewelry and possessions taken by serial killer Rafael (Angel) Resendez-Ramirez was evidence he was motivated by theft. I stated I felt some theft might be incidental as in the case of Aileen Wuornos, but my feeling was the primary motivation was the taking of trophies.

Rick was very specific about the use of the word trophies. He felt serial murderers took these items specifically for use in reliving and re-enjoying the rush of the crimes. While I understood this, I thought there could also be a proof of accomplishment dimension to them, much like the common concept of a trophy. Rick strongly disagreed, and said the items were for the connection to the emotion of the time, and that's it. I asked if a better word could be used, such as a "totem," a physical connection to a psychological state. He agreed.

Rick also explained there was no excitement in the idea of getting caught. There was no rush, no thrill. Rick had learned his desires mostly watching them on a movie screen, and later fantasizing about them at his leisure. He told me the best scenario would have been to "watch himself," like it was a movie. He understood the attraction to filming crimes, as done by other killers, because watching himself with no anxiety, or fear or distraction was the best situation. He said he often felt he was "too close" to the sexual assault or murder to enjoy it.

One of the ways he thought different cases prove the differences between individuals was that some killers really did find an end point, like Edmund Kemper. Kemper killed his mother and her friend after a string of co-ed killings, then turned himself in. Rick disagreed with the common notion that all serial killers will always continue and never reach a point where they stop. I agreed, although I had to specify that it was the minority, like Kemper, who were done.

Rick did reiterate that "once blood is spilled, you never come back from there." He says the serial murderer is changed forever. He said, "I think Dahmer was being honest if he said he'd continue on if he got out. Once you've opened the primitive door, it never closes."

A Diverse and Exhausting Conversation

We certainly spoke about an amazing array of topics for three and a half hours. We talked about family, and mundane interests and other issues that will not find their way into these pages.

Within the conversation about the crimes (or "cases" as he always put it), he mentioned various law enforcement agents following him and proving to be very unsuccessful in apprehending him sooner. The way he was overtly followed reminded him of Gacy. He mentioned various mistakes made by law enforcement and the system that did eventually result in, more cases. Rick said he continued the way he did because he was just lucky. He seemed legitimately conflicted that some of the cases could have been avoided.

Rick did provide some humor. He said once he was arrested he took law enforcement agents on ride-alongs—various field trips to at least two states, in supposed errands related to cases and victims. He said he thought of places he liked to eat and decided where to take them on the next wild-goose chase that way. He said he got the idea from "that guy in Texas," which of course was Henry Lee Lucas. Rick added that he felt the trips almost seemed like a setup, a way to provide him with an opportunity to attempt an escape so they could shoot him, but this was just an observation.

I spoke to an admitted serial murderer within the prison for hours, after months of correspondence in which we built trust and mutual understanding. The experience was intellectually, physically, and emotionally draining. I was truly surprised at the amount of information I had to digest. Rick is very clear that I am not here to make excuses or apologies for him, nor am I here to defend him. I made it clear from the outset that in these pages I am searching for a way to explain some of the most fascinating psychological criminals in history. I was incredibly fortunate to finally connect with a person who was as interested in the same construction and journey of a mind, albeit for decidedly different reasons. I'm not sure I have any answers yet, but this exchange has helped us both get closer to what lies within.

10

Conclusion

You feel the last bit of breath leaving their body. You're looking into their eyes. A person in that situation is God. You possess them and they shall forever be a part of you.

—Ted Bundy

A CRITICAL LOOK AT THIS ANALYSIS

A weakness that stands out in this study is the lack of detail concerning biological factors. There is an inconsistency to the data available, mainly owing to the patchwork design of testing. If a greater proportion of offenders were given the extensive biological analysis that Shawcross received, rather than the minimal consideration Chikatilo was given, this dimension could be either strengthened or disputed.

The inadequacy of data here reduces the biological component to one of intuition, based on the correlational nature of the research. This study would be strengthened and supported with greater quantitative credible data for biological determinants.

Another weakness is the anecdotal nature of case studies. However, as previously discussed, this type of research is most appropriate for limited samples such as this. The actual statistical data are limited and difficult to extract, so the case study approach allows for a look at the complete picture of a killer's development, even if it's a patchwork of related reports.

It should be noted that the case study method does weed out inconsistencies during its accumulation of facts. For example, it was questioned whether Jeffrey Dahmer actually committed cannibalism during his active period.

A look at other serial killers shows that they also did commit cannibalism, most notable Dennis Nilsen, a killer often paralleled with Dahmer. Admittedly, it is possible that many of these subjects are lying and/or embellishing, but as more reports accumulate, this becomes less likely.

Does consistency of reports prove unequivocally that cannibalism occurred? No, but the possibility appears much more likely, given the circumstances. This is especially true when viewed in the context of the control and acceptance issues that the act of cannibalism implies. Other issues such as the role of pornography, evidence of attachment, and other items are reviewed with a fresh perspective with a history of showing up in additional cases.

ISSUES FOR FUTURE ANALYSIS

The aspect of control is a topic needing further development. Issues of control are pervasive and consistent, but a closer look at this dimension has merit. For example, control-related behaviors during the offenses might be identified and examined. Similar backgrounds could also be considered.

It also would be interesting to see a more extensive analysis of prior criminality. Many of the crimes—breaking and entering, burglary, exhibitionism, arson—have a sexual or control drive element to them. Robert Ressler often refers to "fetish burglaries," or crimes committed with an "acting-out" motivation regarding control and sexual issues. This type of psychological crime, with all its implications, would make a worthwhile study.

Further analysis of the linear relationship between dissociation and the role of fantasy also would be productive. This book assumes a relationship between the two as a reasonable developmental observation; however, as Dr. Richard Kraus notes,

> these phenomena, while often contiguous, are nevertheless separate and distinct from each other. Dissociative experiences are altered mental states occurring beyond one's conscious control while fantasy denotes the conscious use of imagination which seeks to relieve one's personal distress or frustration or as in the case of serial killers, a substitute for action or preparation for subsequent action.

(personal communication, December 2, 1997)

Regarding biological factors, studies linking serotonin levels, impulsive violence, and suicide suggest possible analyses of suicidal behavior or ideation in serial killers. Additionally, studies continue to report correlations between genetics and behavior. Dopamine effects on thrill seeking and excitability ("Studies find," 1996), as well as the effects of nitric oxide on violent and sexually aggressive behavior (Toufexis, 1995) have been cited. These findings and others point to a need for exploration of the biological arena. Neurological studies, consideration of infections, genetic analyses, and even brain examinations after death, as have been suggested regarding John Wayne

Gacy and Jeffrey Dahmer, would likely offer additional insight into this issue. A fresh look at the idea of a revised XYY theory is another thought.

On the personality side, I'd like to see a fresh consideration of overall immaturity in the adult serial offender personality. As referenced in Chapter 2, there seems to be a similarity of a narcissistic individual with no developed sense of attachment or empathy to an arrested emotional development. An almost childlike quality comes out in the case studies of many multiple killers who cannot get past the high that killing brings them. They act like kids with their hands in the cookie jar when caught, falling back on the sociopathic excuses and deferrals of blame.

METHODOLOGICAL CHANGES

The most important methodological change or improvement to this analysis would be in the realm of biological study. Ideally, each subject would receive a complete workup similar to that done for Arthur Shawcross. This is unlikely. However, performing standardized measures of key elements such as kryptopyrrole levels or other genetic markers on more offenders would be beneficial.

Another possibility is to analyze in detail exactly what points might best characterize a biological predisposition. Certain particulars, such as kryptopyrrole levels, brain trauma, or heredity, might be examined or measured for consistency among offenders. Along the same lines, those specific behaviors discussed in this book, such as prior crimes or dissociative episodes, could be narrowed and analyzed as separate studies.

ADDITIONAL CASE TESTING

Additional case studies could further test this theory to include varied types of serial killers, such as females or those with a venue outside the United States other than Chikatilo. This volume has specifically added a female killer, an African American killer, and two others studied more recently. Still, this very limited sample cannot be considered representative at any level. A separate study concerning only female killers would likely be of great interest, by examining the similarities and differences with their male counterparts—the matter of biological influence could be a key issue. Another study could categorize killers by type of victims, similar background, or time period. A fascinating suggestion could be the grouping of killers by IQ testing, in order to try to separate the effects of actual intelligence versus sheer skill in manipulativeness.

A study similar to this one could be constructed using a much larger selection of case histories. Going beyond doubling the cases from four to eight, but a much higher number with elemental analysis would be interesting. Given the extensive literary review necessary to formulate this preliminary model, more than four cases would have been unworkable at the outset. However, if another study replicated and measured the theory suggested here, the majority of time and effort could be spent on obtaining a larger sample.

PROTOCOLS FOR VALIDATION THROUGH INTERVIEWS

In-depth, complete interviews with offenders would be an excellent way to further validate this theory. The data would be less secondhand and anecdotal, and interpretation would be consistent. The interviews would include:

1. Investigation of biological factors
2. Questions regarding fantasies
3. Questions regarding the sexual nature of early crimes
4. Inquiry into sexual problems and proclivities
5. Complete examination of the environmental situation
6. Examination of clinical psychological background
7. Discussion of an obsessive or cyclical pattern of crime
8. A minimum experience level or standard outline for the interviewer
9. Control-related questions
10. A determination of the offender's relative acceptance of responsibility

Structure would be the key component of the interview. It would be necessary to conduct repeated interviews, neither too long as to cause the subject to lose interest, nor too short as to ensure the subject has opportunity to elaborate as much as possible with open-ended questions. Repetition is necessary to weed out possible embellishments and lies, and to establish consistent stories and histories. Consistency is also important as is similar experience levels in interviewers.

As seen in my interview of Rick, many of these questions will result in answers that fall right in line with some theory, whereas others will not. They will certainly result in an interpretation issue as well as an assessment of truth and motivation.

Interviewers would also be wise to consider the offenders within a prison setting a *nonemotional offender* type, as regarded within the Reid Nine Steps interrogation method, give careful thought to exactly how inquiries are formulated, and to prepare open questions that call for narrative, ahead of time (Inbau, Reid, Buckley, & Jayne, 2004).

It would also be advantageous to interview family and acquaintances. Former teachers, psychologists, and employers would provide an interesting dimension. The interviews should, however, be conducted by the same interviewer to ensure continuity. However, a key element would be careful standardization of data to allow inference across cases.

CONCLUSIONS AND DISCUSSION

It would be unrealistic to assume that the theoretical model suggested in this book is all-inclusive; even the FBI's Behavioral Sciences Unit assumes its rules of profiling to be applicable in about 75 percent of situations (Ressler, 1992, p. 129). Often, profiling attempts during investigations are revised according to additional data as it is received. This, along with the considerable overlap of many organized and disorganized offenders, and individual variables, makes it difficult to generalize.

I've generally stayed away from the temptation to categorize or provide typologies for serial murderers, acknowledging this is common practice in such study. While it's possible to create subgroups of various serial killers, it's my position that there is more value in the identification of the serial killer personality, essence, and motivation than to paint oneself into a corner trying to force an offender into a pattern that's too restrictive.

This was touched on in my conversations with Rick chronicled in Chapter 9. He said that "once there's an accepted typology, everyone MUST FIT! To me it makes sense to use it as a base but then break it down further." Rick summarized this position with, "there's nothing simple about this."

As Katherine Ramsland states in regard to the Andrea Yates murders, "serious mental illness can be camouflaged" (Paradis, 2010, p. ix). This is even more true of the offender who does not own a clinically diagnosable disorder, but is compelled from within to murder repeatedly with success. Models and assumptions are helpful, but cannot be restrictive in their inflexibility.

THE PROFILE OF THE SERIAL MURDERER

Quite a bit of energy has been spent explaining the various traits, psychological tendencies, and makeup of the serial killer. In addition, many assumptions are made within the study of these monsters, and several issues are included in the majority of profiles used within law enforcement. Let's look at a few.

Serial killers are recognizable suspects. Simply not true; there are more examples of relatively normal looking people hiding in plain sight like Jeffrey Dahmer, Anthony Sowell, Ted Bundy, Dennis Rader, and Wayne Williams than any of the drooling monsters some people might have in their nightmares. A Canadian Air Force pilot who flew for the Queen certainly didn't look like a serial killer. These people are more often quiet predators, who operate within their environment without detection. They are generally patient psychopaths and sociopaths, who get better at what they do.

Serial killers have extremely high IQs. Another concept permeated by Hollywood. Case histories show several high IQs, but just as many that aren't. While many serial killers are reasonably intelligent, they are somewhat clever and manipulative, often appearing more intelligent than they are. This is prototypical sociopathic behavior, although I cannot imagine most offenders being capable of the complicated, multifaceted crimes, and elaborate plans and games with the authorities you see in TV and the movies. Occasionally, it is hard to keep up with it on-screen. Sometimes they look smarter simply compared to ineffective investigations.

Serial killers secretly want to get caught. Not sure of the statistics here, but I have to believe that this is more pop psychology. Edmund Kemper turned himself in when he felt he'd reached the end of the line after his mother's murder. Some people think Ted Bundy escalated to the point of forcing his own capture. However, anyone who followed Bundy's many escape attempts and ideas to defeat the court system would doubt he wanted anything but freedom. Some killers may be tortured by their proclivities, but unconsciously allowing themselves to be caught just doesn't seem like the answer.

Serial killers usually kill within their own race. Here's a basic rule of Hunting Serial Killers 101, right? Is this point not made in every single movie? Repeated in textbooks? I will take the position that this is basically incorrect. Serial killers often interact primarily within their own race due to comfort and ease (Wayne Williams), whereas some almost exclusively kill their own race (Ted Bundy), but the key here is to ask "why?"

The fact is, the study of victimology tells us that serial murder victims generally fall into two categories: (1) Convenient, disposable victims who either might not be readily missed or at least easily explained (such as prostitutes, street people, high-risk lifestyles, residents in high-crime areas, hospital patients). (2) Targets who could be considered suitable or attractive sexual partners or conquests for the killer. They could be attractive young women (Bundy), or men (Dahmer), children (Dodd, Chikatilo), or prostitutes that agree to play dead (Shawcross, finding victims that fit both categories).

Considering this, it's understandable many victims could be the same race as the killer due to location, convenience, comfort, or personal sexual preference. However, there are other cases including Jeffrey Dahmer and a much-less famous killer, Larry Bright of Peoria, Illinois, whose victims were mostly the opposite race, reflecting these men's personal sexual preferences. It is fair to say the race assumption often made might statistically happen more often than not, but is a mistake to get locked into.

Serial killers kill at least three to four victims or more. Arbitrary numbers are often used in criminology texts in defining the serial murderer. It seems like such an obvious question: Why are they serial killers after three kills, but not two? I often ask students in my classes what the difference is between Andrei Chikatilo, who killed more than 50 young people in Russia over a period of years and Westley Dodd, who killed only two. The answer? Luck. Dodd picked the wrong child to kidnap. Chikatilo operated in an area that combined incompetent law enforcement and a society who kept embarrassing stories suppressed. One point I hope this book communicates is, the serial killer is a distinct psychological entity, a monster who kills because he or she needs to and wants to. This is why we exclude motivations like money in our definitions. There may be financial gains involved or personally known victims included, but these pre-programmed repetitive killing machines kill and kill and kill some more because they have to. This is why I often make the controversial declaration that I believe an offender can be what I am describing as a serial killer personality, and might have only killed one person so far in his history.

While the above issues beg for debate, there still seems to be facets of the serial killer profile that are consistent: most are men, but not all. Most are white, but again, not all. Attempts at nailing down age ranges are often confused in cases such as the BTK Killer and Arthur Shawcross. Reports of a developing profile in the 2011 hunt for the Long Island area serial killer included the facts that he's "most-likely a white male in his mid 20's to mid 40's" ("Long Island," 2011). Could this guess at race and gender and a 20-year age range be any less helpful?

Power and control as motivators seems critical, and sexual issues are almost always prevalent, so including assumptions of these features in a profile may sound insightful, but are they going to help law enforcement weed out suspects? Possibly. Still, while the Hollywood films or the latest episode of *CSI* will present a helpful profile very often in a true-crime drama that enables the protagonists to nab that genius-IQ killer in a neat 60 minutes, the fact is there simply is no such thing as a "typical serial killer," according to Former FBI profiler Robert Ressler (Sunde, 2002). Many profiles are general enough to include many of a population involved in a serial spree. Former FBI Agent Gregg McCrary, involved in profiling cases including the Shawcross case, stated, "There's nothing you can say is always true. If I was ever 100% right on a case, that's just dumb luck" (Wagner, 2006). It cannot be ignored that while some segments of some profiles are accurate, the list of complete errors are rarely publicized. While profiling can certainly be a helpful tool in law enforcement, it's no more than that. It's clearly not as effective as it's portrayed in the media.

MEDIA AND POP CULTURE

Speaking of the media, it remains an interesting subject considering the role of the media and of pop culture in the behavior of the serial killer. More studies have popped up on this subject, but it remains to be seen what the final impact might be.

Serial killers who crave interest from the media are the stuff of movies. The Zodiac Killer sent taunting notes to the newspapers. Jack the Ripper's letters are legendary, although the authenticity will always be questioned. Dennis Rader, the BTK Killer, might have missed killing some, but obviously missed the attention more, actually leading to his arrest years after his last murder. The Son of Sam's interactions will the media are well known.

A classic *Rolling Stone* cover shows Charles Manson's face. Many years later it was Jeffrey Dahmer on *People*. The rock-star status of Richard Ramirez, The Night Stalker, drew marriage proposals and horror alike.

Does this exacerbate the serial murderer? It would seem to be a case -by-case basis, as there are even more examples of offenders who clearly wanted to stay under the radar. However, the rush, the excitement, and the demonstration of power and control over authorities evidenced by behaviors like The Hillside Stranglers posing bodies in public view are obvious. Even killers who are less public about their behaviors like Alcala and Desalvo have felt a need to demonstrate their power by their signature posing of victims.

Media often motivates killers. According to Gibson (2006), the media motivated spree killer Andrew Cunanan on a sexual level, as reported by the opinion of a Chicago Police Captain. The connection to the celebrity of victim Gianni Versace also played into this. Gibson also noted the statements by the Hillside Strangler Kenneth Bianchi to this effect: "Wait till they find her. It'll make the papers. It'll be on every channel" (p. 86). It was also noted that, "the more the news reports increased, the more pleased with themselves they became" (p. 87). There are also many reports of killers expressing frustration and even anger that they were not getting the media attention they craved. This is probably best summed up by Dennis Rader: "How many do I have to kill before I get my name in the paper or some national attention?"

It's also fair to say the pop culture of the day has to contribute in some small way. High-profile murderers are stars in a world driven by celebrity. Teenagers get pregnant just to be on a reality show about pregnant teenagers. Adults have 20 children or force their kids into bizarre public behaviors for a chance at a reality show. People with once-hidden personality disorders are now stars of a new cable series while competing networks clamor to copy their success. Every little movement is monitored by the recordings of cell-phone cameras and postings on YouTube, and by the reporting of Twitter, Facebook, and other social media.

Many of these criminals crave the excitement and attention. Killers in the past followed every move of their crimes as reported in the newspapers. How do you think a reality show–driven society affects someone who gets a rush from their rise as a famous murderer?

We also cannot forget the continued popularity of murderabilia, that is, the sale and trade of crime-related artifacts, autographs, paintings, T-shirts, dolls, board games, comic books, and an endless array of collectibles once thought as being the private purview of sports enthusiasts. A collection of serial killer trading cards, complete with stats on the reverse side, is enough to evoke gasps from people who have never seen them before. The sale of John Wayne Gacy paintings, especially his self-portrait as *Pogo the Clown,* and his counterintuitive cartoonish *Hi-Ho* series, continues to demand top dollar. Sites such as eBay say they control for such sales, but in reality attempted postings still manage to connect buyers and sellers. There are also several crime-based memorabilia sites active on the Internet that are very busy.

Interestingly, paintings such as Gacy's that would sell for $100 in the early 1990s have been exploding in price since his execution, even aided by those who wish to suppress it, selling for thousands of dollars just 20 years later. Many killers such as Wayne Henley have had art shows featuring their work, with a tremendous amount of exposure and attention added to them by protestors and people attempting to stop them. In Gacy's case, many of his paintings were destroyed by people trying to limit their sale, but inadvertently enhancing their value. "Even campaigners against Gacy and his crimes would buy his paintings in order to burn them in mass public media invited bonfires," says Steven Scouller, author of *Murderabilia and True Crime Collecting* (2010).

Again, it's not always viewed the same. I've had at least one offender express concern to me that he was worried I was one of those interested in murderabilia when obtaining information and letters from him. He was actually relieved when I freely admitted I did own some true crime artifacts for the purpose of displaying them in my college classroom, but really wasn't interested in that from him. Another answered a letter from me completely typed, including his name at closing in what I took as an obvious attempt to suppress the collection of a marketable autograph. On the other side of the coin, some inmates are more than happy to provide graphic, extreme commentary, and artwork just for the shock value, and routinely produce them for waiting buyers and sellers.

IS A BIOLOGICAL CONNECTION AN EXCUSE?

Dr. Dorothy Otnow-Lewis and her cohort Dr. Jonathan Pincus make compelling arguments connecting brain abnormality and other biological factors to violent criminal behavior, which agrees with the theory asserted in this book, to a point. However, Lewis consistently draws the conclusion that killers who behave as predatory sociopaths simply do not exist without organic origins, psychosis, or brain damage. Dr. Lewis takes the medical model approach "which contrasts sharply with the criminal justice" model (Rowe, 2002, pp. 132–133), which simply addresses the offense as an intentional choice. This perspective naturally leads her to take the side that these killers are essentially all "guilty but mentally ill," and the offenders' physiological makeup is somehow exculpatory of their often repeated violent patterns.

Continued comparison of my research to Otnow-Lewis's findings continues to interest me, as on one hand I feel her general attitude that essentially all killers show a combination of genetic issues and environmental stressors sounds very much like my position on diathesis–stress. However, I do not understand how Dr. Otnow-Lewis retains the belief that murderers are made and not born, with early childhood behaviors like Bundy's and Kemper's that are so pathological and dangerous they seem impossible to be learned. I also have difficulty with the concept that so many of these killers are quite aware their behavior is deviant, dangerous to society, and unacceptable, go to such great lengths to avoid detection (like Dahmer) and yet their crimes are still described as uncontrollable.

ANOTHER DEFINITION

Beyond a profile, the discussion of this book begs the question of the definition of serial murder. Over the years studying this subject, I've come across several definitions of the serial murderer—many I disagree with, many I agree with to a point. Some of these were discussed in detail in Chapter 1. The subject of definition certainly comes up in university classes on Week 1, and generally changes often by Week 16. I've changed my own definition many times over the years. One of the focuses of this book was to attempt to identify the essence of this personality. In considering the most recent research and opinions I've digested, my definition for the serial murderer would be:

A "Serial Murderer" is an offender who actually makes repeated physical affirmative steps towards killing other human beings to satisfy a psychological need. Victims will share a commonality, based on the offenders' sexual interests or control requirements. The pattern of murders or attempted murders will be related to the intended use of these victims and are essential to the psychological motivations.

A PSYCHOLOGICAL MODEL?

Dispute may continue as to the relative weight of factors such as biology, trauma, and sexual deviance. In some cases, biological predisposition has a greater impact; in others, environment plays a larger role. Some may suggest that pornography, pressures from society, or other factors are virtually ignored in this particular study. However, the dynamics suggested in this model are consistent and difficult to deny.

Most, if not all, serial killers display some evidence of the psychological syndromes discussed. Common factors include questionable genetics and biology, as well as emotional problems concerning sense of self and control. There may be questions regarding the relative weights in each case, but both biological and traumatic factors seem to exist in the majority of serial killers, whereas a dispute regarding the presence of either one or the other does not.

Sexual dysfunction and deviance are pervasive themes, as is the link between mental and physical influences. Finally, the obsessive-compulsive cycle of serial murders is well documented.

The focal points in this proposal centered on and circulated about two issues: (1) the serial murderer as a diagnosable syndrome that should be clinically recognized, and (2) a theory of violence based on the diathesis-stress model, with identifying features as applied to the serial killer.

THE SYNDROME OF SERIAL MURDER

Robert Ressler once asked Edmund Kemper where he thought he would fit in the *Diagnostic and Statistical Manual of Mental Disorders*. He replied that he didn't find a description that fit him, and didn't expect to until psychiatry had obtained sufficient information to understand people like him.

He felt this might be by the sixth or seventh edition, probably sometime in the next century (Ressler, 1992, p. 248).

The analysis of the eight cases, along with the literature review, suggests very strongly that there is a clustering of behaviors and traits consistent enough to be recognized and categorized in a diagnostic manual such as the *Diagnostic and Statistical Manual of Mental Disorders-IV-TR* (APA, 2000). The serial murderer displays a pattern of behavior no less diagnosable than the antisocial or borderline personalities, or someone suffering from post-traumatic stress disorder.

This position in no way suggests that an offender diagnosed in this manner is deserving of exculpatory status; in fact, quite the opposite. Insanity, as is well known, is but a legal distinction. It usually refers to a person's ability to appreciate wrongfulness and refrain from certain impulses. A hallmark of the serial murderer is conscious recognition of the illegality of his actions. All the while, he conducts his predatory lifestyle with continued concerns regarding avoidance of detection. So, he is no less alleviated of responsibility than is the antisocial personality, who also continues his criminal ways regardless of existing laws and is not exempt from culpability. Precautions such as Dahmer's security system, Gacy's and Nilsen's disposal methods, or other offenders' proud display of bodies for authorities to find or interactions with the media are not behaviors of people unable to recognize the wrongfulness of their actions.

It makes sense that a diagnostic manual that recognizes patterns such as pathological gambling and intermittent explosive disorder should include this virtually clear-cut set of behaviors. This category would be described and defined much like any other syndrome found in the *DSM-IV-TR*. A suggested diagnostic category, named *Homicidal Pattern Disorder,* and which should be listed under "Impulse-Control Disorders Not Elsewhere Classified" (APA, 2000, p. 663), is detailed in Figure 10.1. The accompanying discussions of etiology would include issues such as biology and environment, as well as sexual dysfunction, intimacy and esteem difficulty, and dissociative process.

This proposed syndrome has been suggested regarding the current authoring of the fifth revision of the *Diagnostic and Statistical Manual.* Feedback has not yet been processed.

A THEORY OF VIOLENCE

The diathesis–stress model combining predisposition and environment is a currently credible theory regarding other mental conditions (e.g., schizophrenia) and is compatible with the most recent studies regarding predisposition and violence. This model can also be applied to the serial killer, initially on an intuitive level but later reinforced by evidence of organic differences among the killers and their dysfunctional heritages.

Many individuals have difficult, even traumatic childhoods. However, most do not develop into serial killers. The continued stressors of social inadequacy

---

Figure 10.1   Suggested *DSM* Diagnostic Listing for Homicidal Pattern Disorder

312.36 Homicidal Pattern Disorder

A. Deliberate and purposeful murder or attempts at murder of strangers on more than one occasion.

B. Tension or affective arousal at some time before the act.

C. Pleasure, gratification, or relief in commission or reflection of the acts.

D. Personality traits consistent with diagnosis of at least one Cluster B personality disorder (antisocial, borderline, histrionic, narcissistic).

E. Understanding the illegality of actions and continuation to avoid apprehension.

F. Murders not motivated by monetary gain, to conceal criminal activity, to express anger or vengeance, in response to a delusion or hallucination, or as a result of impaired judgment (e.g., in dementia, mental retardation, substance intoxication).

---

and sexual dysfunction serve only to exacerbate the situation. It follows that there must be an additional element—a ticking bomb waiting to go off.

The consistent appearance of extreme sexual dysfunction could be taken in an even greater context than is afforded by this study. An argument could be made that sexual motivation is the single most crucial factor in the development of a serial killer. Other factors may reduce the natural checks and balances in a person's life to dissuade him from killing, for whatever reason. However, sexual desires initiate patterns in a person's habits, and cyclical behaviors to fulfill one's desires can be reduced, albeit simplistically, to acts of killing for sex.

This possibility is echoed by Masters (1993, p. 255), in regard to Dennis Nilsen:

> If Nilsen's crimes could be explained in terms of distortion of the sexual need, that might provide sufficient answer in itself. There is certainly no lack of precedents, and any experienced prostitute will confirm that the varieties of sexual stimulation are seemingly endless.

However, we must resist the temptation to label the serial killer as just an extreme collector of sexual paraphilia: The explanation is too simplistic. Kemper's early homicides, Dahmer's obsessions with dead things, as well as many other examples found in the literature preclude the supposition that serial killers kill simply for sex. The relief of tension and the feeling of ultimate control and possession play too great a role.

Stanton E. Samenow underscored the importance of a predeterminant when he stated that criminals who claim they were rejected by everyone of importance in their lives rarely say why (Martingale, 1993). Samenow suggests that it is the criminals who reject their parents, rather than vice versa. He goes on to say, "We ought not to limit our inquiries to what parents have done to children but strive to determine what children have done to their parents" (pp. 153–154). It is then noted that Kemper was freely fantasizing by the time he was incarcerated in the basement, he cut the head and hands off his sister's doll long before puberty, and at age seven said about the teacher he had a crush on: "If I kiss her, I would have to kill her first" (Martingale, 1993, p. 154).

Samenow references the research of psychologist David Cohen when he states the influence of nurture is surprisingly weak (2004, p. 186). He says "there comes a time when parents [of delinquent children] have to face the fact that they are powerless to change the course of events" (p. 36). Florida psychologist Ann McMillan concurs when noting that Gerald Stano, who murdered 35 women, was fostered at six months, raised by a loving couple, and still turned out to be a monster. She observed, "Sometimes it's not going to matter who raises them. If the parents were Mary and Joseph, it would still turn out the same" (Martingale, 1993, p. 154).

This raises another key point. This theory cannot be viewed with each factor always carrying the same weight. Stano's possible biological predisposition may be so great that even just being adopted or some sexual perversions can lead to murder. DeSalvo's and Lucas's environments could have held much more weight. Sadistic sex in the case of Kemper and Chikatilo was very important, but sex appeared to be much less of a factor to Dennis Nilsen, who was obsessed with loneliness and social isolation. However, the appearance of both biological abnormality of some kind and environmental trauma is an established pattern. The key to this theory of violence is the presence of *both* biology and environmental stress.

The degree to which certain factors figure in the development of these killers does appear to vary. Rick certainly underlined that fact. However, a different wiring, problems of personality, pathological retreat to fantasy and dissociation, control-based problems, and sexual dysfunction all are there in some form or another.

Additionally, these case histories dealt with the issue of prior crimes, highlighting the importance and significance of them in each individual's development. The fetish burglaries, the flashings, the pedophilia, and the paraphilia are often signals of bad things to come. Sexual control and obsession themes are red flags for the serial killer. Psychiatrist Robert Brittain (1970) noted: "When sadistic murderers are finally caught, their criminal histories usually reveal they have committed sex offenses of a non-violent nature" (p. 10) and that this type offender should be closely monitored in the future.

THE IRREPLACEABLE DIMENSION OF INTUITION

The theory proposed in this book is admittedly an intuitive assimilation, resulting from case studies and analysis of the literature. The analysis provides clear examples of the constructs, but must be understood in the context of this study's limitations. Surely, eight cases are hardly statistically significant, but when examined in light of available information, are representative of the population described as serial murderers.

Canter (1994, pp. 73, 76) considered the criticisms of intuitive research, and stated:

> As in all intuition, there are recognizable sources that can be brought to the surface for examination and development . . . sensitivity to detail . . . ability to perceive patterns . . . background knowledge with which patterns can be compared. . . . Scientists, though, need intuition too, but are afraid to take it at face value . . . but they be free of intuition. The whole basis of the scientific enterprise is faith that patterns will be found, results will be forthcoming from ideas that have never been asked to stand up to test. This is especially true of psychology when it is believed that ways of thinking about human behavior and experience will reveal shapes and structures that will increase our understanding. The FBI's Behavioral Science Unit strengthened that faith: there were patterns there; the shadows cast by criminals were not arbitrary; they could be read.

The shadows of the serial murderer have been read. It is possible to recognize the pattern, the individual, and some of the ingredients. With further study it may be possible to avoid, if not predict, some of the instances of this criminality and thereby lessen its terrible impact on the society in which he lives.

So Why Do We Care?

A fine question. Why *do* we care? Why write a book detailing the minutia that separates a serial killer from a mass murderer; from a spree killer? Why do we detail a pattern of behavior, able to be listed in the *DSM* instead of saying, "they kill people over and over?" Let's consider a number of reasons.

First, it's fair to say in examining a person's background, an individual could be considered high risk to commit violence as a pattern in the future. A young adult with a history of fire-setting and torturing animals could easily be one who should be watched closely, offered as much therapy and intervention as possible, and also considered in a pool of suspects in a given investigation.

It's also very important to understand the tendencies and types of personalities one may encounter when investigating these type crimes. While I've downplayed the value of profiles in previous segments, I should also offer caution when making assumptions. Here is an example.

When called for a radio interview while the DC Snipers were operating, I fielded a number of profile-related questions. Included in the questioning was the assumption that most of the victims were white, most serial killers were white, and everybody knows most serial killers kill within their own race, so it's safe to say the killer is white. My opinion was, the key here is I did not consider the offender to be a serial killer at all, that it appeared to be more of a spree, and I was not convinced the killings were the type I'd include within a serial killer personality. Therefore, if you accept that serial killers generally kill within their own race (which I do not), I would say that nothing about this spree tells me the killer is white. Actually, contrarily, it seemed to me the killer could more easily be African American, being less noticeable in many of the DC-area neighborhoods involved. Naturally this seemed like an odd observation, but it proved to be appropriate. Of course, this is not to say I offered any sort of useful profile of the killer, who ended up being two killers, John Muhammad and Lee Malvo.

In a 2000 *New York Times* article profiling of 102 "rampage killers," the offenders were found to be far more obviously displaying signs of mental illness. Forty-eight had a formal psychiatric diagnosis. Twenty-four were taking a prescribed psychiatric drug and fourteen had stopped taking their medications just before their attacks. The point here is, it's critical to understand the type of criminal with whom you are dealing. If you appreciate the general psychological state of a serial killer as opposed to a mass murderer, you might look for a different type of offender after a Virginia Tech than you would after the BTK slayings. Jared Loughner, arrested at the 2011 shooting scene of Congresswoman Gabrielle Giffords and mass murder of six others, would look quite a bit different than a quiet serial killer like Anthony Sowell, but no less deadly.

It's important to look at the offender's makeup as opposed to arbitrary qualifiers. I previously mentioned the fact I believe a serial killer is a distinct personality or psychological type—a person who needs to kill to fulfill some compulsion as well as possessing a basic developmental model as outlined in these chapters. I continue to contend, sometimes with opposition, that a serial killer in the most specific psychological sense can be an offender with just one kill. An example is Michael Woodmansee, a convicted child killer who served approximately 28 years in prison for his crime and was scheduled for release in September of 2011, 12 years early.

Woodmansee was a withdrawn 16-year-old boy when he lured a five-year-old boy into his home and stabbed him in the heart. According to his journals, he fantasized that "it would be easy [to kill], easy to get away with it, and some sort of fun" (Lohr, 2011). Woodmansee reportedly removed and ate the child's flesh, shellacked the bones, and kept the skull on his dresser as a trophy. He was detected seven years later after he attempted to lure a 14-year-old paper boy into his home, gave him liquor, and unsuccessfully attempted to strangle him. It matters that we recognize offenders as serial killers when they have the makeup of a Woodmansee rather than overlook this as many arbitrary classification systems would do because he only killed one victim due to his disorganized ineptness.

We care because of the need to understand the differences in personalities. We care because we need to recognize the essence of the monster. Veteran homicide investigator and Duquesne University professor Ronald Freeman told me about a killer he tracked and eventually interviewed. He said:

I asked him to detail his victim selection process. He said that he would start getting a "feeling that I had to do something." Said that he attempted to resist the feelings but they overtook him and off he went. He would usually go to a college campus or an upscale neighborhood as he blended with the environment. Stated he walked through the crowds looking at the faces of the women and would know her when he saw her "because she didn't have a face."

(personal communication, February 7, 2011)

Robert Samsoe, whose little sister was murdered by Rodney Alcala, offered a comment: "The worst part of it is that you have to tell your kids, 'I can protect you,' but in your heart you know that there are monsters out there—and you really can't" (Pelisek, 2010).

It must be understood: regardless of the synthesis of the serial killer personality, we as a society are dealing with a real-life monster—a jungle predator in our midst. Listen to the words of Dennis Rader, the BTK Killer, as he described his behavior:

Well, off hand, I don't know exactly how to say it. I had many, what I call them, "projects," different people I followed, watched.

I was just driving by one day and saw her go into the house with somebody else and I thought that was a possibility– there was many places in the area, College Hill, they are all over Wichita– but anyway, it was just basically a selection process, work toward it, if it didn't work, I just move on to something else. But in my kind of person—stalking and trolling—you go through the trolling stage and then stalking stage. She was in the stalking stage when this happened.

If you read much about serial killers, they go through what they call different phases. That's one of the phases they go through, is a trolling stage. Basically, you are looking for a victim at that time. You could be trolling for months or years, but once you lock in on a certain person, then you become stalking. That might be several of them, but you really hone in that person, they basically become the—that's the victim.

(Rader's testimony, 2007)

This is what a real-life monster sounds like. We must not only catch them, but we must also be able to recognize them if we are to be safe from them.

Appendix A
Case Briefs

Note: these case briefs include dates, locations, and numbers that must be considered approximate. Several sources disagree on many of these details, and items like numbers of cases seem to change as time passes.

Alcala, Rodney James. 1971–1979, California, New York, possibly others. Alias: John Berger. Convicted rapist and killer of five in California, indicted for two in New York in 2011 (believed to be related to many others unverified at this time), known to torture and toy with victims before death. Found with an extensive photo collection of young women, taken personally. Famous for appearing in and winning a TV episode of *The Dating Game* in 1978. Often compared to Ted Bundy. Sentenced to death in 2010. See Case Studies, Chapter 6.

Berdella, Robert. 1984–1988, Missouri. Kidnapped, sadistically raped, tortured, and killed six men. Cut up bodies and put out with trash, keeping various trophies and diaries of torture details. Confessed and sentenced to life. Died in prison in 1992.

Berkowitz, David. 1976–1977, New York. The "Son of Sam." Shot 13 men and women on 8 occasions, 6 fatally. Attacked victims while parked in cars at night. Unsuccessfully attempted insanity defense, stating demon-possessed dogs ordered him to kill. Received 365 years in prison.

Bianchi, Kenneth and Buono, Angelo. 1977–1979, California and Washington. The "Hillside Stranglers," raped, tortured, and killed 12 women, often dumping corpses along the highways. Bianchi, aka "Steve Walker," attempted an elaborate faking of a multiple personality, but was uncovered and convicted, along with Buono. Buono died in prison in 2002. Bianchi denied parole in 2010.

Bittaker, Lawrence and Norris, Roy. 1979, California. The sadistic pair met in prison and planned to rape and kill a girl of each age from 13 to 19. Convicted of five killings, they were believed responsible for many more. Bodies were found brutally mutilated. Norris testified against Bittaker and received 45 years to life, whereas Bittaker got a death sentence plus 199 years.

Boyer, John. 2000–2007 (est.) North Carolina, Tennessee, South Carolina. Suspected of more in additional locations. Admitted to three murders of prostitutes while traveling as a long-haul trucker, and noted by his seething overt hatred for women. Lived with his mother in Georgia. Investigations ongoing.

Brudos, Jerry. 1968–1969, Oregon. Fueled by a long history of foot fetishes and revenge toward women, he sexually assaulted, tortured, and killed four women. He often took pictures and kept severed feet to dress in spiked heels. Reported necrophile. Died in prison in 2006.

BTK Killer. 1974–1991, Kansas. Dennis Lynn Rader, known as the "BTK" (bind, torture, kill) Killer or Strangler, murdered 10 people and was known for his continued sending of letters taunting police and media. Eventually caught when he resumed taunting police in 2004 and was found by modern detection methods. Serving life sentence. See Case Studies, Chapter 6.

Bundy, Ted. 1974–1978, various states. One of the highest-profile serial killers ever, he thoroughly enjoyed his fame and notoriety, up to his execution in 1989. Numbers of victims may have reached 50, as the attractive law student lured women wherever he went. His final rampage, an uncharacteristic set of impulse killings, led to his final arrest. He acted as his own attorney, reveling in the attention before his eventual conviction and death sentence. Executed in 1989.

Buono, Angelo. See Bianchi.

Chase, Richard. 1978, California. The "Vampire Killer," fueled by a schizophrenic belief he needed to drink blood, butchered and mutilated six victims in their homes. A classic disorganized offender, he was the subject of one of the earliest successful attempts by the FBI to utilize psychological profiling. Committed suicide in 1980.

Chikatilo, Andrei. 1978–1990, Russia. Child molester and sadistic murderer of 53 mostly young women and children often lured from bus and train stations. Also known as the Rostov Ripper. Continued long reign of terror mostly due to incompetent investigation. Executed, 1994. See Case Studies, Chapter 6.

Columbine Massacre. 1999, Colorado. High school mass murder carried out by senior students Eric Harris and Dylan Klebold, killing 12 and injuring 24. Both committed suicide on scene. Worst American high school massacre and received a great deal of media and press. Provoked public examination of issues such as violent video games, music, Goth culture, bullying, and access to guns as contributing factors.

Corll, Dean and Wayne Henley. 1970–1973, Texas. With the help of two cohorts who procured young males for him, he sexually abused, tortured, and killed at least 28. Corll was eventually killed by his young partner, Henley, after Corll threatened to shoot him. Henley continues to serve life in prison.

Corona, Juan. 1971, California. Diagnosed schizophrenic in 1956, this Mexican was accused of the homosexual assaults and murders of 25 men after the bodies were found in shallow graves near his home. He was convicted in 1982 after an earlier conviction was overturned.

Cunanan, Andrew. 1997, Minnesota, Illinois, New Jersey, and Florida. Homosexual spree killer murdered five people on a three-month rampage including famous designer Gianni Versace, with whom Cunanan desired a personal relationship. Often misidentified as a serial killer, his spree ended with his suicide.

Dahmer, Jeffrey. 1978–1991, Wisconsin and Ohio. High-profile serial killer of 17 men and boys, including rape, torture, dismemberment, and cannibalism. Expressed a desire to create personal "sex zombies." Beaten to death in prison in 1994. See Case Studies, Chapter 6.

DC Snipers. 2002. Washington, DC, Virginia, and Maryland. Also Beltway Snipers. John Allen Muhammad and a minor, Lee Boyd Malvo, went on a three-week spree killing rampage that left 10 dead and 3 others critically injured. Muhammad's motives were widely speculated on, which included an attempt at extortion through a reign of terror as well as an attempt on the life of his ex-wife. They shot mostly random targets from their modified caprice. Malvo received six life sentences while Muhammad was executed in 2009.

DeSalvo, Albert. 1962–1964, Massachusetts. Also known as the "Boston Strangler" and the "Green Man." After an extensive past of breaking and entering and countless sexual assaults, he conned his way into women's homes, murdered 13, and ritualistically desecrated and posed the corpses. He confessed while in a mental institution and was eventually murdered in prison.

Dodd, Westley Allan. 1989, Washington state. A prolific sadistic pedophile, he killed three young children and was stopped only when caught attempting to abduct another child in public. He kept a detailed diary, complete with torture and killing methods. In 1993, he became the first in 30 years to be executed by hanging.

Eyler, Larry. 1982–1984, Illinois, Ohio, Indiana, Kentucky, Wisconsin. Suspected in at least 22 murders, he was finally convicted of the killing, torture, and dismemberment of a 15-year-old boy whose body parts were dumped out with the trash. He was the prototypical self-hating homosexual, macho acting while torturing and killing other homosexual men. He was given a death sentence and died of AIDs-related illness while awaiting execution.

Ferguson, Colin. 1993, New York. Subway shooter killed 6 people and injured 19. The Jamaican American was one of the few black mass murderers in memory. Suspended from school in 1991 for racially charged violent comments, he appeared to be motivated by rage, race, and mental illness. When arrested, he was found carrying pieces of papers with "reasons for this" written on them, listing various racial issues. Serving 315+ year prison sentence.

Fish, Albert. 1924–1928, New York. This aging pervert took great pride in his extensive experience in sadism, inflicting and receiving pain. He killed and ate a 10-year-old girl and cruelly wrote the parents six years later with details of the crime. He was executed in 1936 at age 65, claiming to anticipate it with glee. Confessed to three killings; suspected of others. Boasted he killed and assaulted more than 100.

Franklin Jr., Lonnie David. See Grim Sleeper.

Fritzl, Josef. 1984–2008, Austria. A multiple sex offender who beat his wife and kidnapped and imprisoned his daughter while pretending she ran away. He held her in an underground dungeon for 24 years, using her as a personal sex slave while impregnating her seven times.

Gacy, John Wayne. 1972–1978, Illinois. Another high-profile killer, the Killer Clown had a history of psychiatric and sexual problems, eventually culminating in 34 murders. A pillar of the community, he lured young men to his home with parties and promises of employment, then sodomized, tortured, and killed them. He buried 29 under his house. He was executed in 1994. Sales of his artwork later became an industry in itself. In 2011, bodies of eight unidentified victims were exhumed in hopes of identification by modern scientific techniques, while dozens of family members of young men lost in the 1970s contacted authorities to provide information and possible testing as totals could rise.

Garrett, Johnny Frank. 1981, Texas. Executed in 1992 for the rape and murder of an elderly nun, committed at age 17. Diagnosed with multiple personalities on death row. Also noted to have brain damage and severe childhood abuse. Another jailhouse killer confessed to the murder at a later date, raising issues of Garrett's guilt, but the fact he confessed to the details of the crime to a defense psychiatrist as an alternate personality are never addressed.

Gein, Ed. 1954–1957, Wisconsin. Used as a model for the movies *Psycho* and *Silence of the Lambs*, he dug up female bodies for experiments and collection of parts. He killed two women who reminded him of his mother. More of a mentally ill grave robber than a serial killer. He was declared criminally insane and died in an institution in 1984.

Green River Killer (Gary Ridgway). 1982–1989, Washington. Admitted to 48 strangulation deaths of women in Washington State in 2003. Believed to be responsible for many more. Nickname derived from dumping ground of several of his first murders. Arrested in 2001, finally connected to the crimes by DNA evidence. Received 48 life sentences plus 480 years for tampering with evidence as part of a plea deal to avoid the death penalty; however, agreed to additional confessions that could be corroborated. Pleaded to a 49th in 2011.

Grim Sleeper. (Franklin Jr., Lonnie David). 1985–2007, Los Angeles. African American retired mechanic, accused of murdering at least 16 young black women as the infamous "Grim Sleeper" in the Los Angeles area. His home contained thousands of photographs and hours of videos of various women. Dubbed the "Sleeper" because of a 14-year lull between killings, he was caught through a DNA sample collected from his son. Kill total continued to rise as of this writing in 2011, including during his lull period.

Gunness, Belle Sorenson. 1900–1909 (estimated), Illinois and Indiana. Born in Norway, was thought to have killed more than 40 victims over many years. Most victims were husbands and lovers, often killed for money reasons. An early black-widow female serial killer. Believed to have faked her own death.

Harris, Eric. See Columbine.

Heirens, William. 1945–1946, Illinois. The "Lipstick Killer" murdered three in their homes, including a six-year-old girl whose body was dismembered. He was diagnosed as a sexual psychopath with maniacal tendencies and tried to blame an imaginary alter-ego named George. After receiving three life sentences, he became the first Illinois prison inmate to be awarded a college degree.

Henley, Wayne. See Corll.

Hennard, George. See Luby's massacre.

Jack the Ripper. 1888, England. At least five savage murders were attributed to this earliest of serial killers. His disemboweled victims were usually accompanied by cheerful notes signed by his famous nickname. An unsubstantiated diary published in 1993 contained many convincing documents and caused great dispute about the veracity of the notes as well as Jack's actual identity, which remains unresolved today.

Jesperson, Keith Hunter. 1990–1995. California, Nebraska, Orgon, Florida, Washington, Wyoming. Also known as the "Happy Face Killer," Jesperson killed eight confirmed victims over a five-year period. Claimed to kill many more than 100. Contacted media when he felt he wasn't getting enough attention and was known to kill animals by strangulation. Most victims were truck stop prostitutes and drifters. Born in Canada; currently incarcerated in Oregon.

Joubert, John. 1982–1983, Nebraska and Maine. Enjoyed stabbing classmates at an early age; felt sexual stimulation. Killed and mutilated three young boys. Subsequently requested crime scene photos to enjoy in his cell. Executed by electric chair in 1996.

Kearney, Patrick. 1965–1977, California. Dubbed the "Trash Bag Killer" for his disposal methods of dismembered victims, he killed between 28 and 40, mostly homosexual men. He received 21 life sentences after signing 28 confessions. In prison in California.

Kemper, Edmund Emil. 1964–1973, California. Also known as the "Co-Ed Killer," the physically enormous (6 feet 9 inches, 300 pounds) Kemper murdered and dismembered six women, in between shooting his grandparents at age 15 and killing his mother and her friend before turning himself in. Serving life in prison. See Case Studies, Chapter 6.

Klebold, Dylan. See Columbine.

Krajcir, Timothy. 1977–1982, Missouri, Pennsylvania and Illinois. Cold case solved by new DNA testing. Long-time sex offender confessed to killing nine in at least two states. Received two 40-year sentences in Illinois. Several rape charges. Received 13 consecutive life sentences in Missouri.

Larson, "Lucky." (pseudonym), 1980s, Florida. Interviewed by Dorothy Otnow-Lewis for her book, *Guilty By Reason of Insanity* on death row in Starke, Florida, home of Ted Bundy at the time. Hacked two separate victims to death during robberies. Used as an example of a violent killer who had both serious brain injuries and a past of severe abuse.

Long, Bobby Joe. 1984, Florida. Cruising in his car, he abducted, assaulted, and murdered at least 10 young women. He had an extensive history of physical abnormalities and head trauma. After confessing, he received 28 life sentences and two death sentences in Florida.

Loughner, Jared Lee. January 8, 2011, Arizona. In broad daylight, he allegedly shot Congresswoman Gabrielle Giffords in the head, killed 6 others, and wounded another 13 in mass murder attack. Found to be mentally incompetent and schizophrenic, prison officials attempted to force him to take anti-psychotic medication to assist in his own defense. Indicted on 49 counts of murder and attempted murder. Awaiting trial.

Luby's Massacre. October 16, 1991, Killeen, Texas. A mass murder committed by George Jo Hennard when he drove his pickup truck into a Luby's Cafeteria and shot 23 people to death while wounding another 20, then committing suicide by shooting himself. It was the deadliest mass murder in the United States until the 2007 Virginia Tech shooting.

Lucas, Henry Lee and Toole, Ottis. 1970–1983, various states. Convicted of 10 killings, Lucas and Toole claimed at one time killing between 350 and 600 victims across the country, with wild stories and details often changing. Victims varied in ages, most were white females, sexually assaulted at some point. Killing methods also varied. Lucas died in prison in 2001.

Malvo, Lee Boyd. See DC Snipers.

Moore, Marie. 1983, New Jersey. Kidnapped and tortured victims along with a 14-year-old lover and killed one. Diagnosed with severe brain injury, trauma, mental illnesses, and multiple personality disorder. Sentenced to death.

Mudgett, Herman. 1888–1894, Pennsylvania and various states. Very early serial murderer, also known as H.H. Holmes. After creating a three-story row of conjoined buildings, he turned them into an elaborate death and torture chamber. He killed anywhere between 20 and more than 100, including men, women, and children, and even sold some of the cadavers to a medical school. He was hanged in 1896.

Muhammad, John Allen. See DC Snipers.

Nance, Wayne. 1974–1986, Montana. The baby-faced deliveryman gained access to people's homes through his job, murdering six and collecting mementos along the way. After developing an obsession with a female coworker, he attacked her and her husband at their home, and was eventually killed in a wild gun battle.

Nelson, Earle Leonard. 1926–1927, California, Oregon, Canada. The notorious "Gorilla Man." Killed more than 20 women in the 1920s, and is used as an example of violent behavior after a significant head injury as a child. Caught in Canada and hanged in 1928.

Nilsen, Dennis. 1978–1983, England. The lonely homosexual often paralleled with Jeffrey Dahmer, killed at least 16 men for company. He was discovered when the cut-up body parts he flushed down the toilet started backing up. He received life in prison in the United Kingdom.

Norris, Roy. See Bittaker.

Rader, Dennis Lynn. See BTK Killer.

Ramirez, Richard. 1984–1985, California. The infamous "Night Stalker" was unique among serial killers, in that the only thing linking the victims was that they were killed in their homes. He killed, raped, mutilated, and terrorized indiscriminately. His satanic connection was believed less important than his enjoyment for killing. Found guilty of 13 and was found eligible for the death penalty; upheld in 2006.

Resendez-Ramirez, Rafael. Also Angel Resendiz and other close spellings. 1986–1999. Texas, Florida, Illinois, Georgia, and other locations in the United States, Mexico, and Canada. Mexican serial killer murdered approximately 15, also committing sexual assault and robbery. Referred to as the "Railroad Killer" for his behavior of committing crimes near railroad tracks and escaping on trains. Executed in Texas in 2006.

Ridgway, Gary. See Green River.

Rifkin, Joel. 1989–1993, New York. During a routine traffic stop, he was discovered to have the corpse of a victim in his pickup truck. He finally confessed to 17 killings, mostly prostitutes. An outcast as a child, he was obsessed with violent fantasy and strangling women. Serving a 203-year sentence at Clinton Correctional Facility.

Rissell, Monte. 1975–1976, various states. Raped 12, committed rape by the age of 14, and killed 5 women before the age of 19. He kept trophies and attacked victims of all types, fueled by a hatred of women. Given five life sentences.

Rogers, Dayton Leroy. 1984–1987, Oregon. A mild-mannered, respected businessman, he killed eight women, reveling in bondage and mutilation. He was caught after slashing to death his last victim in plain view. Sentenced to death by lethal injection. Sentences overturned for various reasons, but sentenced to death row in Oregon again in 2006.

Rolling, Danny. 1989–1990, Florida. The "Gainesville Ripper." A Ted Bundy fan, he decided to kill eight people for each year he served in prison. After three murders the prior year, he killed five Gainesville-area college students, raping three, mutilating, and posing their bodies. Unsuccessful insanity claims. Already serving four life sentences in Florida State Prison when sentenced to death. Executed in 2006.

Runge, Paul. 1995–1997, Illinois. Convicted of two murders in the Chicago area, reportedly confessed to seven total; possibly others. All sexually assaulted and later bodies dismembered. Unsuccessful insanity defense for sexual sadism. Sent to death row until Illinois abolished capital punishment in 2011.

Shawcross, Arthur. 1972–1989, New York. Killer of two children as a young man, then murdered 12 more women, mostly prostitutes, often asking them to play dead. Caused public outcry after resuming killings after being paroled. Also known as the "Genesee River Killer." Found to have brain structure damage. Died in prison in 2008. See Case Studies, Chapter 6.

Sowell, Anthony. 2007–2009 (estimated), Ohio. Convicted of murdering 11 women in July 2011, raped scores of women and was found with bodies in and buried around his Cleveland home on Imperial Avenue. Most recently named the "Cleveland Strangler." An African American murderer, lured homeless and vulnerable women to his home. Received death penalty. See Case Studies, Chapter 6.

Speck, Richard. 1966, Illinois. Committed systematic assault and mass murder of eight nursing students at a Chicago Hospital dormitory. Later the subject of outrage after films of him in prison were released, enjoying sex, drugs, and female hormone treatments while incarcerated. Death penalty eventually commuted to eight consecutive sentences of 50–150 years. Died in prison in 1991.

Stano, Gerald. 1969–1983, Florida, New Jersey. Confessed to 25 killings of young women, possibly linked to 40 or more. Sexual assaults after death. Born to a mother who lost five children owing to abuse and neglect. Horrific childhood; graduated high school at age 21. Executed by electric chair in 1998.

Stewart, Robert. 2009. North Carolina. Mass murderer gunned down eight helpless nursing home patients while searching for his wife, who had left him two weeks prior. The disabled painter was found guilty of murder in 2011 and was sentenced to prison for a period ranging between 141 and 177 years.

Toole, Ottis. See Lucas.

Virginia Tech Massacre. 2007, Virginia. The single worst mass murder by a single gunman in U.S. history. Shooter Seung-Hui Cho, suffering from a variety of anxiety and personality disorders, killed 32 people, and wounded several others over two separate attacks on the Virginia Tech campus. Committed suicide on scene. Sent rambling videos to local media.

Whitman, Charles. 1966, Texas. Committed the mass murder of 16 people and wounded 32 others from the Observation Deck at the University of Texas, after he killed his wife and mother. He was shot and killed by Austin Police. Whitman was found to have an aggressive brain tumor, suffered tremendous headaches, and displayed severe mental illness.

Williams, Russell. 2009, Ontario, Canada. Royal Air Force Colonel, once entrusted to fly Queen Elizabeth II, committed home invasions, sexual assaults, and the murders of at least two women in Canada. Photographed himself wearing stolen undergarments of women as young as 12 in their homes.

Williams, Wayne. 1979–1981, Atlanta. Convicted of two murders and believed responsible for 23 of the additional 29 killings in the Atlanta Child Murders. A local DJ who was caught impersonating a police officer, was also an accused pedophile. One of few black serial killers. Some tried to dispute his guilt in later years, including trying to blame the deaths within the predominately black neighborhood on KKK members, but no credible evidence was ever offered. Serving two life sentences.

Wuornos, Aileen. 1989–1990, Florida. A lesbian drifter, she fueled her hunts with alcohol and a mounting rage against men. She killed at least seven along the Florida interstates, luring them with promises of sex and hard-luck stories. She eventually confessed and was convicted and executed in 2002. See Case Studies, Chapter 6.

Zodiac Killer. 1968–1969, California. Still unidentified serial killer active in California, killing five men and women and wounding two, while suspected of other attacks. Enjoyed sending cryptic messages to the media in the Bay Area. Coded messages reportedly included plans for collecting slaves for the afterlife and called himself "Zodiac" while signing with a familiar symbol. Zodiac's identity remains a popular project for amateur investigators.

Zwanziger, Anna. 1809, Bavaria (estimated). Convicted of poisoning two women and a child while attempting many others, she regarded arsenic as her truest friend. She was executed by beheading in 1811.

Appendix B
Glossary/Explanation of Terms

It is necessary to define exactly what is meant by the terms used this book. There is little agreement among researchers regarding many of the issues discussed here, let alone the meaning of each term. Therefore, the following explains how each term is used in the context of this book.

Anger excitation (sadistic): One of Hazelwood's rapist typologies, this rapist, who is usually very organized and more psychopathic than other sexual offenders, displays that sadistic violence more important than actual rape. This person will have a history of violence to women in personal life. This offender should not be confused with an attacker who offends just for violence; he is sexually stimulated by the violence.

Anger retaliation (displaced): Another of Hazelwood's rapist typologies, this offender dislikes women in general. He is impulsive and angry. Serious injury to the victim is common with this offender. It is also not uncommon for the offender to experience sexual performance problems during the assault. The violence toward the woman is the point of the attack.

Clinically antisocial behavior: Behavior possibly described within the psychiatric community as more problematic than is found in the average person's usual process of growing up. This includes features of the MacDonald triad—namely, animal abuse, late enuresis, and fire setting. It also includes behavior clusters recognized by the *DSM-IV*, such as childhood, adolescent, or adult antisocial behavior, sociopathology, and other disorders.

Cooling-off period: The period of time after a serial killer's murder, when he or she reflects on the crime, usually enjoys mental reenactment while sometimes using trophies. There may be a relation to a lull based on avoiding detection or struggling with anxiety in trying to resist repeating murderous activity. Stress builds up to the next kill during this period. The presence of a cooling-off period is one major detail that differentiates this offender from a spree killer or a mass murderer.

Diathesis–stress: A hybrid theory often associated with schizophrenia, it combines two factors of etiology. Diathesis or pre-disposition (usually biological) combining with stress or a trigger or significant event, often traumatic, relative to the subject.

Dissociative episodes: Displays of a temporary loss of consciousness or withdrawal within the subject's own mind. The term is closely related to flights of fantasy, and an individual's becoming deeply immersed in fantasy is considered a dissociative episode.

Doubling: Term coined by Robert J. Lifton describing the personal psychological compartmentalizing of extreme behaviors they would not have been expected to be capable of in normal circumstances, such as psychopathic behavior or the actions of doctors in Nazi Germany.

DSM: Short for the *Diagnostic and Statistical Manual of Mental Disorders* (*DSM-III, DSM-IV, DSM-IV-TR*), published by the American Psychiatric Association. Common reference used in applying clinical labels and diagnoses on those with mental illnesses, personality disorders, and other syndromes. Often used in terms of crime, insanity, and descriptions of mental function and abnormal behavior.

Early age: Refers to the subject's age before turning 18, although emotional immaturity can cloud this distinction. The idea is to recognize moments of development that can be viewed as irregular. The MacDonald triad of behaviors occurs at an early numeric age, but lesser crimes committed prior to the beginning of a murderous pattern may also apply.

Environmental trauma: Any out-of-the-ordinary significant event(s) the subject may have experienced when growing up. This term includes emotional and physical experiences ranging from those that damage a person's developing ego to those that render the person deeply disturbed and even dangerous. The trauma is relevant to the individual and may not affect all people the same way.

Evidence: The appearance, at least once, of an incident in the case history of a subject. This does not indicate there is or was only one incident of whatever is being discussed, only that some instance has been noted in the study. When there are several instances of a particular nature, it is noted, as well as is minimal appearance of said instance. However, there are no set parameters regarding minimum and maximum occurrences.

Less dead: A term coined by serial murder expert Dr. Steven Egger, describing a large group of targets within serial killer victimology. It describes the more disposable members of society—prostitutes, runaways, minorities, those who live in the worst neighborhoods—who are simply not as easily missed as other members of society.

Lesser (or early) crimes: Crimes committed prior to the subject's first serial murder, usually such as breaking and entering, or arson, and may include serious offenses as well.

MacDonald triad: A three-pronged set of behaviors in youth, which indicate a developing antisocial or pathological personality. The theory was postulated by MacDonald in 1961 and 1963 and Hellman and Blackman in 1966. Also referred to as "ego triad." The combined behaviors include enuresis (late bed-wetting), fire setting, and cruelty to animals and are often used as an indicator of future violence.

Mass murderer: The FBI's term to describe an offender who kills multiple victims in basically a single episode—such as, a sniper or a shooter killing indiscriminately at a public location. This offender usually displays an overt mental imbalance and is the emotional opposite of the serial killer, described in this book as a cold, calculated predator. Like a spree killer, there is no cooling-off period.

Murderabilia (sometimes murderbilia): A descriptor for true-crime collectibles. Similar to sports memorabilia, collectibles such as comic books, trading cards, autographs, and especially artwork by killers have become extremely popular among collectors. Obviously evokes emotional response from victim advocates and a mixed protection by Son of Sam laws. Not likely to die out in a pop culture-driven society. Protestors often inadvertently enhance the interest in such items.

Physiological anomalies: Any physical or biological marker or event that could label the subject physically different from what is considered average. These could include actual physical injury, illness, vitamin deficiency, genetic makeup, chromosomal or chemical measurements, or conditions connected to a genetic link or disposition; also, evidence of certain aspects of the family that suggest factors of heredity and predisposition.

Power assertive (exploitative): According to Roy Hazelwood's rapist typologies, this offender will appear self-assured and demonstrate no empathy for his victim. He is most often violent, and his main focus is power, control, and dominance of his target.

Power reassurance (compensatory): The opposite of the power assertive within Hazelwood's rapist typologies, this offender actually would like to believe his victim is a willing participant. He lacks self-assurance, usually targets a stranger, and likes to use a minimum of force. He is often complimentary, considerate, and apologetic.

Predatory murders: Murders committed in a calculated, selective manner with no apparent motive other than the killer's enjoyment. Killings may be driven by interest in sadism or sex, but not by reasons rendering the murder incidental, such as monetary gain.

Problematic: A relative term, similar to severe, refers to a factor's impact on the subject's life and its importance within that individual's context.

Psychopath: A severe personality type, not officially recognized in the *DSM* at this time. Often erroneously confused with antisocial personality disorder, the psychopathic personality is far more severe and habitually predatory. The psychopath is a classic serial killer personality, an aggressive narcissist, but does not have to commit serial murder to be a psychopath. They (male or female) will have a history of used, manipulated, and damaged victims. Their main trait is the complete absence of empathy, a total lack of remorse, and a feeling of entitlement. They will do anything to achieve their short-term self-ish desires. Key research on the psychopath has been done by Robert Hare and Reid Meloy. Very similar to the sociopath in behavior, generally differen-tiated by the fact a psychopath is considered born, whereas the sociopath is often thought of as a product of his or her environment.

Rapist typologies: A series of descriptive classification of basic personality types of rapists, developed by Roy Hazelwood of the FBI. See power asser-tive, power reassurance, anger excitation, and anger retaliation.

Serial killer: Repetitive, cyclical activity, usually associated with a buildup of tension, committing the crime, and a cooling-off period. Actual numbers are unimportant; what is relevant is the compulsion to repetitively commit the crime and that murder is a psychological necessity, not incidental to other crime. This precludes the mass murderer or spree killer, as the serial killer's interest in murder is a continual, life-long obsessive cycle.

Severe: A subjective term, refers to whether something may have affected the subject excessively, within the individual's context. For example, many 18-year-olds may not have been excessively distressed when left on their own, but for Jeffrey Dahmer it may have been too much for his already fragile psyche. Usually, severity is self-explanatory and applicable to the majority of the population, so exceptions are to be noted and explained.

Sexual deviance: Any sexual preference, interest, or obsession that could be considered out of the ordinary and problematic, where it interferes with the individual's functioning in daily life. For example, a foot fetish becomes devi-ant and problematic when it leads to fetish burglaries and assaults; homosexu-ality becomes deviant and problematic when the subject develops a loathing for himself and others like him.

Sociopath: See psychopath.

Spree killer: An FBI term referring to offenders who go on a rampage of crime, often including multiple murders, but usually during an extension of one basic episode. The description may encompass more time than the fren-zied explosion of typical mass murderer, however. This offender differs from the serial killer in time of activity, emotional disposition, and lack of a cooling-off period.

References

Abdo, J. (1994, March 24). Jury returns unanimous sentence for Rolling. *Independent Florida Alligator, 87*(137), 1.

Abel, G. G., & Blanchard, E. B. (1974). The role of fantasy in the treatment of sexual deviation. *Archives of General Psychiatry, 30,* 467–475.

ADHD: New evidence of crime link. (2007). *Crime Times.* Retrieved from http://www.crimetimes.org/00a/w00ap1.htm

Alcala, R. J. (1994). *You, the jury.* Fremont, CA: Buquor Books.

American Psychiatric Association [APA]. (2000). *Diagnostic and statistical manual of mental disorders, text revision* (4th ed.). Washington, DC: Author.

Andreasen, N. C. (1984). *The broken brain: The biological revolution in psychiatry.* New York, NY: Harper & Row.

Apsche, J. A. (1993). *Probing the mind of a serial killer.* Morrisville, PA: International Information Association.

Atassi, L. (2010, October 11). Judge reins in spending on Anthony Sowell's defense; experts warn order could prompt appeal. *The Plain Dealer.* Retrieved from http://www.cleveland.com/anthony-sowell/

Atassi, L. (2011a, July 15). Suspected serial killer Anthony Sowell told police he "punished" drug-addicted women, interrogation video reveals. *The Plain Dealer.* Retrieved from http://www.cleveland.com/anthony-sowell/index.ssf/2011/07/suspected_serial-killer_anthony_sowell_told_police_he_punished_drug_addicted_women_interrogation_vid.html

Atassi, L. (2011b, August 9). Jury deliberating on death penalty or lifetime behind bars for serial killer Anthony Sowell. *The Plain Dealer.* Retrieved from http://www.cleveland.com/anthony-sowell/index.ssf/2011/08/jury_deliberating_on_death_penalty_or_lifetime_behind_bars_for_serial_killer_anthony_sowell.html

Athens, L. H. (1992). *The creation of dangerous violent criminals.* Urbana, IL: University of Illinois Press.

ATTACh website. (2011). Association for treatment and training in the attachment of children. Retrieved from http://www.attach.org/

Attachment disorder site. (2011). Retrieved from www.attachmentdisorder.net

Ayers, C. (2010, April 1). Rodney Alcala could be the US's most prolific serial killer. *The Times.* Retrieved from http://www.timesonline.co.uk/tol/news/world/us_and_americas/article7083519.ece

Baird, G. (2009, November 5). Anthony Sowell was considered unlikely to attack again according to 2005 evaluation. *The Plain Dealer.* Retrieved from http://blog.cleveland.com/metro/2009/11/anthony_sowell_was_considered.html

Bandura, A. (1969). *Principles of behavior modification.* New York, NY: Holt, Rinehart & Winston.

Bardsley, M., Bell, R., & Lohr, D. (2010, March). *The BTK story.* Retrieved from http://www.trutv.com/library/crime/serial_killers/unsolved/btk/index_1.html

Baron-Cohen, S. (2011). *The science of evil: On empathy and the origins of cruelty.* New York, NY: Basic Books.

Barr, M., & Sheeran, T.J. (2011, August 4). *Expert: Ohio serial killer has sexual compulsions.* Retrieved from http://abcnews.go.com/US/wireStory?id=14230890

Bartol, C., & Bartol, A. (2008). *Introduction to forensic psychology: Research and application.* Los Angeles, CA: Sage.

Benoit's brain showed severe damage from multiple concussions, doctor and dad say. (2007, September 5). *ABC News.* Retrieved from http://abcnews.go.com/GMA/story?id=3560015&page=1#.T2VO7dmNOuI

Berg, B. (1995). *Qualitative research methods for the social sciences* (2nd ed.). Boston, MA: Allyn and Bacon.

Berry-Dee, C. (2002). *Talking with serial killers.* London: John Blake.

Bipolar disorder does not increase risk of violent crime, Swedish study suggests. (2010, September 7). *Science Daily.* Retrieved from http://www.sciencedaily.com/releases/2010/09/100907103613.htm

Blair, M., Mitchell, D., & Blair, K. (2005). *The psychopath: Emotion and the brain.* Malden, MA: Blackwell Publishing.

Bliss, E.C. (1986). *Multiple personality, allied disorders & hypnosis.* New York, NY: Oxford University Press.

Brady, E., & Allen, K. (2011, September 7). Did job pressure help kill NHL enforcers? *USA Today,* 10C.

Brantley, A.C., & Kosky, R.H. (2005, January). Serial murder in the Netherlands: A look at motivation, behavior, and characteristics. *FBI Law Enforcement Bulletin,* 26–32.

Brittain, R.P. (1970). The sadistic murderer. *Medicine, Science and the Law, 10,* 198–207.

Brown, T. (2010, January 24). The road to Imperial Avenue. *The Plain Dealer.* Retrieved from http://blog.cleveland.com/metro/2010/01/post_192.html

Bruno, F.J. (1993). *Psychological symptoms.* New York, NY: John Wiley.

Burgess, A.W., Hartman, C.R., & Ressler, R.K. (1986). Sexual homicide: A motivational model. *Journal of Interpersonal Violence, 1,* 251–272.

Cahill, T. (1986). *Buried dreams.* New York, NY: Bantam Books.

Campbell, D.T., & Stanley, J.C. (1963). *Experimental and quasi experimental designs for research.* Chicago, IL: Rand McNally.

Canter, D. (1994). *Criminal shadows.* Hammersmith, London: HarperCollins.

Cartel, M. (1985). *Disguise of sanity: Serial mass murder.* Toluca Lake, CA: Pepperbox Books.

Casey, M.D., Segall, L.J., Street, D.R.K., & Blank, C.E. (1966). Sex chromosome abnormalities in two state hospitals for patients requiring special security. *Nature, 209,* 641.

Castaneda, C. (1993a, May 22). 2 pictures emerge of teens accused in slayings. *USA Today,* 1D.

Castaneda, C. (1993b, June 11). Report: Rituals of rape, death in mutilation case. *USA Today,* 1D.

Cheney, M. (1992). *Why?: The serial killer in America.* Saratoga, CA: R & E Publishers.

Chin, P., & Tamarkin, C. (1991, August 12). The door of evil. *People,* 34.

Cleckley, H. (1941). *Mask of sanity.* Saint Louis, MO: C. V. Mosby.

Coen, J. (2006, February 12). Runge is convicted in 2 deaths. *The Chicago Tribune.* Retrieved from http://articles.chicagotribune.com/2006–02–12/news/0602120231_1_paul-runge-insanity-defense-boughton

Collins, J., & Dalesio, E.P. (2011, September 18). John Boyer, trucker, killed 3 prostitutes across south: Police. Retrieved from http://www.huffingtonpost.com/2011/09/18/john-boyer- trucker-killed-prostitutes_n_968462.html

Costello, T.W., & Costello, J.T. (1992). *Abnormal psychology.* New York, NY: HarperCollins.

Coston, J. (1992). *To kill and kill again.* New York, NY: Penguin Books.

Court-Brown, W.M., Price, W.H., & Jacobs, P.A. (1968, November 23). The XYY male. *British Medical Journal,* 513, doi: 10.1136/bmj.4.5629.513-a

Court clears Dutch nurse jailed for murdering patients. (2010, April 14). Retrieved from http://www.guardian.co.uk/world/2010/apr/14/dutch-nurse-murder-patients-cleared

Court Psychiatric Clinic. (2005, September 7). *Sexual predator evaluation;* RE: Dockett No.:244471-ZA. Cleveland, OH.

Cullen, R. (1993). *The killer department.* New York, NY: Pantheon Books.

Dahmer, L. (1994). *A father's story.* New York, NY: William Morrow.

Davids, D. (1992, February). The serial murderer as superstar. *McCalls,* 150.

Davis, D. (1991). *The Milwaukee murders.* New York, NY: St. Martin's Press.

Denzin, N.K. (1970). *Sociological methods: A sourcebook.* Chicago, IL: Aldine.

Denzin, N.K. (1978). *The research act.* New York, IL: McGraw-Hill.

Dietz, P.E. (1992a, February 12). Court testimony at trial of Jeffrey Dahmer. *Court TV.*

Dietz, P.E. (1992b, February 15). Statement in reaction to Dahmer verdict. Letter in author's possession.

Dietz, P.E., Harry, B., & Hazelwood, R.R. (1986). Detective magazines: Pornography for the sexual sadist? *Journal of Forensic Sciences, 31*(1), 197–211.

Dietz, P.E., Hazelwood, R.R., & Warren, J. (1990). The sexually sadistic criminal and his offenses. *Bulletin of the American Academy of Psychiatry and the Law, 18,* 163–178.

Dodd, W.A. (1992). *When you meet a stranger.* Unpublished pamphlet, in author's possession.

Doherty, S. (2010, June 8). Wisc. researchers find similar behavior in psychopathic prisoners and people with brain damage. *CorrectionsOne.com.* Retrieved from http://www.correctionsone.com/correctional-psychology/articles/2079969-Wisc-researchers-find-similar-behavior-in-psychopathic-prisoners-and-people-with-brain-damage/

Douglas, J., & Dodd, J. (2008). *Inside the mind of BTK.* San Francisco, CA: Jossey-Bass.

Douglas, J.E., Ressler, R.K., Burgess, A.W., & Hartman, C.R. (1986). Criminal profiling from crime scene analysis. *Behavioral Sciences & the Law, 4*(4), 367–393.

Duclos, S. (2008, April 4). Fetus-snatching murderer, Lisa Montgomery, sentenced to death. Retrieved from http://www.digitaljournal.com/article/252727

Durham III, A. M. (1986). Pornography, social harm and legal control: Observations on Bart. *Justice Quarterly, Academy of Criminal Justice Sciences, 3*(1), 95–102.

Dutch family provides new proof of genetic link to behavior. (1993, October 25). *Springfield (IL) State Journal-Register,* 18.

Dvorchak, R. J., & Holewa, L. (1991). *Milwaukee massacre.* New York, NY: Dell Publishing.

Editors of Time-Life Books. (1992). *Serial killers.* Richmond, VA: Time-Life Books.

Effron, L., Sher, L., & Karlinsky, N. (2010, December 16). New "Grim Sleeper" photos released. *ABC News.* Retrieved from http://abcnews.go.com/TheLaw/grim-sleeper-serial-killer-victim-photos-released-la/story?id=12412994&tqkw=&tqshow=NL

Eftimiates, M. (1993). *Garden of graves.* New York, NY: St. Martin's Press.

Egger, S. A. (1985). *Serial murder and the law enforcement response.* Unpublished dissertation, College of Criminal Justice, Sam Houston State University, Huntsville, TX.

Egger, S. A. (1990). *Serial murder: An elusive phenomenon.* New York, NY: Praeger.

Egger, S. A. (2002). *The killers among us* (2nd ed.). Upper Saddle River, NJ: Prentice-Hall.

Elias, M. (1994, July 19). Violence is linked to brain deficiency. *USA Today,* 8D.

Ellroy, J. (1991). *Murder & mayhem.* Lincolnwood, IL: Publications International.

Ewing, C. P. (1990). *Kids who kill.* New York, NY: Avon.

Expert tells of Dahmer's twisted acts. (1992, February 5). *Boston Herald-American,* 3.

Farkas, K. (2010, August 8). Anthony Sowell did not understand his legal rights so statements to police should not be admitted in trial, his lawyers say. *The Plain Dealer.* Retrieved from http://blog.cleveland.com/metro/2010/08/anthony_sowell_was_incapable_o.html

Fessenden, F. (2000, April 9). They threaten, seethe and unhinge, then kill in quantity. *New York Times,* 28.

Focus on the Family Films, Dr. James Dobson. (1989). *Fatal addiction: Ted Bundy's final interview.* (VHS) Pomona, CA.

Frank, G. (1967). *The Boston strangler.* New York, NY: Signet.

Freud, S. (1938). Splitting of the ego in the process of defense. *Standard Edition, 23,* 271–278.

Friedman, E. (2009, November 4). First victim in Cleveland house of horrors identified. *ABC News.* Retrieved from http://abcnews.go.com/WN/anthony-sowell-victim-identified/story?id=8994164#.T2VNc9mNOuI

Fromm, E. (1973). *The anatomy of human destructiveness.* New York, NY: Holt, Rinehart & Winston.

Galbincea, P. (2010, August 12). Anthony Sowell murder trial moved to Valentine's Day. *The Plain Dealer.* Retrieved from http://blog.cleveland.com/metro/2010/08/anthony_sowell _murder_trial_mo.html

Garelik, G., & Maranto, G. (1984). Multiple murderers. *Discover,* 28.

Giannangelo, S. J. (1996). *The psychopathology of serial murder: A theory of violence.* Westport, CT: Praeger.

Gibb, D. A. (2011). *Camouflaged killer.* New York, NY: Berkley Publishing.

Gibbons, D. C. (1987). *Society, crime & criminal behavior.* Englewood Cliffs, NJ: Prentice-Hall.

Gibson, D. (2006). *Serial murder and media circuses.* Westport, CT: Praeger.

Glaser, B., & Strauss, A. L. (1967). *The discovery of grounded theory.* Chicago, IL: Aldine.

Goode, E. (2008). *Deviant behavior* (8th ed.). Upper Saddle River, NJ: Pearson Prentice-Hall.

Gottesman, I.I., & Shields, J. (1982). *Schizophrenia: The epigenetic puzzle.* Cambridge, MA: Cambridge University Press.

Grossman, W. (1991). Pain, aggression, fantasy & concepts of sadomasochism. *Psychoanalytic Quarterly, 60,* 22–52.

Grotstein, J.S. (1979). The soul in torment: An older and newer view of psychopathology. *Bulletin of the National Council of Catholic Psychologists, 25,* 36–52.

Hall, A. (2008). *Monster.* London: Penguin Books.

Hans, S., & Marcus, J. (1987). A process model for the development of schizophrenia. *Psychiatry: Interpersonal and Biological Processes, 50,* 361–370.

Hare, R. (1993). *Without conscience: The disturbing world of the psychopaths among us.* New York, NY: Pocket Books.

Hare, R. (2003). *Hare psychopathy checklist revised: PCL-R* (2nd ed.). Toronto: Multi-Health Systems.

Hare, R., McPherson, L., & Forth, A. (1988). Male psychopaths & their criminal careers. *Journal of Consulting Clinical Psychology, 56,* 710–714.

Hargrove, T. (2011, March 2). How many unsolved homicides are due to serial killers? Retrieved from http://www.kshb.com/dpp/news/local_news/special_reports/ How-many-unsolved-homicides-are-due-to-serial-killers_47076783

Harper's biochemistry. (22nd ed.). (1990). Norwalk, CT: Appleton & Lange.

Harrison, S., & Barrett, M. (1993). *The diary of Jack the Ripper: The discovery, the investigation, the debate.* New York, NY: Hyperion. (First published in Great Britain by Smith Gryphon Limited.)

Hazelwood, R., & Douglas, J. (1980, April). The lust murderer. *FBI Law Enforcement Bulletin,* 18–22.

Hellman, D., & Blackman, N. (1966). Enuresis, firesetting, and cruelty to animals. *American Journal of Psychiatry, 122,* 1431–1435.

Hickey, E.W. (1991). *Serial murderers and their victims.* Pacific Grove, CA: Brooks-Cole.

Hickey, E.W. (1997). *Serial murderers and their victims* (2nd ed.). Belmont, CA: Wadsworth.

Holewa, L. (1992, February 18). Dahmer is given life in prison. *Boston Globe,* 3.

Holmes, R.M., & DeBurger, J. (1988). *Serial murder.* Newbury Park, CA: Sage.

Holmes, R.M., & Holmes, S. (2009). *Profiling violent crimes* (4th ed.). Los Angeles, CA: Sage.

Honeycombe, G. (2009). *Murders of the black museum.* London: John Blake.

Illinois General Assembly. (2012) *Illinois Compiled Statutes,* 730 ILCS 5/5-1-11. Retrieved from http://www.ilga.gov/legislation/ilcs/ilcs4.asp?DocName=07300 0050HCh%2E+V+Art%2E+1&ActID=1999&ChapterID=55&SeqStart=19200 000&SeqEnd=21900000

Inbau, F.E., Reid, J.E., Buckley, J.P., & Jayne, B.C. (2004). *Criminal interrogation and confessions* (4th ed.). Sudbury, MA: Jones and Bartlett.

Ingram, R.E., & Price, J.M. (eds.) (2010). *Vulnerability to psychopathology* (2nd ed.). New York, NY: Guilford Press.

Inside Edition. (1993). Interviews with Jeffrey Dahmer and Richard Ramirez.

Jackman, T., & Cole, T. (1992). *Rites of burial.* New York, NY: Windsor.

Jacobs, P.A., Brunton, M., & Melville, M.M. (1965). Aggressive behavior, mental subnormality and the XYY male. *Nature, 208,* 1351–1352.

Jaffe, P., Wolfe, D., Wilson, S., & Zak, L. (1986). Similarities in behavioral and social maladjustment among child victims and witnesses to family violence. *American Journal of Orthopsychiatry, 56*, 142–146.

Joel Rifkin biography. (2011). A & E Television Networks. Retrieved from http://www.biography.com/people/joel-rifkin-11930477

Juror: Dahmer is a con artist. (1992, February 16). *Springfield (IL) State Journal Register*, 1, 5.

Karpen, L. (1993, March 14). I've always gravitated to crime. *The New York Times.* Retrieved from JackOlsen.com

Kendall, E. (1981). *The phantom prince: My life with Ted Bundy.* Seattle, WA: Madrona.

King, G. C. (1992). *Blood lust.* New York, NY: Penguin Books.

King, G. C. (1993). *Driven to kill.* New York, NY: Pinnacle Books.

Knowles, D. (2010, April 22). 2 women confirm they are in serial killer's photos. AOLnews.com. Retrieved from http://www.aolnews.com/2010/04/22/2-women-confirm-they-are-in-serial-killers-photos/

Kohut, H. (1971). *Analysis of the self.* New York, NY: International Universities Press.

Kolko, D. (2002). *Handbook on firesetting in children and youth.* San Diego, CA: Academic Press.

Kraus, R. T. (1995). An enigmatic personality: Case report of a serial killer. *Journal of Orthomolecular Medicine, 10*(1), 11–24.

Krivich, M., & Ol'gin, O. (1993). *Comrade Chikatilo: The psychopathology of Russia's most notorious serial killer.* Fort Lee, NJ: Barricade Books.

Lasseter, D. (2004). *Perfect justice: Death row and the appeals courts.* Santa Ana, CA: Seven Locks Press.

Levi Aron, charged with killing 8-year-old Leiby Kletzky, has personality disorder. (2011, August 10). Retrieved from http://www.huffingtonpost.com/2011/08/10/levi-aron-charged-with-ki_n_923723.html?icid=maing-grid10%7Chtmlws-main-bb%7Cdl12%7Csec1_lnk3%7C85373

Levin, J., & Fox, J. A. (1985). *Mass murder: America's growing menace.* New York, NY: Plenum Press.

Lewine, R.R.J., Gulley, L. R., Risch, S. C., Jewart, R., & Houpt, J. (1990). Sexual dimorphism, brain morphology and schizophrenia. *Schizophrenia Bulletin, 16*(2), 195–203.

Leyton, E. (1986). *Hunting humans: Inside the minds of mass murderers.* New York, NY: Pocket Books.

Lieb, D. (2012a, February 6). Mo. Teenager describes knife killing of 9-year-old as amazing, enjoyable. Retrieved from: http://bangordailynews.com/2012/02/06/news/nation/mo-teen-describes-knife-killing-of-9-year-old-as-amazing-enjoyable/

Lieb, D. (2012b, February 8). Mo. Teen gets life with possible parole in killing. Retrieved from: http://news.yahoo.com/mo-teen-gets-life-possible-parole-killing-141938731.html

Lifton, R. J. (2000). *The Nazi doctors: Medical killing and the psychology of genocide.* New York, NY: Basic Books.

Lincoln, Y. S., & Guba, A. L. (1985). *Naturalistic inquiry.* Beverly Hills, CA: Sage Publications.

Lindsey, R. (1984, January 21). Officials cite a rise in killers who roam the US for victims. *New York Times*, 1, 7.

Lohr, D. (2011, March 7). Murderer and accused cannibal to be freed in August. Retrieved from http://www.aolnews.com/2011/03/07/murderer-and-accused-cannibal-michael-woodmansee-to-be-freed-in/

Long Island serial killer: Police begin to build profile of killer. (2011, April 22). Retrieved from http://www.huffingtonpost.com/2011/04/22/long-island-serial-killer_n_852536.html

Lourie, R. (1993). *Hunting the devil.* New York, NY: HarperCollins.

MacCulloch, M. J., Snowden, P. R., & Wood, P. J. and Mills, H. E. (1983). Sadistic fantasy, sadistic behaviour & offending. *British Journal of Psychiatry, 143,* 20–29.

MacDonald, J (1961). *The murderer and his victim.* Springfield, IL: Charles C. Thomas.

MacDonald, J. (1963). The threat to kill. *American Journal of Psychiatry, 120,* 125–130.

Man reportedly confesses to 17 murders. (1993, June 29). *Springfield (IL) State-Journal Register,* 3.

Mann, D. (2005, July 1). The BTK killer: Portrait of a psychopath. Retrieved from FoxNews.com (WebMD).

Martinez, E. (2009, November 2). Anthony Sowell cruised sex fetish site while dead bodies rotted in his Cleveland home. Retrieved from http://www.cbsnews.com/8301–504083_162–5495923–504083.html

Martingale, M. (1993). *Cannibal killers: The history of impossible murderers.* New York, NY: Carroll & Graf Publishers.

Mason, P. (1998). Magnesium deficiency apparently increases violent crime. Retrieved from http://www.mgwater.com/violence.shtml

Masters, B. (1992, November). Dahmer's inferno. *Vanity Fair,* 269.

Masters, B. (1993). *Killing for company.* New York, NY: Random House.

McKay, S. (1985, July 8). Coming to grips with random killers. *MacLean's,* 44–45.

Mellish, P. (1989). Serial killers & porn. *The Backlash Times,* 5.

Meloy, J. R. (1988). *The psychopathic mind: Origins, dynamics, & treatment.* Northvale, NJ: Jason Aronson.

Meloy, J. R. (1992). *Violent attachments.* Northvale, NJ: Jason Aronson.

Meloy, J. R. (1993). *Assessment of violence potential: The psychopathic personality.* Seminars held in St. Louis, MO, June 7 and 8.

Merz-Perez, L., & Heide, K. (2004). *Animal cruelty: Pathway to violence against people.* Lanham, MD: AltaMira Press.

Miller, T. (2010, March 9). Serial killer Rodney Alcala won "the dating game" just before murder spree. *The New York Daily News.* Retrieved from http://www.nydailynews.com/news/national/2010/03/09/2010–03–09

Milwaukee Police Department. (1991). *Homicide incident report: Jeffrey Dahmer's arrest and subsequent confession.* Milwaukee Police. (In author's possession.)

Money, J. (1970). Behavior genetics: Principles, methods and examples from XO, XXY and XYY syndromes. *Seminar in Psychiatry, 2,* 11.

Monteleone, J. (2010, November 8). Researchers find psychopaths know right from wrong. Retrieved from http://www.correctionsone.com/correctional-psychology/articles/2867485

Morrison, B. (2010, October 5). Along highways, signs of serial killings. *USA Today,* 1, 2A.

Moyer, K. E. (1968). *Kinds of aggression and their biological basis. Communication in behavioral biology* (Vol. 2). New York, NY: Academic.

Nadelmann, J. (2009, October 28). Study links ADHD to crime. *Yale Daily News.* Retrieved from http://www.yaledailynews.com/news/2009/oct/28/study-links-adhd-to-crime/

Neilsen, J. (1970). Criminality among patients with Kleinfelter's syndrome and the XYY syndrome. *British Journal of Psychiatry, 117,* 365.

5333939

36393

3939339393

Neilsen, J., Tsuboi, T., Turver, B., Jensen, J. T., & Sachs, J. (1969). Prevalence and incidence of the XYY syndrome and Kleinfelter's syndrome in an institution for criminal psychopaths. Horsens, Denmark. *Acta Psychiatrica Scandinavica, 45,* 402.

Newton, M. (1992). *Hunting humans.* New York, NY: Avon Books.

Newton, M. (2000). *The encyclopedia of serial killers.* New York, NY: Checkmark Books.

Noronha, C. (2010, October 18). Russell Williams, top Canadian military commander, pleads guilty to murder, sexual assault. Retrieved from http://www.huffington post.com/2010/10/18/russell-williams-top-cana_0_n_766710.html

Norris, J. (1992). *Walking time bombs.* New York, NY: Bantam Books.

O'Brien, D. (1985). *Two of a kind: The hillside stranglers.* New York, NY: Penguin Books.

O'Donnell, M. (1992, January 28). A horror warning for Dahmer trial. *Chicago Sun Times,* 14.

Olsen, J. (1993). *The misbegotten son.* New York, NY: Delacorte Press.

Ono, D. (2005, March 17). Who is the BTK killer? Retrieved from http://www.msnbc.msn.com/id/8929452/

O'Reilly, P. O., Hughes, R. T., Russell, S., & Ernest, M. B. (1965). The mauve factor: An evaluation. *Diseases of the Nervous System, 26,* 562.

Osborn, A. (2003, March 25). Serial killer nurse to spend life in jail. *Guardian London,* 13.

Otnow-Lewis, D. (1998). *Guilty by reason of insanity.* New York, NY: Ivy Books.

Packer, I. K. (2009). *Evaluation of criminal responsibility.* New York, NY: Oxford University Press.

Palmer, K. (2011, August 1). Serial killer Sowell weeps during sentencing phase of trial. Retrieved from http://www.reuters.com/article/2011/08/01/us-crime-sowell-idUSTRE7705U620110801

Paradis, C. (2010). *The measure of madness.* New York, NY: Kensington.

Pelisek, C. (2010, January 21). Rodney Alcala: The fine art of killing. One man's murderous romp through polite society. *The L A Weekly News.* Retrieved from http://www.laweekly.com/2010-01-21/news/rodney-alcala-the-fine-art-of-killing/

Pervin, L. A. (1989). *Personality: Theory & research.* New York, NY: John Wiley.

Pfeiffer, C. C. (1974). Observations on the therapy of the schizophrenias. *Journal of Applied Nutrition, 26*(4), 29.

Pfeiffer, C. C., Sohler, A., Jenny, C. H., & Iliev, V. (1974). Treatment of pyroluric schizophrenia and a dietary supplement of zinc. *Journal of Orthomolecular Psychiatry, 3*(4), 1.

Pincus, J. (2001). *Base instincts: What makes killers kill.* New York, NY: W. W. Norton & Company.

Prentky, R. A., Burgess, A. W., Rokous, F., Lee, A., Harman, C., Ressler, R., & Douglas, J. (1989). The presumptive role of fantasy in serial sexual homicide. *American Journal of Psychiatry, 146*(7), 887–891.

Price, W. H., & Jacobs, P. A. (1970). The 47,XYY male with special reference to behavior. *Seminars in Psychiatry, 117,* 365.

Price, W. H., & Whatmore, P. B. (1967). Behavior disorder and patterns of crime among XYY males identified at a maximum security hospital. *British Medical Journal, 1,* 533.

Prince, M. (1975). *Psychotherapy & multiple personality: Selected essays.* Cambridge, MA: Harvard University Press.

Prisoners and Detainees of Ohio: Maurice Clarett, Anthony Sowell. (2010). Memphis, TN: Books LLC.

Rader's testimony. (2007, March 12). Transcript of Dennis Rader's 2005 court admissions. *The Wichita Eagle.* Retrieved from http://www.kansas.com/2005/06/28/16541/raders-testimony.html#ixzz13cv3mghw

Raine, A. (2011). Faculty profile, University of Pennsylvania, Department of Criminology. Retrieved from http://www.crim.upenn.edu/faculty/profiles/raine.html

Raine, A., & Sanmartin, J., (2001). *Violence and psychopathy.* New York, NY: Kluwer Academic/Plenum Publishers.

Ramsland, K. (2005a). *Inside the minds of mass murderers: Why they kill.* Westport, CT: Praeger.

Ramsland, K. (2005b). *The human predator.* New York, NY: Berkley Publishing.

Ramsland, K. (2006). *Inside the minds of serial killers: Why they kill.* Westport, CT: Praeger.

Reinhardt, J. J. (1992). *Sex perversions & sex crimes.* Springfield, IL: Charles C. Thomas.

Relatives' joy as serial killer is sentenced to death after bizarre self-defence featuring clip of U.S. TV show "the dating game" (2010, March 11). *The Mail Online.* Retrieved from http://www.dailymail.co.uk/news/worldnews/article-1256827/

Research and Education Association. (1982). *Behavioral genetics.* New York, NY: Author.

Researchers: Bob Probert had CTE. (2011, March 5). *ESPN NHL.* Retrieved from http://sports.espn.go.com/nhl/news/story?id=6177474

Ressler, R. (1992). *Whoever fights monsters.* New York, NY: St. Martin's Press.

Ressler, R., Burgess, A., Depue, R., Douglas, J., & Hazelwood, R. (1985, August). The men who murdered: The split reality of murder. *FBI Law Enforcement Bulletin, 54*(8), 1–11.

Ressler, R., Burgess, A., D'Agostino, R., & Douglas, J. E. (1984). *Serial murder: A new phenomenon of homicide.* Paper presented at the annual meeting of the International Association of Forensic Sciences, Oxford, UK.

Ressler, R., & Shachtman, T. (1997) *I have lived in the monster.* New York, NY: St. Martin's Press.

Revitch., E., & Schlesinger, L. B. (1981). *The psychopathology of homicide.* Springfield, IL: Charles C. Thomas.

Reynolds, M. (1992). *Dead ends.* New York, NY: Warner Books.

Rolling, D., & London, S. (1996). *The making of a serial killer.* Portland, OR: Feral House.

Rowe, D. (2002). *Biology and crime.* Los Angeles, CA: Roxbury Publishing.

Ryzuk, M. (1994). *The Gainesville ripper.* New York, NY: Donald Fine, Inc.

Samenow, S. (2004). *Inside the criminal mind.* New York, NY: Crown Publishers.

Sands, S. (2011). *The dating game killer.* New York, NY: St. Martin's Press.

Schaefer, G. J., & London, S. (1997). *Killer fiction.* Venice, CA: Feral House.

Schechter, H. (2003). *The serial killer files.* New York, NY: Ballantine Books.

Schechter, H., & Everitt, D. (1997). *The A to Z encyclopedia of serial killers.* New York, NY: Pocket Books.

Schurman-Kauflin, D. (2000). *The new predator: Women who kill.* New York, NY: Algora.

Scott, M. (2011a, August 5). Mental health expert: Anthony Sowell heard voices; military expert: He was a good soldier. *The Plain Dealer.* Retrieved from http://www.cleveland.com/anthony-sowell/index.ssf/2011/08/mental_health_expert_a_disturbed_anthony_sowell_heard_voices_1.html

Scott, M. (2011b, August 5). Mental health expert's testimony challenged by prosecutors in Anthony Sowell capital murder trial. *The Plain Dealer.* Retrieved from http://www.cleveland.com/anthony-sowell/index.ssf/2011/08/mental_health_experts_testimony_challenged_by_prosecutors_in_anthony_sowell_capital_murder_trial.html

Scouller, S. R. (2010). *Murderabilia and true crime collecting.* Central Milton Keynes, UK: Author House.

Sears, D. J. (1991). *To kill again: The motivation and development of serial murder.* Wilmington, DE: Scholarly Resources.

Second Boston strangler eyed. (1993, May 11). *Boston Herald,* 3.

Seewer, J., & Sheeran, T. J. (2011, August 11). Jurors to judge: Execute Ohio man who killed 11. Retrieved from http://news.yahoo.com/jurors-judge-execute-ohio-man-killed-11-081936935.html

Serial killer Anthony Sowell: I'm sorry. (2011, August 8). *19 Action News.* Retrieved from http://www.woio.com/story/15226541/sowell-speaks

Serial killer Sowell's mother whipped him naked with electrical cords. (2011, August 4). *International Business Times.* Retrieved from http://www.ibtimes.com/articles/192205/20110804/serial-killer-anthony-sowell-convict-murder-rape-sexual-abuse-sex-offender-ohio-violence-testimony-j.htm

Sex offender confesses to killing 9 in Missouri, Illinois and elsewhere. (2007, December 11). Retrieved from http://www.foxnews.com/story/0,2933,316450,00.html

Sheeran, T. J. (2011a, July 14). Anthony Sowell case: Ohio murder suspect tells police "I guess I did that." Retrieved from http://www.huffingtonpost.com/2011/07/16/anthony-sowell-case-i-guess-i-did-that_n_900578.html

Sheeran, T. J. (2011b, August 3). Anthony Sowell weeps as rapist pal begs judge to spare Ohio serial killer the death penalty. Retrieved from http://www.huffingtonpost.com/2011/08/03/anthony-sowell-rapist-begs-judge-death-penalty_n_917573.html

Sheeran, T. J. (2011c, August 8). Anthony Sowell: State argues serial killer's brain function normal following apology. Retrieved from http://www.huffingtonpost.com/2011/08/09/state-ohio-killer-sane-apology-video_n_922177.html

Silcox, C. (2010, September 14). Owen Thomas brain autopsy reveals disease. *The Daily Pennsylvanian.* Retrieved from http://www.thedp.com/node/68278

Silverton, L., Mednick, S., Schulsinger, F., Parnas, J., & Harrington, M. (1988). Genetic risk for schizophrenia, birthweight, & cerebral ventricular enlargement. *Journal of Abnormal Psychology, 97*(4), 496–498.

Slavkin, M. K. (2001). Enuresis, firesetting, and cruelty to animals: Does the ego triad show predictive validity? *Adolescence, 36*(143), 461–466.

Sloan, M. P., & Meyer, J. H. (1983). Typology for parents of abused children. *Child Abuse and Neglect, 7,* 443–450.

Smith, S. R., & Meyer, R. G. (1987). *Law, behavior & mental health: Policy & practice.* New York, NY: New York University Press.

Snider, M. (1993, October 22). Genetic flaw makes some men violent. *USA Today,* 1D.

Solotaroff, I. (1993). The terrible secret of Citizen Ch. *Esquire,* 95–99.

Sowell jury: death sentence. (2011, August 10). *WTAM 1100 Newsradio Cleveland.* Retrieved from http://www.wtam.com/cc-common/news/sections/newsarticle.html?feed=122520&article=8945926

Sproull, N. L. (1988). *Handbook of research methods: A guide for practitioners and students in the social sciences.* Metuchen, NJ: Scarecrow Press.

Stout, M. (2005). *The sociopath next door.* New York, NY: Broadway Books.

Studies find link between gene and personality. (1996, January 2). *Springfield (IL) State Journal-Register,* 1.

Sunde S. (2002, January 18). Ex-FBI profiler: No such thing as a "typical" serial killer. *Seattle Post- Intelligencer.* Retrieved from http://www.seattlepi.com/local/54980_profilers18.shtml

Toufexis, A. (1992, February 3). Do mad acts a madman make? *Time,* 17.

Toufexis, A. (1995, December 4). Monster mice. *Time,* 76.

Vronsky, P. (2004). *Serial killers: The method and madness of monsters.* New York, NY: Berkley Publishing.

Vronsky, P. (2007). *Female serial killers: How and why women become monsters.* New York, NY: Berkley Publishing.

Wagner, D. (2006, August 25). Criminal profiling "between science and art." *USA Today,* 9A.

Walker, E., Downey, G., & Bergman, A., (1989). The effects of parental psychopathology and maltreatment on child behavior: A test of the diathesis-stress model. *Child Development, 60,* 15–24.

Ward, J. L. (1975). Relationship of kryptopyrrole, zinc and pyridoxine in schizophrenia. *Journal of Orthomolecular Psychiatry, 4,* 27.

Weber, S. (2011, January 27). Serial killer Rodney Alcala indicted in New York slayings. Retrieved from http://www.nbclosangeles.com/news/local-beat/Serial-Killer-Rodney-Alcala-Reportedly-Indicted-in-New-York-Slayings-114735604.html

Welborn, L. (2010a, March 5). Alcala claims he does not remember 4 murders. *The Orange County Register.* Retrieved from http://articles.ocregister.com/2010–03–04/crime/24646197_1

Welborn, L. (2010b, March 10). Prosecutor worries Alcala might have killed others. *The Orange County Register.* Retrieved from http://articles.ocregister.com/2010–03–10/crime/24651759_1

Wenzl, R., Potter, T., Kelly, L., & Laviana, H. (2007). *Bind, torture, kill.* New York, NY: Harper.

West, D. J. (1987). *Sexual crimes and confrontations: A study of victims and offenders.* Brookfield, VT: Gower.

Williams III, F., & McShane, M. (1999). *Criminological theory* (3rd ed.). Upper Saddle River, NJ: Prentice-Hall.

Wilson, C. (1989). *Written in blood: The criminal mind and method.* New York, NY: Warner Books.

Wilson C. (2010, October 16). Teenager who strangled brother gets life in prison. *Springfield (IL) State Journal-Register,* 6.

Wilson, C., & Seaman, D. (1991). *The serial killers: A study in the psychology of violence.* Washington, DC: U.S. Department of Justice.

Wisconsin serial killer gets 7 life terms. (2011, February 24). Retrieved from http://www.upi.com/Top_News/US/2011/02/24/Wis-serial-killer-gets-7-life-terms/UPI-51761298595212/

Witness: Dahmer said he'd "eat my heart." (1992, February 1). *Springfield (IL) State Journal-Register,* 3.

World Health Organization. (2008). *ICD-10 International statistical classification of diseases and related health problems.* (10th rev.). Geneva, Switzerland: WHO Press.

Wright, J., & Hensley, C. (2003). From animal cruelty to serial murder: Applying the graduation hypothesis. *International Journal of Offender Therapy and Comparative Criminology, 47*(1), 71–88.

Yin, R. K. (1984). *Case study research: Design & methods.* Thousand Oaks, CA: Sage.

Yin, R. K. (2008). *Case study research: Design & methods* (4th ed.). Thousand Oaks, CA: Sage.

Young, J. (2010, April 12). *ADHD and crime: Considering the connections.* Retrieved from http://cme.medscape.com/viewarticle/719862

Zeuthen, E., Hansen, M., Christensen, A. L., & Neilsen, J. (1975). A psychiatric-psychological study of XYY males found in a general male population. *Acta Psychiatrica Scandinavica, 51*, 3–18.

Zimbardo, P. (2007). *The Lucifer effect.* New York, NY: Random House.

Index

About the Author

STEPHEN J. GIANNANGELO is currently a special agent supervisor for the Illinois Department of Revenue's Bureau of Criminal Investigation. He was formerly a senior special agent with the same agency, and also served on Task Forces for the Illinois State Police and the Federal Bureau of Investigation. He holds a master's degree in forensic psychology from the University of Illinois at Springfield (Illinois) and graduated from the Illinois State Police Academy. He is also an adjunct instructor at the University of Illinois at Springfield. He previously published *The Psychopathology of Serial Murder: A Theory of Violence* in 1996.

CPSIA information can be obtained
at www.ICGtesting.com
Printed in the USA
BVOW06*2130150917
494918BV00008B/23/P

9 780313 397844